AF217976

Political Writings

DAVID HUME

Political Writings

Edited, with Introduction and Notes, by

Stuart D. Warner
&
Donald W. Livingston

Hackett Publishing Company
Indianapolis/Cambridge

David Hume: 1711–1776

Copyright © 1994 by Hackett Publishing Company, Inc.
All rights reserved
Printed in the United States of America

14 13 12 11 10 09 3 4 5 6 7 8

Text design by Dan Kirklin
Cover by Listenberger Design & Associates

For further information, please address
Hackett Publishing Company, Inc.
P.O. Box 44937
Indianapolis, Indiana 46244-0937

www.hackettpublishing.com

Library of Congress Cataloging-in-Publication Data

Hume, David, 1711–1776.
[Selections. 1994]
Political writings/David Hume: edited, with introduction and notes, by Stuart D. Warner & Donald W. Livingston.
p. cm.
Includes bibliographical references (p.) and index.
ISBN 0-87220-161-9 (cloth: alk. paper).
ISBN 0-87220-160-0 (pbk.: alk. paper)
1. Political science—Early works to 1800. I. Warner, Stuart D., 1955– . II. Livingston, Donald W. III. Title.
JC176.H892 1994
320'.01—dc20 93-50572
CIP

ISBN-13: 978-0-87220-161-3 (cloth)
ISBN-13: 978-0-87220-160-6 (pbk.)

The paper used in this publication meets the minimum requirements of American National Standard for Information Sciences—Permanence of Paper for Printed Library Materials, ANSI Z39.48–1984.

Contents

INTRODUCTION vii

EDITORS' NOTE xxvii

SELECTED BIBLIOGRAPHY xxix

PART I: JUSTICE AND THE STRUCTURE OF CIVIL SOCIETY 1

From *A Treatise of Human Nature,* Bk. III, Pt. II

Book III: Of Morals

Part II: Of justice and injustice

SECT.

I. Justice, whether a natural or artificial virtue? 1
II. Of the origin of justice and property 7
III. Of the rules which determine property 20
IV. Of the transference of property by consent 31
V. Of the obligation of promises 33
VI. Some further reflections concerning justice and injustice 40
VII. Of the origin of government 47
VIII. Of the source of allegiance 51
IX. Of the measures of allegiance 59
X. Of the objects of allegiance 62
XI. Of the laws of nations 73
XII. Of chastity and modesty 76

From *An Enquiry concerning the Principles of Morals*

III. Of Justice 80

PART II: POLITICAL INTIMATIONS 98

From *Essays, Moral, Political, and Literary*

ESSAY
I. Of the Liberty of the Press 98
II. That Politics may be reduced to a Science 101
III. Of the Independency of Parliament 113
IV. Whether the British Government inclines more to Absolute Monarchy, or to a Republic 117
V. Of the Parties of Great Britain 121
VI. Of Civil Liberty 127
VII. Of the Balance of Power 135
VIII. Of the Coalition of Parties 142
IX. Of the Protestant Succession 149

PART III: THE CRITIQUE OF SPECULATIVE POLITICS 157

From *Essays, Moral, Political, and Literary*

X. Of Parties in General 157
XI. Of the Original Contract 164
XII. Of Passive Obedience 182
XIII. Of Superstition and Enthusiasm 184
XIV. Of Moral Prejudices 189

PART IV: THE EVOLUTION OF CIVILIZATION AND SOCIETY 194

From *Essays, Moral, Political, and Literary*

XV. Of the Origin of Government 194
XVI. Of the Rise and Progress of the Arts and Sciences 197
XVII. Of Commerce 219
XVIII. Of Refinement in the Arts 230
XIX. Idea of a Perfect Commonwealth 240

Variant Readings 253

Introduction

Though David Hume's reputation as one of the greatest philosophers in history is contested by virtually no one, few regard him as a major *political* philosopher. Histories of political philosophy typically pay him scant attention,[1] and courses in the history of political thought often ignore him altogether. Whether thus dispensing with Hume's political reflections can be justified, however, is another matter. We believe that it cannot. Indeed, far from having been discounted after having been duly considered, Hume's political writings have yet to receive a fair hearing. This thematic collection of Hume's political writings is offered both as evidence of the genius of those writings and as a practical remedy to the problem of their neglect.

* * * *

Hume's first book was *A Treatise of Human Nature*,[2] a work divided into three books: "Of the Understanding," "Of the Passions," and "Of Morals." The first two books of the *Treatise* were published in January of 1739, when Hume was almost twenty-eight years of age, and the third twenty-two months later. In an important sense, the work was never completed. Hume suggests in the introduction to the *Treatise* that he intended it to include a book on criticism and a book on politics, one that would involve more than the analyses of "justice" and "allegiance to government" that are contained in "Of Morals." One reason why Hume did not "complete" the *Treatise* was that upon its original publication it received mixed reviews at best, and also produced poor sales. Hume himself commented that the *Treatise* "fell *dead-born from the press*."[3]

The last work that Hume prepared for publication was *Essays and Treatises on Several Subjects*, which appeared in 1777, the year after his death. In an advertisement that he appended to that work, Hume again

1. For example, Thomas I. Cook in his excellent seven-hundred-page *History of Political Philosophy from Plato to Burke* (New York: Prentice-Hall, Inc., 1936), the first extensive work on the subject in this century, devotes seven pages to the work of Juan de Mariana (1536–1623), yet Hume's name only appears once, and then in a footnote.

2. *A Treatise of Human Nature*, second edition, with text revised and notes by P. H. Nidditch (Oxford: at the Clarendon Press, 1978).

3. David Hume, "My Own Life," in *The Letters of David Hume*, edited by J.Y.T. Greig, 2 vols. (Oxford: At the Clarendon Press, 1932), vol. I, p. 2.

downplayed the *Treatise*, calling it "juvenile," and he requested that the *Essays and Treatises on Several Subjects* "alone be regarded as containing his philosophical sentiments and principles."[4] Nevertheless, we should recognize that Hume never repudiated the substance of the *Treatise*, only its manner of presentation, and, whatever differences might exist, there is a fundamental, philosophical unity between the *Treatise*, the pieces that make up the *Essays and Treatises on Several Subjects*, and the rest of Hume's writings.

The *Essays and Treatises on Several Subjects* is a two volume collection of materials from 1741 to 1776. One volume includes *An Enquiry concerning Human Understanding*, *An Enquiry concerning the Principles of Morals*, *The Natural History of Religion*, and the *Dissertation on the Passions*;[5] and the other volume consists of *Essays, Moral, Political, and Literary*. This latter volume is *the* central work for understanding and appreciating his political philosophy. Together with Hume's *A Treatise of Human Nature*, these works contain some two thousand pages. However, these works constitute substantially less than half of the total of Hume's writings; for casting a large shadow over all of them is his three-thousand-page *The History of England*, published from 1754 to 1762, a six-volume work that tells the story of the nature and development of civilization and liberty in England.

Although the title *Essays, Moral, Political, and Literary* suggests a somewhat equal division into three subjects, the *Essays* overwhelmingly inquires into political subjects. In total, Hume wrote forty-nine essays between 1741 and 1776, of which thirty-nine were included in the *Essays and Treatises on Several Subjects* of 1777. Hume first published fifteen essays under the title *Essays, Moral and Political* in 1741, followed the next year by twelve more published under the same title. Hume issued another large collection in 1752 under the title *Political Discourses*.[6] Not only was Hume writing these essays, but he was revising them for later editions, sometimes in significant ways. Given the charac-

4. *The Philosophical Works of David Hume*, edited by T. H. Green and T. H. Grose, new edition, 4 vols. (London: Longmans, Green and Co., 1882), vol. III, p. v.

5. The two *Enquiries* were first published in 1748 and 1751, respectively, and Hume revised them somewhat for later printings. *An Enquiry concerning the Principles of Morals*, like the *Treatise*, contains important discussions of things political. *The Natural History of Religion* and the *Dissertation on the Passions* were first published in 1757.

6. The subject of many of these essays is what today would be called political economy or economics.

ter of the *Essays* and *The History of England* and Hume's continuous attention to them, it is only fair to say that throughout most of his mature life, Hume's intellectual energies were principally devoted to things political.[7]

Correspondingly, in the eighteenth and for much of the nineteenth century, Hume's reputation as a master thinker had its source in his *Essays, Moral, Political, and Literary* and *The History of England*.[8] Things appear different, however, to the twentieth-century audience, for during most of this century Hume's reputation has rested on the *Treatise*, and no small part of this reputation is based on a common reading of that work. This reading understands the *Treatise* as a work primarily animated by metaphysical and, especially, epistemological questions. Here Hume is taken to be vitally interested in questions such as: What is cause and effect? What is personal identity? What is knowledge? and, Can human beings know the external world? On this understanding of the *Treatise*, it is the first book—"Of the Understanding"—that is singled out for special attention. And this attention paid to Book I of the *Treatise* is, for several reasons, all too frequently accompanied by a neglect of the last two books as well as of the *Essays, Moral, Political, and Literary*. Unfortunately, this common reading of the *Treatise* is an impoverished one that neither succeeds in penetrating to the core of the fundamental question that Hume is asking nor grasps the unity of the three books that constitute the work.

The fundamental question that informs the *Treatise* begins to reveal itself in the concluding part of Book I. The title of this part is "Of the sceptical and other systems of philosophy," and the question Hume explores is: What is philosophy? In pursuing this question, he discovers that the practice of philosophy has historically been guided by two principles: What we will call the ultimacy and autonomy principles.[9] The first principle holds that philosophy should attempt to ascertain the ultimate principles of reality. The second principle requires that philosophy endeavor to be a radically autonomous inquiry, one that understands itself as transcending, by critical reflection, all of the habits, customs, traditions, and opinions of common life. These habits, customs, traditions, and opinions that constitute the common life of a

7. This is also evidenced by an examination of Hume's letters.

8. The catalog at the British Library refers to Hume as "the Historian."

9. This point was originated and developed in detail in Donald W. Livingston, *Hume's Philosophy of Common Life* (Chicago: University of Chicago Press, 1984).

society are viewed as having no authority of any kind. Governed by the autonomy principle, philosophy accepts only that which is demonstrated by autonomous reason operating independently of the world of common life in which the philosopher *qua* human being lives and participates. In the *Treatise*, Hume shows that the autonomy principle is incompatible with other principles of our nature and leads to a hopeless and absolute skeptical doubt that no one can actually accept. Hume writes, "Reason first appears in possession of the throne, prescribing laws, and imposing maxims with an absolute sway and authority."[10] However, reason "when it acts alone . . . entirely subverts itself, and leaves not the lowest degree of evidence in any proposition in philosophy or common life."[11] Philosophy guided by the autonomy principle, therefore, bankrupts itself. The autonomy principle must be reformed if philosophy is to be possible at all. Philosophy must recognize that not all opinions, habits, customs, and traditions, that is, not all practices, can be called into question at once without leading to a self-stultifying doubt. Philosophical inquiry can begin and proceed only by recognizing the provisional autonomy of the habits, customs, traditions, and opinions that constitute the practices of common life. It is only within the order of common life that the elements of this order can be subjected to critical, philosophical reflection. There is, in other words, no Cartesian or Archimedian point outside of this order to guide us in our judgments of it, either as a whole or in part. The critical reflection on which philosophy prides itself rests on an order of habit, custom, tradition, and opinion and cannot operate independently of it. Therefore, Hume concludes, "philosophical decisions are nothing but the reflections of common life, methodized and corrected."[12]

Hume's findings regarding the limits of philosophical understanding yield a more profound understanding of what reason is. For by relocating reason within the order of common life, Hume forces us to recognize those elements of human nature that constitute rationality, properly understood; and foremost among these are imagination, memory, opinion, custom, the passions, and our moral sentiments. By deflating the pretensions of a false conception of reason, Hume brings to light the

10. *A Treatise of Human Nature*, p. 186.

11. *A Treatise of Human Nature*, pp. 267–68.

12. *An Enquiry Concerning Human Understanding*, edited by Eric Steinberg, revised edition (Indianapolis: Hackett Publishing, 1993), p. 112.

full significance of these other faculties, now locating them in the capital of human nature and not in the outlying provinces. And it is here that we can find *the* unifying theme of the *Treatise*. The *Treatise* is a work that puts out to sea[13] in order to discover how and in what manner the diverse elements of our human nature constitute an intelligible human world, a world consisting of things moral, political, social, legal, and aesthetic.

* * * *

There is a dramatic difference between the treatment of political subjects in *A Treatise of Human Nature* and that in *Essays, Moral, Political, and Literary*. While the *Treatise* advances an understanding of justice and allegiance to government that has an abstract character, the *Essays* reveals an understanding of things political that has its home in the concrete; and while the *Treatise* advances an understanding of justice and allegiance to government in long, tightly knit arguments, the *Essays* reveals an understanding in which the truth lies, in part, in the nuances. This difference between the works is important, but not because one work is—given its abstract or concrete character—philosophically more worthy than the other. We will gradually begin to uncover the significance of the difference by turning to certain features of Hume's theory of justice in the *Treatise*.[14]

Hume belongs to the philosophical tradition going back at least to Plato that understands justice as a virtue or moral excellence. However, where Plato uses the term 'justice' in a broad manner, referring to a well-ordered soul governed by the unity of wisdom, courage, and temperance, Hume uses the term in a much more limited way. On Hume's understanding, the principal—although not exclusive—meaning of 'justice' has to do with private property and ownership: the just individual is the person who abides by the legal rules governing private property and ownership in his society. This conception of justice postulates a pluralistic understanding of virtue: There are many virtues—for example, benevolence and courage—and these virtues are not reducible to one, in this case justice. Justice is, then, not synonymous with all of the right or all of the good.

13. See *A Treatise of Human Nature*, pp. 263–64.

14. There is a similar structure in Hume's analyses of justice and allegiance to government and, therefore, we omit the latter from our discussion.

Near the beginning of Hume's account of justice in the *Treatise* is an extensive discussion on the origin of justice.[15] Hume's pursuit of this matter rests on the conception that justice is not a natural virtue; that is, justice is not a virtue for which there is an original disposition or motive within the human frame leading us to refrain from taking the possessions or property of others.[16] Nevertheless, justice does exist, and a motive must have been *invented* out of the original dispositions and motives of human nature to bring it into being. Justice is thus an artificial virtue because its ground is human artfulness. To show how justice has originated in that artfulness, Hume moves into the domain of conjectural history.[17]

Hume constructs an account of certain features of human nature and human circumstances that human beings had to overcome in order to live successfully with one another, and a hypothetical or conjectural historical account elucidating the means by which they might have done it. Hume's account begins with the recognition that human beings are selfish and have a love of gain, and although we are also benevolent, that benevolence is limited. Furthermore, human beings live in a world of scarce resources in which the beneficial possessions of one individual can easily be taken by force by another for his own benefit. In the light of human nature and circumstances, the likelihood for repeated human conflict is great, and it is Hume's understanding that the pervasive desire for material things is the focal point of a great deal of violence and conflict in the world. Hume conjectures that human beings, living in a primitive society that was primarily animated by the natural appetites between the sexes, could not have initially discovered by reason a way to escape the predicament we have just sketched. Instead, for human beings there must have gradually *emerged* over some period of time a rudimentary understanding that they could best pursue their own inter-

15. See Hume, *Political Writings*, edited by Stuart D. Warner and Donald W. Livingston (Indianapolis: Hackett Publishing, 1994) pp. 7–20. All further citations to this work will be by page number only.

16. For Hume, mere possession becomes property in civil society under the rubric of justice.

17. This expression was coined by the Scottish thinker Dugald Stewart (1753–1828). See his "Account of the Life and Writings of Adam Smith, L.L.D.," edited by I. S. Ross, in Adam Smith, *Essays on Philosophical Subjects*, in *The Glasgow Edition of the Works and Correspondence of Adam Smith* (Oxford: Clarendon Press, 1980), p. 293. Conjectural history is the activity of trying to reconstruct the past in broad strokes largely on the basis of general principles of human nature.

ests and further the interests of those closest to them by refraining from taking the possessions of others. And this understanding was possible only insofar as in acting, individuals were actually refraining from taking the possessions of others (for example, members of an extended family and individuals with whom one had regular contact) and slowly seeing the beneficial results. An additional factor at play here, Hume conjectures, is the growth of a new affection disposing human beings to an even wider range of company and conversation. We thus over some time learned to redirect artfully our own interested passions in order to further them: Our passion of self-interest learned to counterbalance itself. The pursuit of interest redirected led ultimately and unintentionally to the rules of justice, and therefore it is correct to say that, for Hume, justice is the result of human action, but not of human design.

Even though Hume counts justice as an artificial virtue, there is also a sense in which the three fundamental rules of justice, namely, stability of possession, transfer by consent, and keeping of promises,[18] are *laws of nature*. Hume most perspicuously comments on this when he writes:

> Most of the inventions of men are subject to change. They depend upon humour and caprice. They have a vogue for a time, and then sink into oblivion. It may, perhaps, be apprehended, that if justice were allow'd to be a human invention, it must be plac'd on the same footing. But the cases are widely different. The interest, on which justice is founded, is the greatest imaginable, and extends to all times and places. It cannot possibly be serv'd by any other invention. . . . All these causes render the [fundamental] rules of justice stedfast and immutable. . . .[19]

Justice possesses a universal quality which rests on the passion of interest; it pertains to all human beings in all civil societies; it is what makes civil society possible. Hume understands private property, the separation of material goods into mine and thine, as an essential condition for civil society; therefore, justice—and its three fundamental rules in particular—is a necessary element of the basic structure of civil society. Furthermore, we can say that Hume's use of conjectural history aims at highlighting this universalistic feature of justice by postulating an unchanging human nature over the long course of history.

18. See pp. 40–41.

19. *A Treatise of Human Nature*, p. 620.

It is perhaps tempting to ignore Hume's use of conjectural history and present his theory of justice in a very different idiom, one that recognizes justice as a solution to a coordination problem that is set forth in the now-fashionable game theory. We should, however, resist such a temptation. Central to all of Hume's reflections on things political is the concept of time. And we can see this in the present context by briefly referring to Hume's discussion "Of the rules which determine property."[20] The point of this section in the *Treatise* is to show how the three fundamental rules of justice are made manifest in the world. Hume indicates five specific rules that determine this: Present possession, Occupation, Prescription, Accession, and Succession. These rules which spring from the imagination have an essentially temporal component to them; as such, the concept of justice cannot be divorced from its temporal dimension without distorting its character. Hume, in no small measure, places his theory of justice within the domain of conjectural history to underscore the idea that critical to the normative authority of justice is its emergence in history over time.[21] Justice is not, and should not be thought of as being, the discovery and recommendation of autonomous reason.

* * * *

In his *Essays, Moral, Political, and Literary*, Hume turns his philosophical eye to an activity that is *found in* civil society, namely, the activity of politics, and in so doing, Hume attempts to illuminate the character of this activity and to highlight how it can be corrupted and deformed. Hume's political essays can give the appearance of being haphazard; however, they are carefully tied and united by a distinctive and complex vision of the nature of politics that threads its way through the essays.

Central to Hume's thinking about politics is his understanding of political principles or maxims.[22] The principles or maxims that Hume advances in his *Essays* are strikingly different from what one finds in many other important political philosophers, as attention to the following samples suggests:

20. See pp. 20–31.

21. For Hume's understanding of how justice acquires its normative authority, see pp. 18–20.

22. In the context of morals and politics, Hume uses the terms 'principles' and 'maxims' synonymously.

• In politics, "every man must be supposed a knave."[23]
• "It is impossible for the arts and sciences to arise, at first, among any people unless that people enjoy the blessing of a free government."[24]
• "There is nothing more favourable to the rise of politeness and learning than a number of neighbouring and independent states, connected together by commerce and policy."[25]
• "It is . . . on opinion only that government is founded."[26]
• "An hereditary prince, a nobility without vassals, and a people voting by their representatives, form the best Monarchy, Aristocracy and Democracy."[27]

These principles are nothing like the principle of liberty that is found in Mill or the principles expressive of natural rights that one finds in Locke; and, indeed, what they truly evidence is a fundamentally different understanding of politics.

To achieve a deeper sense of the character of Humean political principles, it is imperative to notice that alongside Hume's declaration of various principles, one finds a deep mistrust of political principles generally. In his essay, "Of Civil Liberty," Hume warns us against being precipitous in concluding that we have arrived at something appropriately called a principle of politics.

> I am apt . . . to entertain a suspicion, that the world is still too young to fix many general truths in politics, which will remain true to the latest posterity. We have not as yet had experience of three thousand years; so that not only the art of reasoning is still imperfect in this science, as in all others, but we even want sufficient materials upon which we can reason.[28]

Significantly, this is not the only cautionary note that Hume sounds. In "Whether the British Government inclines more to Absolute Monarchy, or to a Republic," he offers the following advice:

> It affords a violent prejudice against almost every science, that no prudent man, however sure of his principles, dares prophesy concerning any event,

23. P. 113.

24. P. 200.

25. P. 203.

26. Hume, *Essays, Moral, Political, and Literary*, edited by Eugene F. Miller, revised edition (Indianapolis: Liberty Fund, 1987), p. 32.

27. Pp. 103–4.

28. P. 127.

> or foretel the remote consequences of things. A physician will not venture to pronounce concerning the condition of his patient a fortnight or month after: And still less a politician foretel the situation of public affairs a few years hence.[29]

In part, this caution is reminiscent of that above—do not form principles hastily. However, Hume intends something more, namely, that even well-formed principles—especially political principles—are problematic in their application to the realm of things human.

Hume's appeal here in the context of politics may be seen as sounding a note of moderation—and, indeed, moderation finds a close friend in Hume—but we need to listen more carefully to his warning. What he is directing our attention to is the extraordinarily fragile, precarious, and contingent character of political life, a character that makes the formation of political principles immeasurably difficult. Moreover, all political matters are "infinitely complicated,"[30] and the unintended and unanticipated consequences that result from our choices continually cloud our political world.

Hume's political essays are marked by a profound and recurring understanding of the almost hopeless tangle of incidents and circumstances that shape and make up the world of politics, and the echoes of this understanding are heard on almost every page of the *Essays*. Indeed, in examining Hume's *Essays* (and *The History of England*), one cannot help being impressed with how often he refers to the affairs of politics as "surprising" and "remarkable" and "extraordinary."

We must be careful, however, not to give the wrong impression: Hume *does* advance a good number of political principles or maxims, especially in the realm of political economy. At the same time, we must take notice of his suspicious disposition about political principles in general. Indeed, his political writings celebrate the tension between the political principles he does introduce and his general skepticism about political principles.

Hume's conception of political principles is shaped by his understanding of what especially gives life and substance to the activity of politics: passions, opinions, and the imagination. The world of politics, for Hume, is generated by our passions, opinions, and imagination, which themselves give rise to customs, traditions, and habits. In his

29. Pp. 116–17.
30. P. 152.

essay "Of Eloquence," he observes, "Interest and ambition, honour and shame, friendship and enmity, gratitude and revenge, are the prime movers in all public transactions; and these passions are of a very stubborn and intractable nature."[31] As we have already seen, he remarks that government rests on opinion only. In "Of the Original Contract," he makes the more sweeping judgment that in matters of politics, opinion is the only standard. And in the *Treatise*, he argues that the exercise of imagination is a decisive factor in a society's particular rules of justice.

In our discussion of Hume's theory of justice, we underlined the idea that justice is universal in human affairs, based as it is on the everpresent passion of interest. However, the interplay of various passions—including interest—compounded by a myriad of opinions and the fancy of the imagination, can produce what is shared by only some political orders, and not others. Furthermore, this interplay can produce elements of a political order acutely different from those which are to be found anywhere else. And although these elements may hold generally within that particular order, some of them may rarely make an appearance. There is, then, for Hume, a continuum of things political ranging from the universal to the particular. And whereas Hume's *A Treatise of Human Nature* is almost entirely at home on one side of this continuum, the *Essays, Moral, Political, and Literary* are likely to be found in the middle range or at the other end. And though the political essays *are* concerned to draw general and universal conclusions, they are just as solicitous of the particular features of various political worlds. So while the *Treatise* can proceed abstractly in pursuit of the universal, the political essays relish the pursuit of the concrete, and, accordingly, they embrace a style appropriate to that pursuit.

For Hume, the attempt to discover political principles—either universal or general—is the attempt to discover some constancy or regularity in the tangle of circumstances that is largely generated by the intertwining of passion, opinion, and imagination. The political philosopher must, then, examine the character of particular political worlds and inquire into how they are generated, maintained, and changed by a *melange* of various opinions and passions and the fancy of the imagination. On the surface this would seem to be an exclusively explanatory or descriptive enterprise, but it is not. To invoke a convenient idiom,

31. *Essays, Moral, Political, and Literary*, p. 97.

the political philosopher is engaged in the enterprise of reconstructing the *practices* of a political order. And it is Hume's considered judgment that these practices, which are facts about the world of things moral and political, have a normative character. Thus, the political principles at which the philosopher aims delineate the character of a political order, a character that in some respects is normative.

It is at this point in Hume's political philosophy that the argument of the *Treatise* which establishes a reformed version of the autonomy principle informs Hume's political essays. For his understanding of philosophy demands that in politics we begin with the provisional autonomy of the practices of our current political order. These practices can, of course, be criticized, but only in terms of other features of our practices: There is nothing else to which one can appeal.

The world of politics, for Hume, is a whirligig; there is no stasis. This is a world in which it is inappropriate to use the idiom of problem and solution, for this idiom, at home in mathematics, suggests the possibility of satisfying all claims and all interests. On Hume's account, this is illusory because the world of politics within civil society is animated fundamentally by competing interests. As part and parcel of this, Hume rejects the claim that we should view political decisions as a Manichaean choice between good and evil. In fact, he maintains throughout the body of his writings that it is impossible to separate the good from the ill in human affairs: Even our best choices are tainted.

Hume recognizes politics to be principally concerned with what to do next. For Hume, in large measure, this means pursuing the intimations that we find contained in our practices,[32] and our understanding of these intimations is greatly aided by those universal and general principles that we are able to discover, and even an ideal that we might imaginatively cull from our practices.[33] Central to the pursuit of intimations is the attempt to weigh the advantages and disadvantages that might result from the choices that we are considering. And, on his analysis, something counts as an advantage or disadvantage only

32. Here and elsewhere we believe there is a close affinity between many of the views of Hume and Michael Oakeshott. See Oakeshott's *Rationalism in Politics and Other Essays*, edited by Timothy Fuller, new and expanded edition (Indianapolis: Liberty Fund, 1991).

33. To provide this ideal is the goal of Hume's essay "Idea of a Perfect Commonwealth." See pp. 240–53.

in terms of our practices and what they intimate. For Hume, the activity of politics, then, involves careful judgment, and nothing in the world of politics *determines* what that judgment should be.

* * * *

Alongside Hume's own understanding of political principles lies a critique of principles run amok. This is a critique of the attempt to employ what he terms abstract speculative principles in political life, and he presents it most powerfully in "Of Parties in General," "Of Superstition and Enthusiasm," and "Of the Original Contract." In the first of these essays, Hume makes a distinction between three kinds of political parties: parties of interest, affection, and speculative principle. He judges parties of interest, such as parties based on the division between landed and trading interests, as the most reasonable; and parties of affection, such as attachment to a particular ruling family, though not quite as reasonable, are still understandable. However, parties based on speculative principle are absurdities and, remarkably, unique to modern times: "Parties from *principle*, especially abstract speculative principle, are known only to modern times, and are, perhaps, the most extraordinary and unaccountable *phenomenon* that has yet appeared in human affairs."[34]

Why are *philosophical* political parties unique to modern times? Hume's answer ultimately rests on a distinction between religion prior to the widespread appearance of philosophy in human affairs and religion after its appearance. Prephilosophic religion consisted "mostly of traditional tales and fictions, which may be different in every sect, without being contrary to each other; and even when they are contrary, every one adheres to the tradition of his own sect, without much reasoning or disputation." But Christianity arose when "philosophy was widely spread over the world." The teachers of this new sect were, therefore, "obliged to form a system of speculative opinions; to divide, with some accuracy, their articles of faith; and to explain, comment, confute, and defend with all the subtilty of argument and science."[35] Hume concludes this line of thought by remarking that, "Sects of philosophy, in the ancient world, were more zealous than parties of religion; but in modern times, parties of religion are more furious and

34. P. 161.
35. P. 163.

enraged than the most cruel factions that ever arose from interest and ambition."[36]

We must be careful to observe that it is the *philosophical* content of modern religion, due to the historic merger of philosophy and Christianity, that renders modern religion fanatical. And so Hume can say in *An Enquiry concerning Human Understanding* that "religion . . . is nothing but a species of philosophy."[37] Religion thus infused by philosophy furiously enters political life in the modern world and attempts to remake it by abstract speculative principles. Indeed, in the fifth and sixth volumes of *The History of England*, Hume attempts to delineate how religion so understood helped to bring about the English Civil War (1642–52). Nevertheless, Hume recognizes various appeals to abstract speculative principles that do not reflect a concern with religion at all. As "Of the Original Contract" makes clear, Hume regards social contract theory as one example of an appeal to abstract speculative principles, and his resistance to the idiom of rights points to natural rights theory as yet another example.

For Hume, the distinguishing trait of abstract speculative principles is that they make no difference in conduct, they are incapable of providing any guidance to conduct, that is, they are vacuous. Symptomatic of these principles is that they postulate an unreformed autonomy principle and putatively, on that basis, attempt to transcend the practices of common life. However, in the domain of politics, such principles rarely even hint at their vacuity; in fact, the defenders of social contract theory or natural rights theory are quick to recommend some course of conduct on the basis of their respective theories. Hume believes that what happens here is that the abstract speculative theorist has either knowingly or unknowingly smuggled in—without any fanfare—some favorite and thus privileged feature of common life to animate the theory.

Hume's critique aims at revealing speculative politics as a corrupt form of politics, one in which abstract speculative political principles can undermine a public order without being capable of offering anything in its stead. This critique surely cuts against the grain of many political philosophers who lament that politics is typically actuated by interest and passion and not by abstract speculative principles. Indeed, it is a pervasive view that the world of politics can in fact be guided

36. P. 163.

37. *An Enquiry Concerning Human Understanding*, p. 101.

by abstract speculative principles, thereby transfiguring politics from a debased into a noble enterprise: After all, it is such principles that many political philosophers see themselves as contributing to the world. Hume would not deny that politics can be a noble enterprise, but not under the direction of those who trade in abstract speculative political principles. What renders politics noble is not the alleged purity and goodness of abstract speculative principles, but legislators who, knowledgeable of their time and circumstances and moved by moderation, are able to effect a delicate balance amongst various competing interests and passions. Nobility can be achieved in politics not by rejecting the supposed underbelly of the human condition, but by accepting and perhaps even embracing it.

* * * *

The eighteenth century was not only a witness to but a participant in the quarrel between the ancients and the moderns. Central to this quarrel was the question whether the ancient world was superior to the modern—superior from the perspective of literature, morality, law, politics, and nearly everything else in the human domain. Hume was profoundly interested in this quarrel, especially as it concerned things moral and political. His political essays reveal a persistent effort to exhibit the superior achievement of the modern political world compared to that of the ancient. And Hume's remarks in this regard are important not only because of what they reveal about his judgment of the modern political situation itself but also because of the light they shed on what his judgment might be on many of our own quarrels.

Hume's reflections on the quarrel between the ancients and the moderns center on commerce and luxury. Indeed, at the core of Hume's defense of modern political life lies a quite different understanding of commerce and luxury from what he finds in the ancients. At the heart of the ethos of the ancient world, as Hume understands it, one discovers honor, glory, and martial virtue. And although the ancients may have believed that commerce and luxury were important in certain respects, they regarded them as suspect, if not contemptible, features of their own world. In the ancient vision of life, politics is most usually upheld as the highest and noblest form of human activity. Commerce and luxury, far from being inconsequential to human affairs, are understood as anathema to human excellence, enervating the souls of individuals and corrupting and weakening political orders.

Hume's critique of the ancient conception of politics and commerce is intertwined with his defense of modern political life. Since Hume believes that the prevalence of commercialism is one of the distinguishing traits of the modern world, his arguments in favor of modern political life are inseparable from his defense of the propriety of commercial societies. And Hume advances his most penetrating case for commercial societies and against the ancients in "Of Commerce," "Of Refinement in the Arts," and "Of the Populousness of Ancient Nations."[38]

"Of Commerce" inquires into the relationship between the opulence and extensive commerce of private individuals and the greatness of a state. Ultimately, Hume draws the general maxim that, as the former increase, so does the latter. However, before doing so, Hume carefully considers the cases of Rome and, especially, Sparta, two small ancient republics.[39] In these two instances, Hume believes, the greatness of the state depended upon the absence of commerce and luxury; indeed, Hume maintains that Sparta was more powerful than any modern state with the same number of people.

The historically commanding examples of Sparta and Rome tempt us into thinking that modern sovereigns can and should return to a policy predicated upon the ancient maxim that the greatness of the state depends upon a want of commerce and luxury. However, Hume contends that this is a temptation we should resist, and he points us in the direction of human nature as the ground for our resistance. Hume remarks that the "ancient policy was violent, and contrary to the more natural and usual course of things."[40] In the natural course of things, the human disposition is such that the absence of commerce and luxury leads to sloth and barbarity, which in turn lead to poverty and indolence; and the impoverishment and indolence of individuals do not support greatness of state. On the contrary, the possibility of

38. We have not included this latter essay in this collection. See *Essays, Moral, Political, and Literary*, pp. 377–464.

39. In part, "Of Commerce" is a contribution to the theory of republicanism insofar as it moves us to reflect on the relative merits of small-scale and large, extended republics. It is no coincidence that Hume's "Idea of a Perfect Commonwealth," an essay that portrays a large, extended republic as an ideal, originally appeared in the same collection of essays (*Political Discourses*, 1752) as "Of Commerce." Moreover, it is instructive that "Of Commerce" was the first essay in that collection and "Idea of a Perfect Commonwealth" was the last.

40. P. 223.

commerce and luxury provides for the development of industry, ambition, skill, and wealth—all things that support and further individual happiness and a powerful state. Only special circumstances made it possible for Sparta and Rome to flourish, Hume argues, circumstances that are almost impossible to replicate in the modern political situation. Furthermore, Hume claims, Rome did not fall into disorder because of the spread of commerce and luxury, as defenders of the ancients believe; instead the cause was an ill-modelled government and unlimited conquest.

"Of Refinement in the Arts" is Hume's most sustained effort at understanding the effects of luxury—that is, "great refinement in the gratification of the senses"[41]—upon the human condition. Here, as in many essays, Hume attempts to steer a middle course between two extremes: those who think that all luxury is innocent and those who think that it is entirely pernicious. Hume considers luxury in most instances to be more than merely innocent, since it has the effect of being beneficial both to individuals and the public. Indeed, in "Of Refinement in the Arts," Hume assigns himself the task of proving that "ages of refinement are both the happiest and most virtuous."[42] To prove this, Hume adduces three principal effects of an age of luxury. First, luxury encourages commerce, and when commerce thrives, individuals are constantly busy, enjoying both their labor and the fruit of their labor. As a result, "The mind acquires new vigour; enlarges its powers and faculties and by an assiduity in honest industry, both satisfies its natural appetites, and prevents the growth of unnatural ones, which commonly spring up, when nourished by ease and idleness."[43] Second, extensive commerce also produces advances in what Hume calls the mechanical arts, and, Hume claims, such advances commonly produce advances in the liberal arts. There is a "spirit of the age,"[44] which when animated by commerce and luxury, undermines lethargy, banishes ignorance, and thereby enables individuals to "enjoy the privilege of rational creatures, to think as well as to act, to cultivate the pleasures of the mind as well as those of the body."[45] Third, as the liberal arts advance, individuals become more sociable, wanting to

41. P. 230.
42. P. 231.
43. P. 232.
44. P. 232.
45. Pp. 232–33.

exchange ideas and reveal their wit and taste concerning all manner of things. And as individuals become more sociable, they become more humane: "So that, beside the improvements which they receive from knowledge and the liberal arts, it is impossible but they must feel an encrease of humanity from the very habit of conversing together, and contributing to each other's pleasure and entertainment."[46] Thus, Hume concludes that "*industry*, *knowledge*, and *humanity* are linked by an indissoluble chain" and are "peculiar to the more polished, and . . . more luxurious ages."[47]

For the ancients, commerce and luxury are at odds with the noble life of politics, for such a life requires citizens to immerse themselves in the activity of politics, and a concern for commerce and luxury deforms the soul and the political order. Hume does not dispute that politics can be a noble activity, although he locates nobility more in the activity of legislators than citizens. However, Hume provides a ringing and powerful endorsement for commerce and luxury, seeing them as momentous civilizing elements. For Hume, even if the activity of commerce is not the hallmark of nobility, it has a vastly more elevated place in the domain of things human than the ancients would have us understand: Commerce is not an activity for which one should apologize, and it can serve as an emblem for certain virtues.

Vitally connected with Hume's quarrel with the ancient conception of politics and commerce is his admiration of the liberty that he finds (in places) in the modern world, and his abhorrence of the slavery that he believes was rampant in the ancient.[48] Slavery is contemptible, despoiling both slave and master. Slavery violates an original demand of human nature, namely, liberty: "The heart of man delights in liberty: the very image of constraint is grievous to it. . . . For my part, I esteem liberty so invaluable a blessing in society, that whatever favours its progress and security, can scarce be too fondly cherished by every one who is a lover of human kind."[49] For Hume, human beings are fit for liberty: "It has also been found, as the experience of mankind increases, that the *people* are no such dangerous monster as they have been represented, and that it is in every respect better to guide them, like

46. P. 233.

47. P. 233.

48. See "Of the Populousness of Ancient Nations," in *Essays, Moral, Political, and Literary*, especially pp. 383–96.

49. *Essays, Moral, Political, and Literary*, p. 187; p. 259.

rational creatures, than to lead or drive them, like brute beasts."[50] Hume's embrace of liberty informs "Of Commerce" and "Of Refinement in the Arts," for in those essays, Hume signals the importance of freedom of trade, freedom of contract, freedom of association, and toleration.

However, Hume does not have any grand, speculative theory of liberty to offer. For Hume, there is no timeless object called liberty that can be discovered by autonomous reason. Rather, liberty refers to a complex set of conventions or practices that have been hammered out over time. Thus, one will not find in Hume a set of necessary and sufficient conditions for applying the term 'liberty.' Instead, he presents his understanding of liberty through a narrative of the evolution of the experience of liberty. For this reason, a study of Hume's *The History of England* is ultimately indispensable for appreciating Hume's understanding of liberty.

As Hume surveys the human world, his eyes constantly come to rest on the conditions necessary for civilizing human beings. Being civilized is not something that is given to human beings: It is something that has to be learned. And Hume's interest is less in how particular individuals learn to become civilized—Hume never wrote extensively on education—but more on how countries and societies achieve a civilized condition and escape from barbarism. Indeed, as we have noted, *The History of England* is a work on the English achievement in becoming civilized. "Of the Rise and Progress of the Arts and Sciences" is also extremely important in this regard. In that essay Hume describes the elements in a country's life that make it tend toward being civilized. And it should come as no surprise that at the top of his list are the development of the arts (including the polite arts), the sciences, commerce, liberty and law. These elements hint at what serves to distinguish the barbarous from the civilized society: A civilized society is marked by the disposition to engage in critical reflection about the conventions or practices that constitute the very fabric of a society. The arts and sciences of a country provide the tools for critical reflection, while commerce, liberty, and law provide the time and security.

Hume fully recognizes, however, that critical reflection can become distorted, leading to a *new* barbarism. Whereas a barbarous society is one in which critical reflection is relatively absent, the new barbarism is possible only within a civilized society. The new barbarians unsus-

50. P. 253.

pectingly remove critical reflection from its moorings in common life. As a result, the new barbarians acquire the strangest of maladies—an ignorance of the conventions or practices of their own world. This can be amusing, but also dangerous—especially when the new barbarians are philosophers. For the moral, social, political, and legal conventions or practices of a society rest on opinion; and opinion can be deformed by false or wrongheaded critical reflection. In this manner, the critical reflection that constitutes and generates a civilized order can be a destroyer of the order it helped to create.

* * * *

The most important political writings have a teaching that bears on times and places other than the author's own. Even when Hume's political writings are most obviously a response to local circumstances—for example, "Of the Protestant Succession"—they enunciate a teaching germane to circumstances quite different from Hume's own. As one reads and reflects on the writings in this collection, it is important to ask whether, in fact, they improve and cultivate our understanding of our own time and place. We hope the reader will share our belief that Hume's political writings clarify our own circumstances as few others can, and are thus worthy of serious study.

Editors' Note

The texts used in this edition have been provided to us in electronic files by InteLex Corporation. The selection from *A Treatise of Human Nature* is a corrected version of the edition in the Everyman's Library series (1911). The spelling and the punctuation have been modernized (for example, from " 'tis" to "it is"). This text was checked and corrected against the 1886 edition of the *Treatise* edited by T. H. Green and T. H. Grose and published in *The Philosophical Works of David Hume.* The selection from *An Enquiry concerning the Principles of Morals* is a corrected version of the 1898 Green and Grose edition. The text of the essays from *Essays, Moral, Political, and Literary* is also based on the 1898 Green and Grose edition; these essays were corrected against the edition of *Essays, Moral, Political, and Literary* which Eugene F. Miller edited for Liberty Fund, Inc. (revised edition, 1987).

We have included nineteen of Hume's forty-nine essays in this edition. Seventeen of these nineteen appeared several times each in various collections of his writings during his lifetime. "Of Moral Prejudice" and "Of the Origin of Government" were printed only once in editions supervised by Hume; the former appeared in 1742 and the latter in the posthumous 1777 edition of the *Essays*, the final edition which Hume prepared for publication. Hume continually revised his essays, thus often creating variations in an essay from one published version of it to the next. In following Green and Grose and Miller, we are using the text from the 1777 edition for the above-mentioned seventeen essays; we are also including several of the significant variations from earlier editions collated by Green and Grose. These variations are indicated in the text by superscript lowercase letters, and the variations are found in the back of the text.

Unless otherwise noted, references to and translations of Greek and Latin texts are drawn from the relevant volume in the Loeb Classical Library, published by Harvard University Press. Citations to Hume's writings in the editors' footnotes are given by title and page number; the editions we have used will be found in the selected bibliography.

The editors have provided extensive bracketed material in the footnotes; footnotes and parts of footnotes that are not bracketed are Hume's.

We are indebted to many people in preparing this edition of Hume's political writings. John Danford, Gilbert Goldman, Charles H. Hamilton, Lisa Kaderabek, and Inger Thomsen made helpful suggestions about the introduction; Martine Brownley, Alan Houston, Charles McCracken, and Michael Zuckert kindly answered queries about particular historical matters; Henry Clark was generous enough to comment on all of the editors' footnotes; an anonymous reader for Hackett offered very useful advice about the introduction and the editors' footnotes; Jack Cella of the Seminary Co-op Bookstore and Brad Jonas of Powell's Bookstore were magical in finding books that we needed; and we received invaluable aid from Eugene F. Miller's work on Hume's *Essays*. Also, Stuart D. Warner would like to thank Roosevelt University for providing a Research Leave in the spring of 1993 during which some of the work on this volume was completed.

We dedicate this volume to J. Charles King, a patron and friend of Hume letters.

Selected Bibliography

Editions of Hume's works cited:

A Treatise of Human Nature. Edited by L. A. Selby-Bigge. Second edition by P. H. Nidditch. Oxford: Clarendon Press, 1978.

The Letters of David Hume. Edited by J.Y.T. Greig. 2 vols. Oxford: Clarendon Press, 1932.

"My Own Life." In *The Letters of David Hume*.

The Philosophical Works of David Hume. Edited by T. H. Green and T. H. Grose. New edition. 4 vols. London: Longmans, Green and Co., 1882.

Essays, Moral, Political, and Literary. Edited by Eugene F. Miller. Revised edition. Indianapolis: Liberty Fund, Inc., 1987.

An Enquiry Concerning Human Understanding. Edited by Eric Steinberg. Revised edition. Indianapolis: Hackett Publishing, 1993.

An Enquiry Concerning the Principles of Morals. Edited by J. B. Schneewind. Indianapolis: Hackett Publishing, 1983.

The History of England, from the Invasion of Julius Caesar to The Revolution of 1688. Edited by William B. Todd. 6 vols. Indianapolis: Liberty Classics, 1983.

Writings on Economics. Edited by Eugene Rotwein. Edinburgh: Nelson, 1955.

Selected Secondary Writings:

Baier, Annette C. *A Progress of Sentiments*. Cambridge: Harvard University Press, 1991.

Capaldi, Nicholas, and Donald W. Livingston, editors. *Liberty in Hume's History of England*. Dordrecht: Kluwer Academic Publishers, 1990.

Danford, John W. *David Hume and the Problem of Reason*. New Haven: Yale University Press, 1990.

Forbes, Duncan. *Hume's Philosophical Politics*. Cambridge: Cambridge University Press, 1975.

Livingston, Donald W. *Hume's Philosophy of Common Life*. Chicago: University of Chicago Press, 1984.

Livingston, Donald W., and Marie Martin, editors. *Hume as Philosopher of Society, Politics and History*. Rochester: University of Rochester Press, 1991.

Miller, David. *Philosophy and Ideology in Hume's Political Thought*. Oxford: Clarendon Press, 1981.

Phillipson, Nicholas. *Hume*. New York: St. Martin's Press, 1989.

Stewart, John B. *Opinion and Reform in Hume's Political Philosophy*. Princeton: Princeton University Press, 1992.

Warner, Stuart D., editor. *Reason Papers*. No. 15, Summer 1990. *Essays to Commemorate the 250th Anniversary of David Hume's A Treatise of Human Nature*.

Whelan, Frederick G. *Order and Artifice in Hume's Political Philosophy*. Princeton: Princeton University Press, 1985.

Part I
Justice and the Structure of Civil Society

From *A Treatise of Human Nature,* Bk. III, Pt. II

Book III
Of Morals

Part II
Of Justice and Injustice

Section I
Justice, Whether a Natural or Artificial Virtue?

I have already hinted, that our sense of every kind of virtue is not natural;[1] but that there are some virtues that produce pleasure and approbation by means of an artifice or contrivance, which arises from the circumstances and necessity of mankind. Of this kind I assert *justice* to be; and shall endeavour to defend this opinion by a short, and, I hope, convincing argument, before I examine the nature of the artifice, from which the sense of that virtue is derived.

It is evident that, when we praise any actions, we regard only the motives that produced them, and consider the actions as signs or indications of certain principles in the mind and temper. The external performance has no merit. We must look within to find the moral quality. This we cannot do directly; and therefore fix our attention on actions, as on external signs. But these actions are still considered as

1. [In the preceding section of the *Treatise* (pp. 473–76), Hume raises the question whether all virtue is natural in the context of distinguishing three senses of the term 'nature': nature as distinguished from miracles; nature as distinguished from the rare and unusual; and nature as distinguished from artifice. Also, Hume discusses the identification of the natural with the end of man in a letter of September 17, 1739, written to Francis Hutcheson, an important Scottish Enlightenment thinker (despite his being born in Ireland). See *The Letters of David Hume*, vol. I., p. 33. Also, see Arthur O. Lovejoy and George Boas, *Primitivism and Related Ideas in Antiquity* (Baltimore: Johns Hopkins Press, 1935), pp. 447–56, where Lovejoy identifies sixty-six different meanings of 'nature' that had some philosophical and literary currency in the Ancient and Modern worlds.]

signs; and the ultimate object of our praise and approbation is the motive that produced them.

After the same manner, when we require any action, or blame a person for not performing it, we always suppose that one in that situation should be influenced by the proper motive of that action, and we esteem it vicious in him to be regardless of it. If we find, upon enquiry, that the virtuous motive was still powerful over his breast, though checked in its operation by some circumstances unknown to us, we retract our blame, and have the same esteem for him, as if he had actually performed the action which we require of him.

It appears, therefore, that all virtuous actions derive their merit only from virtuous motives, and are considered merely as signs of those motives. From this principle I conclude, that the first virtuous motive which bestows a merit on any action, can never be a regard to the virtue of that action, but must be some other natural motive or principle. To suppose that the mere regard to the virtue of the action, may be the first motive which produced the action, and rendered it virtuous, is to reason in a circle. Before we can have such a regard, the action must be really virtuous; and this virtue must be derived from some virtuous motive: and, consequently, the virtuous motive must be different from the regard to the virtue of the action. A virtuous motive is requisite to render an action virtuous. An action must be virtuous before we can have a regard to its virtue. Some virtuous motive, therefore, must be antecedent to that regard.

Nor is this merely a metaphysical subtilty; but enters into all our reasonings in common life, though perhaps we may not be able to place it in such distinct philosophical terms. We blame a father for neglecting his child. Why? because it shews a want of natural affection, which is the duty of every parent. Were not natural affection a duty, the care of children could not be a duty; and it were impossible we could have the duty in our eye in the attention we give to our offspring. In this case, therefore, all men suppose a motive to the action distinct from a sense of duty.

Here is a man that does many benevolent actions; relieves the distressed, comforts the afflicted, and extends his bounty even to the greatest strangers. No character can be more amiable and virtuous. We regard these actions as proofs of the greatest humanity. This humanity bestows a merit on the actions. A regard to this merit is, therefore, a secondary consideration, and derived from the antecedent principle of humanity, which is meritorious and laudable.

In short, it may be established as an undoubted maxim, *that no action can be virtuous, or morally good, unless there be in human nature some motive to produce it distinct from the sense of its morality.*[2]

But may not the sense of morality or duty produce an action, without any other motive? I answer, it may: but this is no objection to the present doctrine. When any virtuous motive or principle is common in human nature, a person who feels his heart devoid of that motive, may hate himself upon that account, and may perform the action without the motive, from a certain sense of duty, in order to acquire, by practice, that virtuous principle, or at least to disguise to himself, as much as possible, his want of it. A man that really feels no gratitude in his temper, is still pleased to perform grateful actions, and thinks he has, by that means, fulfilled his duty. Actions are at first only considered as signs of motives: but it is usual, in this case, as in all others, to fix our attention on the signs, and neglect, in some measure, the thing signified. But though, on some occasions, a person may perform an action merely out of regard to its moral obligation, yet still this supposes in human nature some distinct principles, which are capable of producing the action, and whose moral beauty renders the action meritorious.

Now, to apply all this to the present case; I suppose a person to have lent me a sum of money, on condition that it be restored in a few days; and also suppose, that after the expiration of the term agreed on, he demands the sum: I ask, *What reason or motive have I to restore the money?* It will perhaps be said, that my regard to justice, and abhorrence of villainy and knavery, are sufficient reasons for me, if I have the least grain of honesty, or sense of duty and obligation. And this answer, no doubt, is just and satisfactory to man in his civilized state, and when trained up according to a certain discipline and education. But in his rude and more natural condition, if you are pleased to call such a condition natural, this answer would be rejected as perfectly unintelligible and sophistical. For one in that situation would immediately ask you, *Wherein consists this honesty and justice, which you find in restoring a loan, and abstaining from the property of others?* It does not surely lie in the external action. It must, therefore, be placed in the motive from which the external action is derived. This motive can never be a regard to the honesty of the action. For it is a plain fallacy

2. [Hume is following the argument of Cicero (106–43 B.C.) See Cicero's *De Finibus Bonorum ed Malorum*, bk. IV.]

to say, that a virtuous motive is requisite to render an action honest, and, at the same time, that a regard to the honesty is the motive of the action. We can never have a regard to the virtue of an action, unless the action be antecedently virtuous. No action can be virtuous, but so far as it proceeds from a virtuous motive. A virtuous motive, therefore, must precede the regard to the virtue; and it is impossible that the virtuous motive and the regard to the virtue can be the same.

It is requisite, then, to find some motive to acts of justice and honesty, distinct from our regard to the honesty; and in this lies the great difficulty. For should we say, that a concern for our private interest or reputation, is the legitimate motive to all honest actions: it would follow that wherever that concern ceases, honesty can no longer have place. But it is certain that self-love, when it acts at its liberty, instead of engaging us to honest actions, is the source of all injustice and violence; nor can a man ever correct those vices, without correcting and restraining the *natural* movements of that appetite.

But should it be affirmed that the reason or motive of such actions is the *regard to public interest,* to which nothing is more contrary than examples of injustice and dishonesty; should this be said, I would propose the three following considerations as worthy of our attention. *First,* Public interest is not naturally attached to the observation of the rules of justice; but is only connected with it, after an artificial convention for the establishment of these rules, as shall be shewn more at large hereafter. *Secondly,* If we suppose that the loan was secret, and that it is necessary for the interest of the person, that the money be restored in the same manner (as when the lender would conceal his riches), in that case the example ceases, and the public is no longer interested in the actions of the borrower; though I suppose there is no moralist who will affirm that the duty and obligation ceases. *Thirdly,* Experience sufficiently proves that men, in the ordinary conduct of life, look not so far as the public interest, when they pay their creditors, perform their promises, and abstain from theft, and robbery, and injustice of every kind. That is a motive too remote and too sublime to affect the generality of mankind, and operate with any force in actions so contrary to private interest as are frequently those of justice and common honesty.

In general, it may be affirmed, that there is no such passion in human minds as the love of mankind, merely as such, independent of personal qualities, of services, or of relation to ourself. It is true, there is no human, and indeed no sensible creature, whose happiness or misery does not, in some measure, affect us, when brought near to us, and represented in lively colours: but this proceeds merely from sympathy, and is no proof of such an universal affection to mankind, since this concern extends itself beyond our own species. An affection betwixt the sexes is a passion evidently implanted in human nature; and this passion not only appears in its peculiar symptoms, but also in inflaming every other principle of affection, and raising a stronger love from beauty, wit, kindness, than what would otherwise flow from them. Were there an universal love among all human creatures, it would appear after the same manner. Any degree of a good quality would cause a stronger affection than the same degree of a bad quality would cause hatred; contrary to what we find by experience. Men's tempers are different, and some have a propensity to the tender, and others to the rougher affections: but in the main, we may affirm, that man in general, or human nature, is nothing but the object both of love and hatred, and requires some other cause, which, by a double relation of impressions and ideas, may excite these passions. In vain would we endeavour to elude this hypothesis. There are no phenomena that point out any such kind affection to men, independent of their merit, and every other circumstance. We love company in general; but it is as we love any other amusement. An Englishman in Italy is a friend; a European in China; and perhaps a man would be beloved as such, were we to meet him in the moon. But this proceeds only from the relation to ourselves; which in these cases gathers force by being confined to a few persons.

If public benevolence, therefore, or a regard to the interests of mankind, cannot be the original motive to justice, much less can *private benevolence, or a regard to the interests of the party concerned,* be this motive. For what if he be my enemy, and has given me just cause to hate him? What if he be a vicious man, and deserves the hatred of all mankind? What if he be a miser, and can make no use of what I would deprive him of? What if he be a profligate debauchee, and would rather receive harm than benefit from large possessions? What if I be in necessity, and have urgent motives to acquire something to my family? In all these cases, the original motive to justice would fail; and consequently the justice itself, and along with it all property, right, and obligation.

A rich man lies under a moral obligation to communicate to those in necessity a share of his superfluities. Were private benevolence the original motive to justice a man would not be obliged to leave others in the possession of more than he is obliged to give them. At least, the difference would be very inconsiderable. Men generally fix their affections more on what they are possessed of, than on what they never enjoyed: for this reason, it would be greater cruelty to dispossess a man of any thing, than not to give it him. But who will assert that this is the only foundation of justice?

Besides, we must consider, that the chief reason why men attach themselves so much to their possessions, is, that they consider them as their property, and as secured to them inviolably by the laws of society. But this is a secondary consideration, and dependent on the preceding notions of justice and property.

A man's property is supposed to be fenced against every mortal, in every possible case. But private benevolence is, and ought to be, weaker in some persons than in others: and in many, or indeed in most persons, must absolutely fail. Private benevolence, therefore, is not the original motive of justice.

From all this it follows, that we have no real or universal motive for observing the laws of equity, but the very equity and merit of that observance; and as no action can be equitable or meritorious, where it cannot arise from some separate motive, there is here an evident sophistry and reasoning in a circle. Unless, therefore, we will allow that nature has established a sophistry, and rendered it necessary and unavoidable, we must allow, that the sense of justice and injustice is not derived from nature, but arises artificially, though necessarily, from education and human conventions.

I shall add, as a corollary to this reasoning, that since no action can be laudable or blamable, without some motives or impelling passions, distinct from the sense of morals, these distinct passions must have a great influence on that sense. It is according to their general force in human nature that we blame or praise. In judging of the beauty of animal bodies, we always carry in our eye the economy of a certain species; and where the limbs and features observe that proportion which is common to the species, we pronounce them handsome and beautiful. In like manner, we always consider the *natural* and *usual* force of the passions, when we determine concerning vice and virtue; and if the passions depart very much from the common measures on either side, they are always disapproved as vicious. A man naturally loves his children better than his nephews, his nephews better than his cousins, his cousins better than strangers, where every thing else is equal. Hence arise our common measures of duty, in preferring the one to the other. Our sense of duty always follows the common and natural course of our passions.

To avoid giving offence, I must here observe, that when I deny justice to be a natural virtue, I make use of the word *natural*, only as opposed to *artificial*. In another sense of the word, as no principle of the human mind is more natural than a sense of virtue, so no virtue is more natural than justice. Mankind is an inventive species; and where an invention is obvious and absolutely necessary, it may as properly be said to be natural as any thing that proceeds immediately from original principles, without the intervention of thought or reflection. Though the rules of justice be *artificial*, they are not *arbitrary*. Nor is the expression improper to call them *Laws of Nature;* if by natural we understand what is common to any species, or even if we confine it to mean what is inseparable from the species.[3]

Section II: *Of the Origin of Justice and Property*

We now proceed to examine two questions, viz. *concerning the manner in which the rules of justice are established by the artifice of men;* and *concerning the reasons which determine us to attribute to the observance or neglect of these rules a moral beauty and deformity.* These questions will appear afterwards to be distinct. We shall begin with the former.

Of all the animals with which this globe is peopled, there is none towards whom nature seems, at first sight, to have exercised more cruelty than towards man, in the numberless wants and necessities with which she has loaded him, and in the slender means which she affords to the relieving these necessities. In other creatures, these two particulars generally compensate each other. If we consider the lion as a voracious and carnivorous animal, we shall easily discover him to be very necessitous; but if we turn our eye to his make and temper, his agility, his courage, his arms, and his force, we shall find that his advantages hold proportion with his wants. The sheep and ox are deprived of all these advantages; but their appetites are moderate, and their food is of easy purchase. In man alone this unnatural conjunction of infirmity and of necessity may be observed in its greatest perfection. Not only the food which is required for his sustenance flies his search and approach, or at least requires his labour to be produced, but he must be possessed of cloaths and lodging to defend him against the injuries of the weather; though, to consider him only in himself, he is

3. [See n. 1.]

provided neither with arms, nor force, nor other natural abilities which are in any degree answerable to so many necessities.

It is by society alone he is able to supply his defects, and raise himself up to an equality with his fellow-creatures, and even acquire a superiority above them. By society all his infirmities are compensated; and though in that situation his wants multiply every moment upon him, yet his abilities are still more augmented, and leave him in every respect more satisfied and happy than it is possible for him, in his savage and solitary condition, ever to become. When every individual person labours apart, and only for himself, his force is too small to execute any considerable work; his labour being employed in supplying all his different necessities, he never attains a perfection in any particular art; and as his force and success are not at all times equal, the least failure in either of these particulars must be attended with inevitable ruin and misery. Society provides a remedy for these three inconveniences. By the conjunction of forces, our power is augmented; by the partition of employments, our ability encreases; and by mutual succour, we are less exposed to fortune and accidents. It is by this additional *force, ability,* and *security,* that society becomes advantageous.

But, in order to form society, it is requisite not only that it be advantageous, but also that men be sensible of these advantages; and it is impossible, in their wild uncultivated state, that by study and reflection alone they should ever be able to attain this knowledge. Most fortunately, therefore, there is conjoined to those necessities, whose remedies are remote and obscure, another necessity, which, having a present and more obvious remedy, may justly be regarded as the first and original principle of human society. This necessity is no other than that natural appetite betwixt the sexes, which unites them together, and preserves their union, till a new tie takes place in their concern for their common offspring. This new concern becomes also a principle of union betwixt the parents and offspring, and forms a more numerous society, where the parents govern by the advantage of their superior strength and wisdom, and at the same time are restrained in the exercise of their authority by that natural affection which they bear their children. In a little time, custom and habit, operating on the tender minds of the children, makes them sensible of the advantages which they may reap from society, as well as fashions them by degrees for it, by rubbing off those rough corners and untoward affections which prevent their coalition.

For it must be confessed, that however the circumstances of human nature may render a union necessary, and however those passions of lust and natural affection may seem to render it unavoidable, yet there are other particulars in our *natural temper*, and in our *outward circumstances,* which are very incommodious, and are even contrary to the requisite conjunction. Among the former we may justly esteem our *selfishness* to be the most considerable. I am sensible that, generally speaking, the representations of this quality have been carried much too far; and that the descriptions which certain philosophers delight so much to form of mankind in this particular, are as wide of nature as any accounts of monsters which we meet with in fables and romances. So far from thinking that men have no affection for any thing beyond themselves, I am of opinion that, though it be rare to meet with one who loves any single person better than himself, yet it is as rare to meet with one in whom all the kind affections, taken together, do not overbalance all the selfish. Consult common experience; do you not see, that though the whole expence of the family be generally under the direction of the master of it, yet there are few that do not bestow the largest part of their fortunes on the pleasures of their wives and the education of their children, reserving the smallest portion for their own proper use and entertainment. This is what we may observe concerning such as have those endearing ties; and may presume, that the case would be the same with others, were they placed in a like situation.

But though this generosity must be acknowledged to the honour of human nature, we may at the same time remark, that so noble an affection, instead of fitting men for large societies, is almost as contrary to them as the most narrow selfishness. For while each person loves himself better than any other single person, and in his love to others bears the greatest affection to his relations and acquaintance, this must necessarily produce an opposition of passions, and a consequent opposition of actions, which cannot but be dangerous to the new-established union.

It is, however, worth while to remark, that this contrariety of passions would be attended with but small danger, did it not concur with a peculiarity in our *outward circumstances,* which affords it an opportunity of exerting itself. There are three different species of goods which we are possessed of; the internal satisfaction of our minds; the external advantages of our body; and the enjoyment of such possessions as we have acquired by our industry and good fortune. We are perfectly secure in the enjoyment of the first. The second may be ravished from us, but can be of no advantage to him who deprives us of them. The last only are both exposed to the violence of others, and may be transferred without suffering any loss or alteration; while at the same time there is not a sufficient quantity of them to supply every one's desires and necessities. As the improvement, therefore, of these goods is the chief advantage of society, so the *instability* of their possession, along with their *scarcity,* is the chief impediment.

In vain should we expect to find, in *uncultivated nature,* a remedy to this inconvenience; or hope for any inartificial principle of the human mind which might control those partial affections, and make us overcome the temptations arising from our circumstances. The idea of justice can never serve to this purpose, or be taken for a natural principle, capable of inspiring men with an equitable conduct towards each other. That virtue, as it is now understood, would never have been dreamed of among rude and savage men. For the notion of injury or injustice implies an immorality or vice committed against some other person: And as every immorality is derived from some defect or unsoundness of the passions, and as this defect must be judged of, in a great measure, from the ordinary course of nature in the constitution of the mind, it will be easy to know whether we be guilty of any immorality with regard to others, by considering the natural and usual force of those several affections which are directed towards them. Now, it appears that, in the original frame of our mind, our strongest attention is confined to ourselves; our next is extended to our relations and acquaintance; and it is only the weakest which reaches to strangers and indifferent persons. This partiality, then, and unequal affection, must not only have an influence on our behaviour and conduct in society, but even on our ideas of vice and virtue; so as to make us regard any remarkable transgression of such a degree of partiality, either by too great an enlargement or contraction of the affections, as vicious and immoral. This we may observe in our common judgments concerning actions, where we blame a person who either centers all his affections in his family, or is so regardless of them as, in any opposition of interest, to give the preference to a stranger or mere chance acquaintance. From all which it follows, that our natural uncultivated ideas of morality, instead of providing a remedy for the partiality of our affections, do rather conform themselves to that partiality, and give it an additional force and influence.

The remedy, then, is not derived from nature, but from *artifice;* or, more properly speaking, nature provides a remedy, in the judgment and understanding, for what is irregular and incommodious in the affections. For when men, from their early education in society, have become sensible of the infinite advantages that result from it, and have besides acquired a new affection to company and conversation, and when they have observed that the principal disturbance in society arises from those goods, which we call external, and from their looseness and easy transition from one person to another, they must seek for a remedy, by putting these goods, as far as possible, on the same footing with the fixed and constant advantages of the mind and body. This can be done after no other manner, than by a convention entered into by all the members of the society to bestow stability on the possession of those external goods, and leave every one in the peaceable enjoyment of what he may acquire by his fortune and industry. By this means every one knows what he may safely possess; and the passions are restrained in their partial and contradictory motions. Nor is such a restraint contrary to these passions; for, if so, it could never be entered into nor maintained; but it is only contrary to their heedless and impetuous movement. Instead of departing from our own interest, or from that of our nearest friends, by abstaining from the possessions of others, we cannot better consult both these interests than by such a convention; because it is by that means we maintain society, which is so necessary to their well-being and subsistence, as well as to our own.

This convention is not of the nature of a *promise;* for even promises themselves, as we shall see afterwards, arise from human conventions. It is only a general sense of common interest; which sense all the members of the society express to one another, and which induces them to regulate their conduct by certain rules. I observe, that it will be for my interest to leave another in the possession of his goods, *provided* he will act in the same manner with regard to me. He is sensible of a like interest in the regulation of his conduct. When this common sense of interest is mutually expressed, and is known to both, it produces a suitable resolution and behaviour. And this may properly enough be called a convention or agreement betwixt us, though without the interposition of a promise; since the actions of each of us have a reference to those of the other, and are performed upon the supposition that something is to be performed on the other part. Two men who pull the oars of a boat, do it by an agreement or convention, though they have never given promises to each other. Nor is the rule concerning the stability of possession the less derived from human conventions, that it arises gradually, and acquires force by a slow progression, and by our repeated experience of the inconveniences of transgressing it. On the contrary, this experience assures us still more, that the sense of interest has become common to all our fellows, and gives us a confidence of the future regularity of their conduct; and it is only on the expectation of this, that our moderation and abstinence are founded. In like manner are languages gradually established by human conventions, without any promise. In like manner do gold and silver become the common measures of exchange, and are esteemed sufficient payment for what is of a hundred times their value.

After this convention, concerning abstinence from the possessions of others, is entered into, and every one has acquired a stability in his possessions, there immediately arise the ideas of justice and injustice; as also those of *property, right,* and *obligation.* The latter are altogether unintelligible, without first understanding the former. Our property is nothing but those goods, whose constant possession is established by the laws of society; that is, by the laws of justice. Those, therefore, who make use of the words *property,* or *right,* or *obligation,* before they have explained the origin of justice, or even make use of them in that explication, are guilty of a very gross fallacy, and can never reason upon any solid foundation. A man's property is some object related to him. This relation is not natural, but moral, and founded on justice. It is very preposterous, therefore, to imagine that we can have any idea of property, without fully comprehending the nature of justice, and shewing its origin in the artifice and contrivance of men. The origin of justice explains that of property. The same artifice gives rise to both. As our first and most natural sentiment of morals is founded on the nature of our passions, and gives the preference to ourselves and friends above strangers, it is impossible there can be naturally any such thing as a fixed right or property, while the opposite passions of men impel them in contrary directions, and are not restrained by any convention or agreement.

No one can doubt that the convention for the distinction of property, and for the stability of possession, is of all circumstances the most necessary to the establishment of human society, and that, after the agreement for the fixing and observing of this rule, there remains little or nothing to be done towards settling a perfect harmony and concord. All the other passions, beside this of interest, are either easily restrained, or are not of such pernicious consequence when indulged. *Vanity* is rather to be esteemed a social passion, and a bond of union among men. *Pity* and *love* are to be considered in the same light. And as to *envy* and *revenge*, though pernicious, they operate only by intervals, and are directed against particular persons, whom we consider as our superiors or enemies. This avidity alone, of acquiring goods and possessions for ourselves and our nearest friends, is insatiable, perpetual, universal, and directly destructive of society. There scarce is any one who is not actuated by it; and there is no one who has not reason to fear from it, when it acts without any restraint, and gives way to its first and most natural movements. So that, upon the whole, we are to esteem the difficulties in the establishment of society to be greater or less, according to those we encounter in regulating and restraining this passion.

It is certain, that no affection of the human mind has both a sufficient force and a proper direction to counterbalance the love of gain, and render men fit members of society, by making them abstain from the possessions of others. Benevolence to strangers is too weak for this purpose; and as to the other passions, they rather inflame this avidity, when we observe, that the larger our possessions are, the more ability we have of gratifying all our appetites. There is no passion, therefore, capable of controlling the interested affection, but the very affection itself, by an alteration of its direction. Now, this alteration must necessarily take place upon the least reflection, since it is evident that the passion is much better satisfied by its restraint than by its liberty, and that, in preserving society, we make much greater advances in the acquiring possessions, than in the solitary and forlorn condition which must follow upon violence and an universal licence. The question, therefore, concerning the wickedness or goodness of human nature, enters not in the least into that other question concerning the origin of society; nor is there any thing to be considered but the degrees of men's sagacity or folly. For whether the passion of self-interest be esteemed vicious or virtuous, it is all a case, since itself alone restrains it; so that if it be virtuous, men become social by their virtue; if vicious, their vice has the same effect.

Now, as it is by establishing the rule for the stability of possession that this passion restrains itself, if that rule be very abstruse and of difficult invention, society must be esteemed in a manner accidental, and the effect of many ages. But if it be found that nothing can be more simple and obvious than that rule; that every parent, in order to preserve peace among his children, must establish it; and that these first rudiments of justice must every day be improved, as the society enlarges: if all this appear evident, as it certainly must, we may conclude that it is utterly impossible for men to remain any considerable time in that savage condition which precedes society, but that his very first state and situation may justly be esteemed social. This, however, hinders not but that philosophers may, if they please, extend their reasoning to the supposed *state of nature;* provided they allow it to be a mere philosophical fiction, which never had, and never could have, any reality. Human nature being composed of two principal parts, which are requisite in all its actions, the affections and understanding, it is certain that the blind motions of the former, without the direction of the latter, incapacitate men for society; and it may be allowed us to consider separately the effects that result from the separate operations of these two component parts of the mind. The same liberty may be permitted to moral, which is allowed to natural philosophers; and it is very usual with the latter to consider any motion as compounded and consisting of two parts separate from each other, though at the same time they acknowledge it to be in itself uncompounded and inseparable.

This *state of nature,* therefore, is to be regarded as a mere fiction, not unlike that of the *golden age* which poets have invented; only with this difference, that the former is described as full of war, violence, and injustice; whereas the latter is painted out to us as the most charming and most peaceable condition that can possibly be imagined. The seasons, in that first age of nature, were so temperate, if we may believe the poets, that there was no necessity for men to provide themselves with cloaths and houses as a security against the violence of heat and cold. The rivers flowed with wine and milk; the oaks yielded honey; and nature spontaneously produced her greatest delicacies. Nor were these the chief advantages of that happy age. The storms and tempests were not alone removed from nature; but those more furious tempests were unknown to human breasts, which now cause such uproar, and engender such confusion. Avarice, ambition, cruelty, selfishness, were never heard of: cordial affection, compassion, sympathy, were the only movements with which the human mind was yet acquainted. Even the distinction of *mine* and *thine* was banished from that happy race of mortals, and carried with them the very notions of property, and obligation, justice and injustice.

This, no doubt, is to be regarded as an idle fiction; but yet deserves our attention, because nothing can more evidently shew the origin of those virtues, which are the subjects of our present enquiry. I have already observed, that justice takes its rise from human conventions; and that these are intended as a remedy to some inconveniences, which proceed from the concurrence of certain *qualities* of the human mind with the *situation* of external objects. The qualities of the mind are *selfishness* and *limited generosity:* and the situation of external objects is their *easy change,* joined to their *scarcity* in comparison of the wants and desires of men. But however philosophers may have been bewildered in those speculations, poets have been guided more infallibly, by a certain taste or common instinct, which, in most kinds of reasoning, goes further than any of that art and philosophy with which we have been yet acquainted. They easily perceived, if every man had a tender regard for another, or if nature supplied abundantly all our wants and desires, that the jealousy of interest, which justice supposes, could no longer have place; nor would there be any occasion for those distinctions and limits of property and possession, which at present are in use among mankind. Encrease to a sufficient degree the benevolence of men, or the bounty of nature, and you render justice useless, by supplying its place with much nobler virtues, and more valuable blessings. The selfishness of men is animated by the few possessions we have, in proportion to our wants; and it is to restrain this selfishness, that men have been obliged to separate themselves from the community, and to distinguish betwixt their own goods and those of others.

Nor need we have recourse to the fictions of poets to learn this; but, beside the reason of the thing, may discover the same truth by common experience and observation. It is easy to remark, that a cordial affection renders all things common among friends; and that married people, in particular, mutually lose their property, and are unacquainted with the mine and thine, which are so necessary, and yet cause such disturbance in human society. The same effect arises from any alteration in the circumstances of mankind; as when there is such a plenty of any thing as satisfies all the desires of men: in which case the distinction of property is entirely lost, and every thing remains in common. This we may observe with regard to air and water, though the most valuable of all external objects; and may easily conclude, that if men were supplied with every thing in the same abundance, or if *every one* had the same affection and tender regard for *every one* as for himself, justice and injustice would be equally unknown among mankind.

Here then is a proposition, which, I think, may be regarded as certain, *that it is only from the selfishness and confined generosity of men, along with the scanty provision nature has made for his wants, that justice derives its origin.* If we look backward we shall find, that this proposition bestows an additional force on some of those observations which we have already made on this subject.

First, We may conclude from it, that a regard to public interest, or a strong extensive benevolence, is not our first and original motive for the observation of the rules of justice; since it is allowed, that if men were endowed with such a benevolence, these rules would never have been dreamed of.

Secondly, We may conclude from the same principle, that the sense of justice is not founded on reason, or on the discovery of certain connexions and relations of ideas, which are eternal, immutable, and universally obligatory. For since it is confessed, that such an alteration as that above mentioned, in the temper and circumstances of mankind, would entirely alter our duties and obligations, it is necessary upon the common system, *that the sense of virtue is derived from reason,* to shew the change which this must produce in the relations and ideas. But it is evident, that the only cause why the extensive generosity of man, and the perfect abundance of every thing, would destroy the very idea of justice, is, because they render it useless; and that, on the other hand, his confined benevolence, and his necessitous condition, give rise to that virtue, only by making it requisite to the public interest, and to that of every individual. It was therefore a concern for our own and the public interest which made us establish the laws of justice; and nothing can be more certain, than that it is not any relation of ideas which gives us this concern, but our impressions and sentiments, without which every thing in nature is perfectly indifferent to us, and can never in the least affect us. The sense of justice, therefore, is not founded on our ideas, but on our impressions.[4]

Thirdly, We may further confirm the foregoing proposition, *that those impressions, which give rise to this sense of justice, are not natural to the mind of man, but arise from artifice and human conventions.* For, since any considerable alteration of temper and circumstances destroys equally justice and injustice; and since such an alteration has an effect only by changing our own and the public interest, it follows that the first establishment of the rules of justice depends on these different interests. But if men pursued the public interest naturally, and with a hearty affection, they would have never dreamed of restraining each other by these rules; and if they pursued their own interest, without any precau-

4. [For Hume's argument that morality generally is not founded on reason, see the *Treatise*, pp. 456–70.]

tion, they would run headlong into every kind of injustice and violence. These rules, therefore, are artificial, and seek their end in an oblique and indirect manner; nor is the interest which gives rise to them of a kind that could be pursued by the natural and inartificial passions of men.

To make this more evident, consider, that, though the rules of justice are established merely by interest, their connexion with interest is somewhat singular, and is different from what may be observed on other occasions. A single act of justice is frequently contrary to *public interest;* and were it to stand alone, without being followed by other acts, may, in itself, be very prejudicial to society. When a man of merit, of a beneficent disposition, restores a great fortune to a miser, or a seditious bigot, he has acted justly and laudably; but the public is a real sufferer. Nor is every single act of justice, considered apart, more conducive to private interest than to public; and it is easily conceived how a man may impoverish himself by a signal instance of integrity, and have reason to wish, that, with regard to that single act, the laws of justice were for a moment suspended in the universe. But, however single acts of justice may be contrary, either to public or private interest, it is certain that the whole plan or scheme is highly conducive, or indeed absolutely requisite, both to the support of society, and the well-being of every individual. It is impossible to separate the good from the ill. Property must be stable, and must be fixed by general rules. Though in one instance the public be a sufferer, this momentary ill is amply compensated by the steady prosecution of the rule, and by the peace and order which it establishes in society.[5] And even every individual person must find himself a gainer on balancing the account; since, without justice, society must immediately dissolve, and every one must fall into that savage and solitary condition, which is infinitely worse than the worst situation that can possibly be supposed in society. When, therefore, men have had experience enough to observe, that, whatever may be the consequence of any single act of justice, performed by a single person, yet the whole system of actions concurred in by the whole society, is infinitely advantageous to the whole, and to every part, it is not long before justice and property take place. Every member of society is sensible of this interest: every one expresses this sense to his fellows, along with the resolution he has taken of squaring his

5. [Compare Hume's treatment of this subject here in the *Treatise* to his *An Enquiry Concerning the Principles of Morals*, pp. 93–94.]

actions by it, on condition that others will do the same. No more is requisite to induce any one of them to perform an act of justice, who has the first opportunity. This becomes an example to others; and thus justice establishes itself by a kind of convention or agreement, that is, by a sense of interest, supposed to be common to all, and where every single act is performed in expectation that others are to perform the like. Without such a convention, no one would ever have dreamed that there was such a virtue as justice, or have been induced to conform his actions to it. Taking any single act, my justice may be pernicious in every respect; and it is only upon the supposition that others are to imitate my example, that I can be induced to embrace that virtue; since nothing but this combination can render justice advantageous, or afford me any motives to conform myself to its rules.

We come now to the *second* question we proposed, viz. *Why we annex the idea of virtue to justice, and of vice to injustice.* This question will not detain us long after the principles which we have already established. All we can say of it at present will be despatched in a few words: and for further satisfaction, the reader must wait till we come to the third part of this book. The *natural* obligation to justice, viz. interest, has been fully explained; but as to the *moral* obligation, or the sentiment of right and wrong, it will first be requisite to examine the natural virtues, before we can give a full and satisfactory account of it.

After men have found by experience, that their selfishness and confined generosity, acting at their liberty, totally incapacitate them for society; and at the same time have observed that society is necessary to the satisfaction of those very passions, they are naturally induced to lay themselves under the restraint of such rules, as may render their commerce more safe and commodious. To the imposition, then, and observance of these rules, both in general, and in every particular instance, they are at first induced only by a regard to interest; and this motive, on the first formation of society, is sufficiently strong and forcible. But when society has become numerous, and has encreased to a tribe or nation, this interest is more remote; nor do men so readily perceive that disorder and confusion follow upon every breach of these rules, as in a more narrow and contracted society. But though, in our own actions, we may frequently lose sight of that interest which we have in maintaining order, and may follow a lesser and more present interest, we never fail to observe the prejudice we receive, either mediately or immediately, from the injustice of others; as not being in that case either blinded by passion, or biassed by any contrary temptation.

Nay, when the injustice is so distant from us as no way to affect our interest, it still displeases us; because we consider it as prejudicial to human society, and pernicious to every one that approaches the person guilty of it. We partake of their uneasiness by *sympathy;* and as every thing which gives uneasiness in human actions, upon the general survey, is called Vice, and whatever produces satisfaction, in the same manner, is denominated Virtue, this is the reason why the sense of moral good and evil follows upon justice and injustice. And though this sense, in the present case, be derived only from contemplating the actions of others, yet we fail not to extend it even to our own actions. The *general rule* reaches beyond those instances from which it arose; while, at the same time, we naturally *sympathize* with others in the sentiments they entertain of us. *Thus self-interest is the original motive to the* establishment *of justice: but a sympathy with public interest is the source of the* moral approbation, *which attends that virtue.*

Though this progress of the sentiments be *natural,* and even necessary, it is certain that it is here forwarded by the artifice of politicians, who, in order to govern men more easily, and preserve peace in human society, have endeavoured to produce an esteem for justice, and an abhorrence of injustice. This, no doubt, must have its effect; but nothing can be more evident than that the matter has been carried too far by certain writers on morals, who seem to have employed their utmost efforts to extirpate all sense of virtue from among mankind. Any artifice of politicians may assist nature in the producing of those sentiments, which she suggests to us, and may even, on some occasions, produce alone an approbation or esteem for any particular action; but it is impossible it should be the sole cause of the distinction we make betwixt vice and virtue. For if nature did not aid us in this particular, it would be in vain for politicians to talk of *honourable* or *dishonourable, praiseworthy* or *blamable.* These words would be perfectly unintelligible, and would no more have any idea annexed to them, than if they were of a tongue perfectly unknown to us. The utmost politicians can perform, is to extend the natural sentiments beyond their original bounds; but still nature must furnish the materials, and give us some notion of moral distinctions.

As public praise and blame encrease our esteem for justice, so private education and instruction contribute to the same effect. For as parents easily observe, that a man is the more useful, both to himself and others, the greater degree of probity and honour he is endowed with, and that those principles have greater force when custom and education assist interest and reflection: for these reasons they are induced to inculcate on their children, from their earliest infancy, the principles of probity, and teach them to regard the observance of those rules by which society is maintained, as worthy and honourable, and their violation as base and infamous. By this means the sentiments of honour may take root in their tender minds, and acquire such firmness and solidity, that they may fall little short of those principles which are the most essential to our natures, and the most deeply radicated in our internal constitution.

What further contributes to encrease their solidity, is the interest of our reputation, after the opinion, *that a merit or demerit attends justice or injustice,* is once firmly established among mankind. There is nothing which touches us more nearly than our reputation, and nothing on which our reputation more depends than our conduct with relation to the property of others. For this reason, every one who has any regard to his character, or who intends to live on good terms with mankind, must fix an inviolable law to himself, never, by any temptation, to be induced to violate those principles which are essential to a man of probity and honour.

I shall make only one observation before I leave this subject, viz. that, though I assert that, in the *state of nature,* or that imaginary state which preceded society, there be neither justice nor injustice, yet I assert not that it was allowable, in such a state, to violate the property of others. I only maintain, that there was no such thing as property; and consequently could be no such thing as justice or injustice. I shall have occasion to make a similar reflection with regard to *promises,* when I come to treat of them; and I hope this reflection, when duly weighed, will suffice to remove all odium from the foregoing opinions, with regard to justice and injustice.

Section III: *Of the Rules Which Determine Property*

Though the establishment of the rule, concerning the stability of possession, be not only useful, but even absolutely necessary to human society, it can never serve to any purpose, while it remains in such general terms. Some method must be shewn, by which we may distinguish what particular goods are to be assigned to each particular person, while the rest of mankind are excluded from their possession and enjoyment. Our next business, then, must be to discover the reasons which modify this general rule, and fit it to the common use and practice of the world.

It is obvious that those reasons are not derived from any utility or advantage, which either the *particular* person or the public may reap from his enjoyment of any *particular* goods, beyond what would result from the possession of them by any other person. It were better, no doubt, that every one were possessed of what is most suitable to him, and proper for his use: but besides, that this relation of fitness may be common to several at once, it is liable to so many controversies, and men are so partial and passionate in judging of these controversies, that such a loose and uncertain rule would be absolutely incompatible with the peace of human society. The convention concerning the stability of possession is entered into, in order to cut off all occasions of discord and contention; and this end would never be attained were we allowed to apply this rule differently in every particular case, according to every particular utility which might be discovered in such an application. Justice, in her decisions, never regards the fitness or unfitness of objects to particular persons, but conducts herself by more extensive views. Whether a man be generous, or a miser, he is equally well received by her, and obtains, with the same facility, a decision in his favour, even for what is entirely useless to him.

It follows, therefore, that the general rule, *that possession must be stable,* is not applied by particular judgments, but by other general rules, which must extend to the whole society, and be inflexible either by spite or favour. To illustrate this, I propose the following instance. I first consider men in their savage and solitary condition; and suppose that, being sensible of the misery of that state, and foreseeing the advantages that would result from society, they seek each other's company, and make an offer of mutual protection and assistance. I also suppose that they are endowed with such sagacity as immediately to perceive that the chief impediment to this project of society and partnership lies in the avidity and selfishness of their natural temper; to remedy which, they enter into a convention for the stability of possession, and for mutual restraint and forbearance. I am sensible that this method of proceeding is not altogether natural; but, besides that, I here only suppose those reflections to be formed at once, which, in fact, arise insensibly and by degrees; besides this, I say, it is very possible that several persons, being by different accidents separated from the societies to which they formerly belonged, may be obliged to form a new society among themselves; in which case they are entirely in the situation above mentioned.

It is evident, then, that their first difficulty in this situation, after the general convention for the establishment of society, and for the constancy of possession, is, how to separate their possessions, and assign to each his particular portion, which he must for the future inalterably enjoy. This difficulty will not detain them long; but it must immediately occur to them, as the most natural expedient, that every one continue to enjoy what he is at present master of, and that property or constant possession be conjoined to the immediate possession. Such is the effect of custom, that it not only reconciles us to any thing we have long enjoyed, but even gives us an affection for it, and makes us prefer it to other objects, which may be more valuable, but are less known to us. What has long lain under our eye, and has often been employed to our advantage, *that* we are always the most unwilling to part with; but can easily live without possessions which we never have enjoyed, and are not accustomed to. It is evident, therefore, that men would easily acquiesce in this expedient, *that every one continue to enjoy what he is at present possessed of:* and this is the reason why they would so naturally agree in preferring it.[6]

6. No questions in philosophy are more difficult, than when a number of causes present themselves for the same phenomenon, to determine which is the principal and predominant. There seldom is any very precise argument to fix our choice, and men must be contented to be guided by a kind of taste or fancy, arising from analogy, and a comparison of similar instances. Thus, in the present case, there are, no doubt, motives of public interest for most of the rules which determine property; but still I suspect that these rules are principally fixed by the imagination, or the more frivolous properties of our thought and conception. I shall continue to explain these causes, leaving it to the reader's choice whether he will prefer those derived from public utility, or those derived from the imagination. We shall begin with the right of the present possessor.

It is a quality which I have already observed {in Book I. Part IV. Sect. 5} in human nature, that when two objects appear in a close relation to each other, the mind is apt to ascribe to them any additional relation, in order to complete the union; and this inclination is so strong, as often to make us run into errors (such as that of the conjunction of thought and matter) if we find that they can serve to that purpose. Many of our impressions are incapable of place or local position; and yet those very impressions we suppose to have a local conjunction with the impressions of sight and touch, merely because they are conjoined by causation, and are already united in the imagination. Since, therefore, we can feign a new relation, and even an absurd one, in order to complete any union, it will easily be imagined, that if there be any relations which depend

But we may observe, that, though the rule of the assignment of property to the present possessor be natural, and by that means useful, yet its utility extends not beyond the first formation of society; nor would any thing be more pernicious than the constant observance of it; by which restitution would be excluded, and every injustice would be authorized and rewarded. We must, therefore, seek for some other circumstance, that may give rise to property after society is once established; and of this kind I find four most considerable, viz. Occupation, Prescription, Accession, and Succession. We shall briefly examine each of these, beginning with *occupation.*

The possession of all external goods is changeable and uncertain; which is one of the most considerable impediments to the establishment of society, and is the reason why, by universal agreement, express or tacit, men restrain themselves by what we now call the rules of justice and equity. The misery of the condition which precedes this restraint is the cause why we submit to that remedy as quickly as possible; and this affords us an easy reason why we annex the idea of property to the first possession, or to *occupation.* Men are unwilling to leave property in suspense, even

---

on the mind, it will readily conjoin them to any preceding relation, and unite, by a new bond, such objects as have already an union in the fancy. Thus, for instance, we never fail, in our arrangement of bodies, to place those which are *resembling* in *contiguity* to each other, or at least in *correspondent* points of view; because we feel a satisfaction in joining the relation of contiguity to that of resemblance, or the resemblance of situation to that of qualities. And this is easily accounted for from the known properties of human nature. When the mind is determined to join certain objects, but undetermined in its choice of the particular objects, it naturally turns its eye to such as are related together. They are already united in the mind: they present themselves at the same time to the conception; and instead of requiring any new reason for their conjunction, it would require a very powerful reason to make us overlook this natural affinity. This we shall have occasion to explain more fully afterwards, when we come to treat of *beauty.* [Although Hume had at one time planned on writing at length on beauty in the *Treatise,* he never did. However, for a detailed discussion of beauty see his essay "Of the Standard of Taste," in *Essays, Moral, Political, and Literary.*] In the meantime, we may content ourselves with observing, that the same love of order and uniformity which arranges the books in a library, and the chairs in a parlour, contributes to the formation of society, and to the well-being of mankind, by modifying the general rule concerning the stability of possession. And as property forms a relation betwixt a person and an object, it is natural to found it on some preceding relation; and, as property is nothing but a constant possession, secured by the laws of society, it is natural to add it to the present possession, which is a relation that resembles it. For this also has its influence. If it be natural to conjoin all sorts of relations, it is more so to conjoin such relations as are resembling, and are related together.

for the shortest time, or open the least door to violence and disorder. To which we may add, that the first possession always engages the attention most; and did we neglect it, there would be no colour of reason for assigning property to any succeeding possession.[7]

There remains nothing but to determine exactly what is meant by possession; and this is not so easy as may at first sight be imagined. We are said to be in possession of any thing, not only when we immediately touch it, but also when we are so situated with respect to it, as to have it in our power to use it; and may move, alter, or destroy it, according to our present pleasure or advantage. This relation, then, is a species of cause and effect; and as property is nothing but a stable possession, derived from the rules of justice, or the conventions of men, it is to be considered as the same species of relation. But here we may observe, that, as the power of using any object becomes more or less certain, according as the interruptions we may meet with are more or less probable; and as this probability may encrease by insensible degrees, it is in many cases impossible to determine when possession begins or ends; nor is there any certain standard by which we can decide such controversies. A wild boar that falls into our snares, is deemed to be in our possession if it be impossible for him to escape. But what do we mean by impossible? How do we separate this impossibility from an improbability? And how distinguish that exactly from a probability? Mark the precise limits of the one and the other, and shew the standard, by which we may decide all disputes that may arise, and, as we find by experience, frequently do arise upon this subject.[8]

7. Some philosophers account for the right of occupation, by saying that every one has a property in his own labour; and when he joins that labour to anything, it gives him the property of the whole: but, 1. There are several kinds of occupation where we cannot be said to join our labour to the object we acquire: as when we possess a meadow by grazing our cattle upon it. 2. This accounts for the matter by means of *accession;* which is taking a needless circuit. 3. We cannot be said to join our labour to anything but in a figurative sense. Properly speaking, we only make an alteration on it by our labour. This forms a relation betwixt us and the object; and thence arises the property, according to the preceding principles. [Hume is criticizing John Locke's (1632–1704) so-called labor theory of property. See Locke's *Two Treatises of Government*, ed. by P. Laslett, student edition (Cambridge: Cambridge University Press, 1988), pp. 285–302.]

8. If we seek a solution of these difficulties in reason and public interest, we never shall find satisfaction; and if we look for it in the imagination, it is evident that the qualities which operate upon that faculty run so insensibly and gradually into each other, that it is impossible to give them any precise bounds or termination. The difficulties on

this head must encrease, when we consider that our judgment alters very sensibly according to the subject, and that the same power and proximity will be deemed possession in one case, which is not esteemed such in another. A person who has hunted a hare to the last degree of weariness, would look upon it as an injustice for another to rush in before him, and seize his prey. But the same person, advancing to pluck an apple that hangs within his reach, has no reason to complain if another, more alert, passes him, and takes possession. What is the reason of this difference, but that immobility, not being natural to the hare, but the effect of industry, forms in that case a strong relation with the hunter, which is wanting in the other?

Here, then, it appears, that a certain and infallible power of enjoyment, without touch or some other sensible relation, often produces not property: and I further observe, that a sensible relation, without any present power, is sometimes sufficient to give a title to any object. The sight of a thing is seldom a considerable relation, and is only regarded as such, when the object is hidden, or very obscure; in which case we find that the view alone conveys a property; according to that maxim, *that even a whole continent belongs to the nation which first discovered it.* It is however remarkable, that both in the case of discovery and that of possession, the first discoverer and possessor must join to the relation an intention of rendering himself proprietor, otherwise the relation will not have its effect; and that because the connexion in our fancy betwixt the property and the relation is not so great but that it requires to be helped by such an intention.

From all these circumstances, it is easy to see how perplexed many questions may become concerning the acquisition of property by occupation; and the least effort of thought may present us with instances which are not susceptible of any reasonable decision. If we prefer examples which are real to such as are feigned, we may consider the following one, which is to be met with in almost every writer that has treated of the laws of nature. [Two law of nature theorists whom Hume undoubtedly has in mind are Hugo Grotius (1583–1645), *On the Law of War and Peace*, bk. II, ch. 8, sec. 6, and Samuel Pufendorf (1632–94), *On the Law of Nature and Nations in Eight Books*, bk. 4, ch. 6, sec. 8. The source of the example for both Grotius and Pufendorf is Plutarch's (before A.D. 50–after 120) *Greek Questions* (in *Moralia*, vol. IV), ch. 30.] Two Grecian colonies, leaving their native country in search of new seats, were informed that a city near them was deserted by its inhabitants. To know the truth of this report, they despatched at once two messengers, one from each colony, who finding, on their approach, that the information was true, begun a race together, with an intention to take possession of the city, each of them for his countrymen. One of these messengers, finding that he was not an equal match for the other, launched his spear at the gates of the city, and was so fortunate as to fix it there before the arrival of his companion. This produced a dispute betwixt the two colonies, which of them was the proprietor of the empty city; and this dispute still subsists among philosophers. For my part, I find the dispute impossible to be decided, and that because the whole question hangs upon the fancy, which in this case is not possessed of any precise or determinate standard upon which it can give sentence. To make this evident, let us consider, that if these two persons had been simply members of the colonies, and not messengers or deputies, their actions would not have been of any consequence; since in that case their relation to the colonies would have been but feeble and imperfect. Add to this, that nothing determined them to run to the gates rather than the walls or any other part of the city,

But such disputes may not only arise concerning the real existence of property and possession, but also concerning their extent; and these disputes are often susceptible of no decision, or can be decided by no other faculty than the imagination. A person who lands on the shore of a small island that is desert and uncultivated, is deemed its possessor from the very first moment, and acquires the property of the whole; because the object is there bounded and circumscribed in the fancy, and at the same time is proportioned to the new possessor. The same person landing on a desert island as large as Great Britain, extends his property no further than his immediate possession; though a numerous colony are esteemed the proprietors of the whole from the instant of their debarkment.

But it often happens that the title of first possession becomes obscure through time, and that it is impossible to determine many controversies which may arise concerning it; in that case, long possession or *prescription* naturally takes place, and gives a person a sufficient property in any thing he enjoys. The nature of human society admits not of any great accuracy; nor can we always remount to the first origin of things, in order to determine their present condition. Any considerable space of time sets objects at such a distance that they seem in a manner to lose their reality, and have as little influence on the mind as if they never had been in being. A man's title that is clear and certain at present, will seem obscure and doubtful fifty years hence, even though the facts on which it is founded should be proved with the greatest evidence and certainty. The same facts have not the same influence after so long an interval of time. And this may be received as a convincing argument for our preceding doctrine with regard to property and justice. Possession during a long tract of time conveys a title to any object. But as it is certain that, however every thing be produced in time, there is nothing real that is produced by time, it follows, that property being produced by time, is not any thing real in the objects,

---

but that the gates, being the most obvious and remarkable part, satisfy the fancy best in taking them for the whole; as we find by the poets, who frequently draw their images and metaphors from them. Besides, we may consider that the touch or contact of the one messenger is not properly possession, no more than the piercing the gates with the spear, but only forms a relation; and there is a relation in the other case equally obvious, though not perhaps of equal force. Which of these relations, then, conveys a right and property, or whether any of them be sufficient for that effect, I leave to the decision of such as are wiser than myself.

but is the offspring of the sentiments, on which alone time is found to have any influence.[9]

We acquire the property of objects by *accession,* when they are connected in an intimate manner with objects that are already our property, and at the same time are inferior to them. Thus, the fruits of our garden, the offspring of our cattle, and the work of our slaves, are all of them esteemed our property, even before possession. Where objects are connected together in the imagination, they are apt to be put on the same footing, and are commonly supposed to be endowed with the same qualities. We readily pass from one to the other, and make no difference in our judgments concerning them, especially if the latter be inferior to the former.[10]

9. Present possession is plainly a relation betwixt a person and an object; but is not sufficient to counterbalance the relation of first possession, unless the former be long and uninterrupted; in which case the relation is encreased on the side of the present possession by the extent of time, and diminished on that of first possession by the distance. This change in the relation produces a consequent change in the property.

10. This source of property can never be explained but from the imagination; and one may affirm, that the causes are here unmixed. We shall proceed to explain them more particularly, and illustrate them by examples from common life and experience.

It has been observed above, that the mind has a natural propensity to join relations, especially resembling ones, and finds a kind of fitness and uniformity in such an union. From this propensity are derived these laws of nature, *that upon the first formation of society, property always follows the present possession;* and afterwards, *that it arises from first or from long possession.* Now, we may easily observe, that relation is not confined merely to one degree; but that from an object that is related to us, we acquire a relation to every other object which is related to it, and so on, till the thought loses the chain by too long a progress. However the relation may weaken by each remove, it is not immediately destroyed; but frequently connects two objects by means of an immediate one, which is related to both. And this principle is of such force as to give rise to the right of *accession,* and causes us to acquire the property, not only of such objects as we are immediately possessed of, but also of such as are closely connected with them.

Suppose a German, a Frenchman, and a Spaniard, to come into a room where there are placed upon the table three bottles of wine, Rhenish, Burgundy, and Port; and suppose they should fall a quarrelling about the division of them, a person who was chosen for umpire would naturally, to shew his impartiality, give every one the product of his own country; and this from a principle which, in some measure, is the source of those laws of nature that ascribe property to occupation, prescription, and accession.

In all these cases, and particularly that of accession, there is first a *natural* union betwixt the idea of the person and that of the object, and afterwards a new and *moral* union produced by that right or property which we ascribe to the person. But here there occurs a difficulty which merits our attention, and may afford us an opportunity of putting to trial that singular method of reasoning which has been employed on the present subject. I have already observed, that the imagination passes with greater facility from little to great, than from great to little, and that the transition of ideas is always easier and smoother in the former case than in the latter. Now, as the right of accession arises from the easy transition of ideas by which related objects are connected together, it should naturally be imagined that the right of accession must encrease in strength, in proportion as the transition of ideas is performed with greater facility. It may therefore be thought, that when we have acquired the property of any small object, we shall readily consider any great object related to it as an accession, and as belonging to the proprietor of the small one; since the transition is in that case very easy from the small object to the great one, and should connect them together in the closest manner. But in fact the case is always found to be otherwise. The empire of Great Britain seems to draw along with it the dominion of the Orkneys, the Hebrides, the Isle of Man, and the Isle of Wight; but the authority over those lesser islands does not naturally imply any title to Great Britain. In short, a small object naturally follows a great one as its accession; but a great one is never supposed to belong to the proprietor of a small one related to it, merely on account of that property and relation. Yet in this latter case the transition of ideas is smoother from the proprietor to the small object which is his property, and from the small object to the great one, than in the former case from the proprietor to the great object, and from the great one to the small. It may therefore be thought, that these phenomena are objections to the foregoing hypothesis, *that the ascribing of property to accession is nothing but an effect of the relations of ideas, and of the smooth transition of the imagination.*

It will be easy to solve this objection, if we consider the agility and unsteadiness of the imagination, with the different views in which it is continually placing its objects. When we attribute to a person a property in two objects, we do not always pass from the person to one object, and from that to the other related to it. The objects being here to be considered as the property of the person, we are apt to join them together, and place them in the same light. Suppose, therefore, a great and a small object to be related together, if a person be strongly related to the great object, he will likewise be strongly related to both the objects considered together, because he is related to the most considerable part. On the contrary, if he be only related to the small object, he will not be strongly related to both considered together, since his relation lies only with the most trivial part, which is not apt to strike us in any great degree when we consider the whole. And this is the reason why small objects become accessions to great ones, and not great to small.

It is the general opinion of philosophers and civilians, that the sea is incapable of becoming the property of any nation; and that because it is impossible to take possession of it, or form any such distinct relation with it, as may be the foundation of property. Where this reason ceases, property immediately takes place. Thus, the most strenuous advocates for the liberty of the seas universally allow, that friths and bays naturally belong as an accession to the proprietors of the surrounding continent. These have properly no more bond or union with the land than the *Pacific* ocean would have; but having an union in the fancy, and being at the same time *inferior,* they are of course regarded as an accession.

The property of rivers, by the laws of most nations, and by the natural turn of our thought, is attributed to the proprietors of their banks, excepting such vast rivers as the Rhine or the Danube, which seem too large to the imagination to follow as an accession the property of the neighbouring fields. Yet even these rivers are considered as the property of that nation through whose dominions they run; the idea of a nation being of a suitable bulk to correspond with them, and bear them such a relation in the fancy.

The accessions which are made to lands bordering upon rivers, follow the land, say the civilians, provided it be made by what they call *alluvion,* that is, insensibly and imperceptibly; which are circumstances that mightily assist the imagination in the conjunction. Where there is any considerable portion torn at once from one bank, and joined to another, it becomes not his property whose land it falls on, till it unite with the land, and till the trees or plants have spread their roots into both. Before that, the imagination does not sufficiently join them.

There are other cases which somewhat resemble this of accession, but which, at the bottom, are considerably different, and merit our attention. Of this kind is the conjunction of the properties of different persons, after such a manner as not to admit of *separation.* The question is, to whom the united mass must belong.

Where this conjunction is of such a nature as to admit of *division,* but not of *separation,* the decision is natural and easy. The whole mass must be supposed to be common betwixt the proprietors of the several parts, and afterwards must be divided according to the proportions of these parts. But here I cannot forbear taking notice of a remarkable subtilty of the Roman law, in distinguishing betwixt *confusion* and *commixtion.* Confusion is a union of two bodies, such as different liquors, where the parts become entirely undistinguishable. Commixtion is the blending of two bodies, such as two bushels of corn, where the parts remain separate in an obvious and visible manner. As in the latter case the imagination discovers not so entire a union as in the former, but is able to trace and preserve a distinct idea of the property of each; this is the reason why the *civil* law, though it established an entire community in the case of *confusion,* and after that a proportional division, yet in the case of *commixtion,* supposes each of the proprietors to maintain a distinct right; however, necessity may at last force them to submit to the same division.

Quod si frumentum Titii frumento tuo mistum fuerit: siquidem ex voluntate vestra, commune est: quia singula corpora, id est, singula grana, quae cujusque propria fuerunt, ex consensu vestro communicata sunt. Quod si casu id mistum fuerit, vel Titius id miscuerit sine tua voluntate, non videtur id commune esse; quia singula corpora in sua substantia durant. Sed nec magis istis casibus commune sit frumentum quam grex intelligitur esse communis, si pecora Titii tuis pecoribus mista fuerint. Sed si ab alterutro vestrum totum id frumentum retineatur, in rem quidem actio pro modo frumenti cujusque competit. Arbitrio autem judicis, ut ipse aestimet quale cujusque frumentum fuerit. Inst. Lib. II. Tit. 1, Sec. 28. [*Justinian's Institutes*, trans. by P. Birks and G. McLeod (Ithaca: Cornell University Press, 1987), pp. 57, 59 (2.1.28): "But suppose that corn owned by Titius is mixed with yours. If you both wanted the mixing done, you own the mass in common, because every particle you each owned, i.e., every grain of corn, is by your agreement made common to you both. But if the mixture happens accidentally or is done by Titius against your will, the whole is not held in common, because the individual particles retain their own identity. The corn is not made common property here any more than flocks become common if the animals get mixed up. If one of you keeps the whole lot, a real action lies for the quantity of the other's individual contribution. The judge has power to allow for the quality of each contribution in assessing his award."]

Where the properties of two persons are united after such a manner as neither to admit of *division* nor *separation,* as when one builds a house on another's ground, in that case the whole must belong to one of the proprietors; and here I assert, that it naturally is conceived to belong to the proprietor of the most considerable part. For, however the compound object may have a relation to two different persons, and carry our view at once to both of them, yet, as the most considerable part principally engages our attention, and by the strict union draws the inferior along it; for this reason, the whole bears a relation to the proprietor of that part and is regarded as his property. The only difficulty is, what we shall be pleased to call the most considerable part, and most attractive to the imagination.

This quality depends on several different circumstances which have little connexion with each other. One part of a compound object may become more considerable than another, either because it is more constant and durable; because it is of greater value; because it is more obvious and remarkable; because it is of greater extent; or because its existence is more separate and independent. It will be easy to conceive, that, as these circumstances may be conjoined and opposed in all the different ways, and according to all the different degrees, which can be imagined, there will result many cases where the reasons on both sides are so equally balanced, that it is impossible for us to give any satisfactory decision. Here, then, is the proper business of municipal laws, to fix what the principles of human nature have left undetermined.

The superficies yields to the soil, says the civil law: the writing to the paper: the canvas to the picture. These decisions do not well agree together, and are a proof of the contrariety of those principles from which they are derived.

But of all the questions of this kind, the most curious is that which for so many ages divided the disciples of *Proculus* and *Sabinus.* [Proculus and Sabinus were two leading Roman jurists of the first half of the first century A.D. Hume is drawing from the discussion of this issue in *The Institutes of Gaius*. See *The Institutes of Gaius*, trans. by W.M. Gordon and O.F. Robinson (Ithaca: Cornell University Press, 1988), p. 159 (2.79).] Suppose a person should make a cup from the metal of another, or a ship from his wood, and suppose the proprietor of the metal or wood should demand his goods, the question is, whether he acquires a title to the cup or ship. *Sabinus* maintained the affirmative, and asserted, that the substance or matter is the foundation of all the qualities; that it is incorruptible and immortal, and therefore superior to the form, which is casual and dependent. On the other hand, *Proculus* observed, that the form is the most obvious and remarkable part, and that from it bodies are denominated of this or that particular species. To which he might have added, that the matter or substance is in most bodies so fluctuating and uncertain, that it is utterly impossible to trace it in all its changes. For my part, I know not from what principles such a controversy can be certainly determined. I shall therefore content myself with observing, that the decision of *Trebonian* [A sixth-century-A.D. jurist, who collaborated with the Emperor Justinian on the codification of Roman law. Justinian (*c.* A.D. 482–565) was Emperor from 527 until his death.] seems to me pretty ingenious; that the cup belongs to the proprietor of the metal, because it can be brought back to its first form: but that the ship belongs to the author of its form, for a contrary reason. But however ingenious this reason may seem, it plainly depends upon the fancy, which, by the possibility of such a reduction, finds a closer connexion and relation betwixt a cup and the proprietor of its metal, than betwixt a ship and the proprietor of its wood, where the substance is more fixed and unalterable.

The right of *succession* is a very natural one, from the presumed consent of the parent or near relation, and from the general interest of mankind, which requires that men's possessions should pass to those who are dearest to them, in order to render them more industrious and frugal. Perhaps these causes are seconded by the influence of *relation,* or the association of ideas, by which we are naturally directed to consider the son after the parent's decease, and ascribe to him a title to his father's possessions. Those goods must become the property of somebody: but *of whom* is the question. Here it is evident the person's children naturally present themselves to the mind; and being already connected to those possessions by means of their deceased parent, we are apt to connect them still further by the relation of property. Of this there are many parallel instances.[11]

Section IV: *Of the Transference of Property By Consent*

However useful, or even necessary, the stability of possession may be to human society, it is attended with very considerable inconveniences. The relation of fitness or suitableness ought never to enter into consideration, in distributing the properties of mankind; but we must govern ourselves by rules which are more general in their application, and more free from doubt and uncertainty. Of this kind is *present* possession upon the first establishment of society; and afterwards *occupation, prescription, accession,* and *succession.* As these depend very much on chance, they must frequently prove contradictory both to men's wants and desires; and persons and possessions must often be very ill adjusted. This is a grand inconvenience, which calls for a remedy. To apply one

11. In examining the different titles to authority in government, we shall meet with many reasons to convince us that the right of succession depends, in a great measure, on the imagination. Mean while I shall rest contented with observing one example, which belongs to the present subject. Suppose that a person die without children, and that a dispute arises among his relations concerning his inheritance; it is evident, that if his riches be derived partly from his father, partly from his mother, the most natural way of determining such a dispute is, to divide his possessions, and assign each part to the family from whence it is derived. Now, as the person is supposed to have been once the full and entire proprietor of those goods, I ask, what is it makes us find a certain equity and natural reason in this partition, except it be the imagination? His affection to these families does not depend upon his possessions; for which reason his consent can never be presumed precisely for such a partition. And as to the public interest, it seems not to be in the least concerned on the one side or the other.

directly, and allow every man to seize by violence what he judges to be fit for him, would destroy society; and therefore the rules of justice seek some medium betwixt a rigid stability and this changeable and uncertain adjustment. But there is no medium better than that obvious one, that possession and property should always be stable, except when the proprietor consents to bestow them on some other person. This rule can have no ill consequence in occasioning wars and dissensions, since the proprietor's consent, who alone is concerned, is taken along in the alienation; and it may serve to many good purposes in adjusting property to persons. Different parts of the earth produce different commodities; and not only so, but different men both are by nature fitted for different employments, and attain to greater perfection in any one, when they confine themselves to it alone. All this requires a mutual exchange and commerce; for which reason the translation of property by consent is founded on a law of nature, as well as its stability without such a consent.

So far is determined by a plain utility and interest. But perhaps it is from more trivial reasons, that *delivery,* or a sensible transference of the object is commonly required by civil laws, and also by the laws of nature, according to most authors, as a requisite circumstance in the translation of property. The property of an object, when taken for something real, without any reference to morality, or the sentiments of the mind, is a quality perfectly insensible, and even inconceivable; nor can we form any distinct notion, either of its stability or translation. This imperfection of our ideas is less sensibly felt with regard to its stability, as it engages less our attention, and is easily passed over by the mind, without any scrupulous examination. But as the translation of property from one person to another is a more remarkable event, the defect of our ideas becomes more sensible on that occasion and obliges us to turn ourselves on every side in search of some remedy. Now, as nothing more enlivens any idea than a present impression, and a relation betwixt that impression and the idea; it is natural for us to seek some false light from this quarter. In order to aid the imagination in conceiving the transference of property, we take the sensible object, and actually transfer its possession to the person on whom we would bestow the property. The supposed resemblance of the actions, and the presence of this sensible delivery, deceive the mind, and make it fancy that it conceives the mysterious transition of the property. And that this explication of the matter is just, appears hence, that men have invented a symbolical delivery, to satisfy the fancy where the real one is impracticable. Thus the giving the keys of a granary is understood to be the delivery of the corn contained in it; the giving of stone and earth represents the delivery of a manor. This is a kind of superstitious practice in civil laws, and in the laws of nature, resembling the *Roman Catholic* superstitions in religion. As the *Roman Catholics* represent the inconceivable mysteries of the *Christian* religion, and render them more present to the mind, by a taper, or habit, or grimace, which is supposed to resemble them; so lawyers and moralists have run into like inventions for the same reason, and have endeavoured by those means to satisfy themselves concerning the transference of property by consent.

Section V: *Of the Obligation of Promises*

That the rule of morality, which enjoins the performance of promises, is not natural, will sufficiently appear from these two propositions, which I proceed to prove, viz. *that a promise would not be intelligible before human conventions had established it;* and *that even if it were intelligible, it would not be attended with any moral obligation.*

I say, first, that a promise is not intelligible naturally, nor antecedent to human conventions; and that a man, unacquainted with society, could never enter into any engagements with another, even though they could perceive each other's thoughts by intuition. If promises be natural and intelligible, there must be some act of the mind attending these words, *I promise;* and on this act of the mind must the obligation depend. Let us therefore run over all the faculties of the soul, and see which of them is exerted in our promises.

The act of the mind, expressed by a promise, is not a *resolution* to perform any thing; for that alone never imposes any obligation. Nor is it a *desire* of such a performance; for we may bind ourselves without such a desire, or even with an aversion, declared and avowed. Neither is it the *willing* of that action which we promise to perform; for a promise always regards some future time, and the will has an influence only on present actions. It follows, therefore, that since the act of the mind, which enters into a promise, and produces its obligation, is neither the resolving, desiring, nor willing any particular performance, it must necessarily be the *willing* of that *obligation* which arises from the promise. Nor is this only a conclusion of philosophy, but is entirely conformable to our common ways of thinking and of expressing ourselves, when we say that we are bound by our own consent, and that the obligation arises from our mere will and pleasure. The only question then is, whether there be not a manifest absurdity in supposing this act of the mind, and such an absurdity as no man could fall into, whose ideas are not confounded with prejudice and the fallacious use of language.

All morality depends upon our sentiments; and when any action or quality of the mind pleases us *after a certain manner* we say it is virtuous; and when the neglect or nonperformance of it displeases us *after a like manner,* we say that we lie under an obligation to perform it. A change of the obligation supposes a change of the sentiment; and a creation of a new obligation supposes some new sentiment to arise. But it is certain we can naturally no more change our own sentiments than the motions of the heavens; nor by a single act of our will, that is, by a promise, render any action agreeable or disagreeable, moral or immoral, which, without that act, would have produced contrary impressions, or have been endowed with different qualities. It would be absurd therefore, to will any new obligation, that is, any new sentiment of pain or pleasure; nor is it possible that men could naturally fall into so gross an absurdity. A promise, therefore, is *naturally* something altogether unintelligible, nor is there any act of the mind belonging to it.[12]

But, *secondly,* if there was any act of the mind belonging to it, it

12. Were morality discoverable by reason, and not by sentiment, it would be still more evident that promises could make no alteration upon it. Morality is supposed to consist in relation. Every new imposition of morality, therefore, must arise from some new relation of objects; and consequently the will could not produce *immediately* any change in morals, but could have that effect only by producing a change upon the objects. But as the moral obligation of a promise is the pure effect of the will, without the least change in any part of the universe, it follows that promises have no *natural* obligation.

Should it be said, that this act of the will, being in effect a new object, produces new relations and new duties; I would answer, that this is a pure sophism, which may be detected by a very moderate share of accuracy and exactness. To will a new obligation is to will a new relation of objects; and therefore, if this new relation of objects were formed by the volition itself, we should, in effect, will the volition, which is plainly absurd and impossible. The will has here no object to which it could tend, but must return upon itself *in infinitum.* The new obligation depends upon new relations. The new relations depend upon a new volition. The new volition has for object a new obligation, and consequently new relations, and consequently a new volition; which volition, again, has in view a new obligation, relation, and volition, without any termination. It is impossible, therefore, we could ever will a new obligation; and consequently it is impossible the will could ever accompany a promise, or produce a new obligation of morality.

could not *naturally* produce any obligation. This appears evidently from the foregoing reasoning. A promise creates a new obligation. A new obligation supposes new sentiments to arise. The will never creates new sentiments. There could not naturally, therefore, arise any obligation from a promise, even supposing the mind could fall into the absurdity of willing that obligation.

The same truth may be proved still more evidently by that reasoning which proved justice in general to be an artificial virtue. No action can be required of us as our duty, unless there be implanted in human nature some actuating passion or motive capable of producing the action. This motive cannot be the sense of duty. A sense of duty supposes an antecedent obligation; and where an action is not required by any natural passion, it cannot be required by any natural obligation; since it may be omitted without proving any defect or imperfection in the mind and temper, and consequently without any vice. Now, it is evident we have no motive leading us to the performance of promises, distinct from a sense of duty. If we thought that promises had no moral obligation, we never should feel any inclination to observe them. This is not the case with the natural virtues. Though there was no obligation to relieve the miserable, our humanity would lead us to it; and when we omit that duty, the immorality of the omission arises from its being a proof that we want the natural sentiments of humanity. A father knows it to be his duty to take care of his children, but he has also a natural inclination to it. And if no human creature had that inclination, no one could lie under any such obligation. But as there is naturally no inclination to observe promises distinct from a sense of their obligation, it follows that fidelity is no natural virtue, and that promises have no force antecedent to human conventions.

If any one dissent from this, he must give a regular proof of these two propositions, viz. *that there is a peculiar act of the mind annexed to promises;* and *that consequent to this act of the mind, there arises an inclination to perform, distinct from a sense of duty.* I presume that it is impossible to prove either of these two points; and therefore I venture to conclude, that promises are human inventions, founded on the necessities and interests of society.

In order to discover these necessities and interests, we must consider the same qualities of human nature which we have already found to give rise to the preceding laws of society. Men being naturally selfish, or endowed only with a confined generosity, they are not easily induced to perform any action for the interest of strangers, except with a view to some reciprocal advantage, which they had no hope of obtaining but by such a performance. Now, as it frequently happens that these mutual performances cannot be finished at the same instant, it is necessary that one party be contented to remain in uncertainty, and depend upon the gratitude of the other for a return of kindness. But so much corruption is there among men, that, generally speaking, this becomes but a slender security; and as the benefactor is here supposed to bestow his favours with a view to self-interest, this both takes off from the obligation, and sets an example of selfishness, which is the true mother of ingratitude. Were we, therefore, to follow the natural course of our passions and inclinations, we should perform but few actions for the advantage of others from disinterested views, because we are naturally very limited in our kindness and affection; and we should perform as few of that kind out of a regard to interest, because we cannot depend upon their gratitude. Here, then, is the mutual commerce of good offices in a manner lost among mankind, and every one reduced to his own skill and industry for his well-being and subsistence. The invention of the law of nature, concerning the *stability* of possession, has already rendered men tolerable to each other; that of the *transference* of property and possession by consent has begun to render them mutually advantageous; but still these laws of nature, however strictly observed, are not sufficient to render them so serviceable to each other as by nature they are fitted to become. Though possession be *stable,* men may often reap but small advantage from it, while they are possessed of a greater quantity of any species of goods than they have occasion for, and at the same time suffer by the want of others. The *transference* of property, which is the proper remedy for this inconvenience, cannot remedy it entirely; because it can only take place with regard to such objects as are *present* and *individual,* but not to such as are *absent* or *general.* One cannot transfer the property of a particular house, twenty leagues distant, because the consent cannot be attended with delivery, which is a requisite circumstance. Neither can one transfer the property of ten bushels of corn, or five hogsheads of wine, by the mere expression and consent, because these are only general terms, and have no direct relation to any particular heap of corn or barrels of wine. Besides, the commerce of mankind is not confined to the barter of commodities, but may extend to services and actions, which we may exchange to our mutual interest and advantage. Your corn is ripe to-day; mine will be so to-morrow. It is profitable for us both that I should labour with you to-day, and that you should aid me to-morrow. I have no kindness for you, and know you have as little for me. I will not, therefore, take any pains upon your account; and should I labour with you upon my own account, in expectation of a return, I know I should be disappointed, and that I should in vain depend upon your gratitude. Here, then, I leave you to labour alone: you treat me in the same manner. The seasons change; and both of us lose our harvests for want of mutual confidence and security.

All this is the effect of the natural and inherent principles and passions of human nature; and as these passions and principles are inalterable, it may be thought that our conduct, which depends on them, must be so too, and that it would be in vain, either for moralists or politicians, to tamper with us, or attempt to change the usual course of our actions, with a view to public interest. And, indeed, did the success of their designs depend upon their success in correcting the selfishness and ingratitude of men, they would never make any progress, unless aided by Omnipotence, which is alone able to new-mould the human mind, and change its character in such fundamental articles. All they can pretend to is, to give a new direction to those natural passions, and teach us that we can better satisfy our appetites in an oblique and artificial manner, than by their headlong and impetuous motion. Hence I learn to do a service to another, without bearing him any real kindness; because I foresee that he will return my service, in expectation of another of the same kind, and in order to maintain the same correspondence of good offices with me or with others. And accordingly, after I have served him, and he is in possession of the advantage arising from my action, he is induced to perform his part, as foreseeing the consequences of his refusal.

But though this self-interested commerce of men begins to take place, and to predominate in society, it does not entirely abolish the more generous and noble intercourse of friendship and good offices. I may still do services to such persons as I love, and am more particularly acquainted with, without any prospect of advantage; and they may make me a return in the same manner, without any view but that of recompensing my past services. In order, therefore, to distinguish those two different sorts of commerce, the interested and the disinterested, there is a *certain form of words* invented for the former, by which we bind ourselves to the performance of any action. This form of words constitutes what we call a *promise*, which is the sanction of the interested commerce of mankind. When a man says *he promises any thing*, he in effect expresses a resolution of performing it; and along with that, by making use of this *form of words*, subjects himself to the penalty of never being trusted again in case of failure. A resolution is the natural act of the mind, which promises express; but were there no more than a resolution in the case, promises would only declare our former motives, and would not create any new motive or obligation. They are the conventions of men, which create a new motive, when experience has taught us that human affairs would be conducted much more for mutual advantage, were there certain *symbols* or *signs* instituted, by which we might give each other security of our conduct in any particular incident. After these signs are instituted, whoever uses them is immediately bound by his interest to execute his engagements, and must never expect to be trusted any more if he refuse to perform what he promised.

Nor is that knowledge, which is requisite to make mankind sensible of this interest in the *institution* and *observance* of promises, to be esteemed superior to the capacity of human nature, however savage and uncultivated. There needs but a very little practice of the world to make us perceive all these consequences and advantages. The shortest experience of society discovers them to every mortal; and when each individual perceives the same sense of interest in all his fellows, he immediately performs his part of any contract, as being assured that they will not be wanting in theirs. All of them, by concert, enter into a scheme of actions, calculated for common benefit, and agree to be true to their word; nor is there any thing requisite to form this concert or convention, but that every one have a sense of interest in the faithful fulfilling of engagements, and express that sense to other members of the society. This immediately causes that interest to operate upon them; and interest is the *first* obligation to the performance of promises.

Afterwards a sentiment of morals concurs with interest, and becomes a new obligation upon mankind. This sentiment of morality, in the performance of promises, arises from the same principles as that in the abstinence from the property of others. *Public interest, education,* and *the artifices of politicians,* have the same effect in both cases. The difficulties that occur to us in supposing a moral obligation to attend promises, we either surmount or elude. For instance, the expression of a resolution is not commonly supposed to be obligatory; and we cannot readily conceive how the making use of a certain form of words should be able to cause any material difference. Here, therefore, we *feign* a new act of the mind, which we call the *willing* an obligation; and on this we suppose the morality to depend. But we have proved already that there is no such act of the mind, and consequently, that promises impose no natural obligation.

To confirm this, we may subjoin some other reflections concerning that will, which is supposed to enter into a promise, and to cause its obligation. It is evident that the will alone is never supposed to cause the obligation, but must be expressed by words or signs, in order to impose a tie upon any man. The expression being once brought in as subservient to the will, soon becomes the principal part of the promise; nor will a man be less bound by his word, though he secretly give a different direction to his intention, and withhold himself both from a resolution, and from willing an obligation. But though the expression makes on most occasions the whole of the promise, yet it does not always so; and one who should make use of any expression of which he knows not the meaning, and which he uses without any intention of binding himself, would not certainly be bound by it. Nay, though he knows its meaning, yet if he uses it in jest only, and with such signs as shew evidently he has no serious intention of binding himself, he would not lie under any obligation of performance; but it is necessary that the words be a perfect expression of the will, without any contrary signs. Nay, even this we must not carry so far as to imagine, that one, whom, by our quickness of understanding, we conjecture, from certain signs, to have an intention of deceiving us, is not bound by his expression or verbal promise, if we accept of it; but must limit this conclusion to those cases where the signs are of a different kind from those of deceit. All these contradictions are easily accounted for, if the obligation of promises be merely a human invention for the convenience of society; but will never be explained, if it be something *real* and *natural*, arising from any action of the mind or body.

I shall further observe, that, since every new promise imposes a new obligation of morality on the person who promises, and since this new obligation arises from his will; it is one of the most mysterious and incomprehensible operations that can possibly be imagined, and may even be compared to *transubstantiation* or *holy orders*,[13] where a certain form of words, along with a certain intention, changes entirely the nature of an external object, and even of a human creature. But though these mysteries be so far alike, it is very remarkable that they differ widely in other particulars, and that this difference may be regarded as a strong proof of the difference of their origins. As the obligation of promises is an invention for the interest of society, it is warped into as many different forms as that interest requires, and even runs into direct contradictions, rather than lose sight of its object. But as those

13. I mean so far as holy orders are supposed to produce the *indelible character*. In other respects they are only a legal qualification.

other monstrous doctrines are mere priestly inventions, and have no public interest in view, they are less disturbed in their progress by new obstacles; and it must be owned, that, after the first absurdity, they follow more directly the current of reason and good sense. Theologians clearly perceived that the external form of words, being mere sound, require an intention to make them have any efficacy; and that this intention being once considered as a requisite circumstance, its absence must equally prevent the effect, whether avowed or concealed, whether sincere or deceitful. Accordingly they have commonly determined, that the intention of the priest makes the sacrament, and that when he secretly withdraws his intention, he is highly criminal in himself; but still destroys the baptism, or communion, or holy orders. The terrible consequences of this doctrine were not able to hinder its taking place; as the inconvenience of a similar doctrine, with regard to promises, have prevented that doctrine from establishing itself. Men are always more concerned about the present life than the future; and are apt to think the smallest evil which regards the former more important than the greatest which regards the latter.

We may draw the same conclusion concerning the origin of promises, from the *force* which is supposed to invalidate all contracts, and to free us from their obligation. Such a principle is a proof that promises have no natural obligation, and are mere artificial contrivances for the convenience and advantage of society. If we consider aright of the matter, force is not essentially different from any other motive of hope or fear, which may induce us to engage our word, and lay ourselves under any obligation. A man, dangerously wounded, who promises a competent sum to a surgeon to cure him, would certainly be bound to performance; though the case be not so much different from that of one who promises a sum to a robber, as to produce so great a difference in our sentiments of morality, if these sentiments were not built entirely on public interest and convenience.

Section VI: *Some Further Reflections Concerning Justice and Injustice*

We have now run over the three fundamental laws of nature *that of the stability of possession, of its transference by consent, and of the performance of promises*. It is on the strict observance of those three laws that the peace and security of human society entirely depend; nor is there any possibility of establishing a good correspondence among men, where these are neglected. Society is absolutely necessary for the well-being of men; and these are as necessary to the support of society. Whatever restraint they may impose on the passions of men, they are the real offspring of those passions, and are only a more artful and more refined way of satisfying them. Nothing is more vigilant and inventive than our passions; and nothing is more obvious than the convention for the observance of these rules. Nature has, therefore, trusted this affair entirely to the conduct of men, and has not placed in the mind any peculiar original principles, to determine us to a set of actions, into which the other principles of our frame and constitution were sufficient to lead us. And to convince us the more fully of this truth, we may here stop a moment, and, from a review of the preceding reasonings, may draw some new arguments, to prove that those laws, however necessary, are entirely artificial, and of human invention; and consequently, that justice is an artificial, and not a natural virtue.

I. The first argument I shall make use of is derived from the vulgar definition of justice. Justice is commonly defined to be *a constant and perpetual will of giving every one his due.* In this definition it is supposed that there are such things as right and property, independent of justice, and antecedent to it; and that they would have subsisted, though men had never dreamt of practicing such a virtue. I have already observed, in a cursory manner, the fallacy of this opinion, and shall here continue to open up, a little more distinctly, my sentiments on that subject.

I shall begin with observing that this quality, which we call *property*, is like many of the imaginary qualities of the *Peripatetic* philosophy,[14] and vanishes upon a more accurate inspection into the subject, when considered apart from our moral sentiments. It is evident property does not consist in any of the sensible qualities of the object. For these may continue invariably the same, while the property changes. Property, therefore, must consist in some relation of the object. But it is not in its relation with regard to other external and inanimate objects. For these may also continue invariably the same, while the property changes. This quality, therefore, consists in the relations of objects to intelligent and rational beings. But it is not the external and corporeal relation

14. ['Peripatetic' is a name associated with the philosophy of Aristotle (384–322 B.C.) and his followers. As found in modern philosophy—the period roughly from 1600 to 1899—it is frequently a term of abuse.]

which forms the essence of property. For that relation may be the same betwixt inanimate objects, or with regard to brute creatures; though in those cases it forms no property. It is therefore in some internal relation that the property consists; that is, in some influence which the external relations of the object have on the mind and actions. Thus the external relation which we call *occupation* or first possession, is not of itself imagined to be the property of the object, but only to cause its property. Now, it is evident this external relation causes nothing in external objects, and has only an influence on the mind, by giving us a sense of duty in abstaining from that object, and in restoring it to the first possessor. These actions are properly what we call *justice;* and consequently it is on that virtue that the nature of property depends, and not the virtue on the property.

If any one, therefore, would assert that justice is a natural virtue, and injustice a natural vice, he must assert that abstracting from the notions of *property* and *right* and *obligation* a certain conduct and train of actions, in certain external relations of objects, has naturally a moral beauty or deformity, and causes an original pleasure or uneasiness. Thus the restoring a man's goods to him is considered as virtuous, not because nature has annexed a certain sentiment of pleasure to such a conduct with regard to the property of others, but because she has annexed that sentiment to such a conduct, with regard to those external objects of which others have had the first or long possession, or which they have received by the consent of those who have had first or long possession. If nature has given us no such sentiment, there is not naturally, nor antecedent to human conventions, any such thing as property. Now, though it seems sufficiently evident, in this dry and accurate consideration of the present subject, that nature has annexed no pleasure or sentiment of approbation to such a conduct, yet, that I may leave as little room for doubt as possible, I shall subjoin a few more arguments to confirm my opinion.

First, If nature had given us a pleasure of this kind, it would have been as evident and discernible as on every other occasion; nor should we have found any difficulty to perceive that the consideration of such actions, in such a situation, gives a certain pleasure and sentiment of approbation. We should not have been obliged to have recourse to notions of property in the definition of justice, and at the same time make use of the notions of justice in the definition of property. This deceitful method of reasoning is a plain proof that there are contained in the subject some obscurities and difficulties which we are not able to surmount, and which we desire to evade by this artifice.

Secondly, Those rules by which properties, rights, and obligations are determined, have in them no marks of a natural origin, but many of artifice and contrivance. They are too numerous to have proceeded from nature; they are changeable by human laws; and have all of them a direct and evident tendency to public good, and the support of civil society. This last circumstance is remarkable upon two accounts. *First,* Because, though the cause of the establishment of these laws had been a *regard* for the public good, as much as the public good is their natural tendency, they would still have been artificial, as being purposely contrived and directed to a certain end. *Secondly,* Because, if men had been endowed with such a strong regard for public good, they would never have restrained themselves by these rules; so that the laws of justice arise from natural principles, in a manner still more oblique and artificial. It is self-love which is their real origin; and as the self-love of one person is naturally contrary to that of another, these several interested passions are obliged to adjust themselves after such a manner as to concur in some system of conduct and behaviour. This system, therefore, comprehending the interest of each individual, is of course advantageous to the public, though it be not intended for that purpose by the inventors.

II. In the *second* place, we may observe that all kinds of vice and virtue run insensibly into each other, and may approach by such imperceptible degrees as will make it very difficult, if not absolutely impossible, to determine when the one ends, and the other begins; and from this observation we may derive a new argument for the foregoing principle. For, whatever may be the case with regard to all kinds of vice and virtue, it is certain that rights, and obligations, and property, admit of no such insensible gradation, but that a man either has a full and perfect property, or none at all; and is either entirely obliged to perform any action, or lies under no manner of obligation. However civil laws may talk of a perfect *dominion,* and of an imperfect, it is easy to observe, that this arises from a fiction, which has no foundation in reason, and can never enter into our notions of natural justice and equity. A man that hires a horse, though but for a day, has as full a right to make use of it for that time, as he whom we call its proprietor has to make use of it any other day; and it is evident that, however the use may be bounded in time or degree, the right itself is not susceptible of any such gradation, but is absolute and entire, so far as it extends. Accordingly, we may observe that this right both arises and perishes in an instant; and that a man entirely acquires the property of any object by occupation, or the consent of the proprietor; and loses it by his own consent, without any of that insensible gradation which is remarkable in other qualities and relations. Since, therefore, this is the case with regard to property, and rights, and obligations, I ask, how it stands with regard to justice and injustice? After whatever manner you answer this question, you run into inextricable difficulties. If you reply, that justice and injustice admit of degree, and run insensibly into each other, you expressly contradict the foregoing position, that obligation and property are not susceptible of such a gradation. These depend entirely upon justice and injustice, and follow them in all their variations. Where the justice is entire, the property is also entire: where the justice is imperfect, the property must also be imperfect. And *vice versa,* if the property admit of no such variations, they must also be incompatible with justice. If you assent, therefore, to this last proposition, and assert that justice and injustice are not susceptible of degrees, you in effect assert that they are not *naturally* either vicious or virtuous; since vice and virtue, moral good and evil, and indeed all *natural* qualities, run insensibly into each other, and are on many occasions undistinguishable.

And here it may be worth while to observe, that though abstract reasoning and the general maxims of philosophy and law establish this position, *that property, and right, and obligation, admit not of degrees,* yet, in our common and negligent way of thinking, we find great difficulty to entertain that opinion, and do even *secretly* embrace the contrary principle. An object must either be in the possession of one person or another. An action must either be performed or not. The necessity there is of choosing one side in these dilemmas, and the impossibility there often is of finding any just medium, oblige us, when we reflect on the matter, to acknowledge that all property and obligations are entire. But, on the other hand, when we consider the origin of property and obligation, and find that they depend on public utility, and sometimes on the propensities of the imagination, which are seldom entire on any side, we are naturally inclined to imagine that these moral relations admit of an insensible gradation. Hence it is, that in references, where the consent of the parties leave the referees entire masters of the subject, they commonly discover so much equity and justice on both sides as induces them to strike a medium, and divide the difference betwixt the parties. Civil judges, who have not this liberty, but are obliged to give a decisive sentence on some one side, are often at a loss how to determine, and are necessitated to proceed on the most frivolous reasons in the world. Half rights and obligations, which seem so natural in common life, are perfect absurdities in their tribunal; for which reason they are often obliged to take half arguments for whole ones, in order to terminate the affair one way or other.

III. The *third* argument of this kind I shall make use of may be explained thus. If we consider the ordinary course of human actions, we shall find that the mind restrains not itself by any general and universal rules, but acts on most occasions as it is determined by its present motives and inclination. As each action is a particular individual event, it must proceed from particular principles, and from our immediate situation within ourselves, and with respect to the rest of the universe. If on some occasions we extend our motives beyond those very circumstances which gave rise to them, and form something like *general rules* for our conduct, it is easy to observe that these rules are not perfectly inflexible, but allow of many exceptions. Since, therefore, this is the ordinary course of human actions, we may conclude that the laws of justice, being universal and perfectly inflexible, can never be derived from nature, nor be the immediate offspring of any natural motive or inclination. No action can be either morally good or evil, unless there be some natural passion or motive to impel us to it, or deter us from it; and it is evident that the morality must be susceptible of all the same variations which are natural to the passion. Here are two persons who dispute for an estate; of whom one is rich, a fool, and a bachelor; the other poor, a man of sense, and has a numerous family: the first is my enemy; the second my friend. Whether I be actuated in this affair by a view to public or private interest, by friendship or enmity, I must be induced to do my utmost to procure the estate to the latter. Nor would any consideration of the right and property of the persons be able to restrain me, were I actuated only by natural motives, without any combination or convention with others. For as all property depends on morality, and as all morality depends on the ordinary course of our passions and actions, and as these again are only directed by particular motives, it is evident such a partial conduct must be suitable to the strictest morality, and could never be a violation of property. Were men, therefore, to take the liberty of acting with regard to the laws of society, as they do in every other affair, they would conduct themselves, on most occasions, by particular judgments, and would take into consideration the characters and circumstances of the persons, as well as the general nature of the question. But it is easy to observe, that this would produce an infinite confusion in human society, and that the avidity and partiality of men would quickly bring disorder into the world, if not restrained by some general and inflexible principles. It was therefore with a view to this inconvenience that men have established those principles, and have agreed to restrain themselves by general rules, which are unchangeable by spite and favour, and by particular views of private or public interest. These rules, then, are artificially invented for a certain purpose, and are contrary to the common principles of human nature, which accommodate themselves to circumstances, and have no stated invariable method of operation.

Nor do I perceive how I can easily be mistaken in this matter. I see, evidently, that when any man imposes on himself general inflexible rules in his conduct with others, he considers certain objects as their property, which he supposes to be sacred and inviolable. But no proposition can be more evident, than that property is perfectly unintelligible without first supposing justice and injustice; and that these virtues and vices are as unintelligible, unless we have motives, independent of the morality, to impel us to just actions, and deter us from unjust ones. Let those motives, therefore, be what they will, they must accommodate themselves to circumstances, and must admit of all the variations which human affairs, in their incessant revolutions, are susceptible of. They are, consequently, a very improper foundation for such rigid inflexible rules as the laws of nature; and it is evident these laws can only be derived from human conventions, when men have perceived the disorders that result from following their natural and variable principles.

Upon the whole, then, we are to consider this distinction betwixt justice and injustice, as having two different foundations, viz. that of *interest,* when men observe that it is impossible to live in society without restraining themselves by certain rules; and that of *morality,* when this interest is once observed, and men receive a pleasure from the view of such actions as tend to the peace of society, and an uneasiness from such as are contrary to it. It is the voluntary convention and artifice of men which makes the first interest take place; and therefore those laws of justice are so far to be considered as *artificial.* After that interest is once established and acknowledged, the sense of morality in the observance of these rules follows *naturally,* and of itself; though it is certain that it is also augmented by a new *artifice,* and that the public instructions of politicians, and the private education of parents, contribute to the giving us a sense of honour and duty, in the strict regulation of our actions with regard to the properties of others.

Section VII: *Of the Origin of Government*

Nothing is more certain than that men are in a great measure governed by interest, and that, even when they extend their concern beyond themselves, it is not to any great distance; nor is it usual for them, in common life, to look further than their nearest friends and acquaintance. It is no less certain, that it is impossible for men to consult their interest in so effectual a manner, as by an universal and inflexible observance of the rules of justice, by which alone they can preserve society, and keep themselves from falling into that wretched and savage condition which is commonly represented as the *state of nature.* And as this interest which all men have in the upholding of society, and the observation of the rules of justice, is great, so is it palpable and evident, even to the most rude and uncultivated of the human race; and it is almost impossible for any one who has had experience of society, to be mistaken in this particular. Since, therefore, men are so sincerely attached to their interest, and their interest is so much concerned in the observance of justice, and this interest is so certain and avowed, it may be asked, how any disorder can ever arise in society, and what principle there is in human nature so *powerful* as to overcome so strong a passion, or so *violent* as to obscure so clear a knowledge?

It has been observed, in treating of the Passions, that men are mightily governed by the imagination, and proportion their affections more to the light under which any object appears to them, than to its real and intrinsic value. What strikes upon them with a strong and lively idea commonly prevails above what lies in a more obscure light; and it must be a great superiority of value that is able to compensate this advantage. Now, as every thing that is contiguous to us, either in space or time, strikes upon us with such an idea, it has a proportional effect on the will and passions, and commonly operates with more force than any object that lies in a more distant and obscure light. Though we may be fully convinced that the latter object excels the former, we are not able to regulate our actions by this judgment, but yield to the solicitations of our passions, which always plead in favour of whatever is near and contiguous.

This is the reason why men so often act in contradiction to their known interest; and, in particular, why they prefer any trivial advantage that is present, to the maintenance of order in society, which so much depends on the observance of justice. The consequences of every breach of equity seem to lie very remote, and are not able to counterbalance any immediate advantage that may be reaped from it. They are, however, never the less real for being remote; and as all men are, in some degree, subject to the same weakness, it necessarily happens, that the violations of equity must become very frequent in society, and the commerce of men, by that means, be rendered very dangerous and uncertain. You have the same propension that I have in favour of what is contiguous above what is remote. You are, therefore, naturally carried to commit acts of injustice as well as me. Your example both pushes me forward in this way by imitation, and also affords me a new reason for any breach of equity, by shewing me that I should be the cully of my integrity, if I alone should impose on myself a severe restraint amidst the licentiousness of others.

This quality, therefore, of human nature, not only is very dangerous to society, but also seems, on a cursory view, to be incapable of any remedy. The remedy can only come from the consent of men; and if men be incapable of themselves to prefer remote to contiguous, they will never consent to any thing which would oblige them to such a choice, and contradict, in so sensible a manner, their natural principles and propensities. Whoever chooses the means, chooses also the end; and if it be impossible for us to prefer what is remote, it is equally impossible for us to submit to any necessity which would oblige us to such a method of acting.

But here it is observable, that this infirmity of human nature becomes a remedy to itself, and that we provide against our negligence about remote objects, merely because we are naturally inclined to that negligence. When we consider any objects at a distance, all their minute distinctions vanish, and we always give the preference to whatever is in itself preferable, without considering its situation and circumstances. This gives rise to what, in an improper sense, we call *reason,* which is a principle that is often contradictory to those propensities that display themselves upon the approach of the object. In reflecting on any action which I am to perform a twelvemonth hence, I always resolve to prefer the greater good, whether at that time it will be more contiguous or remote; nor does any difference in that particular make a difference in my present intentions and resolutions. My distance from the final determination makes all those minute differences vanish, nor am I affected by any thing but the general and more discernible qualities of good and evil. But on my nearer approach, those circumstances which I at first overlooked begin to appear, and have an influence on my conduct and affections. A new inclination to the present good springs up, and makes it difficult for me to adhere inflexibly to my first purpose and resolution. This natural infirmity I may very much regret, and I may endeavour, by all possible means, to free myself from it. I may have recourse to study and reflection within myself; to the advice of friends; to frequent meditation, and repeated resolution: And having experienced how ineffectual all these are, I may embrace with pleasure any other expedient by which I may impose a restraint upon myself, and guard against this weakness.

The only difficulty, therefore, is to find out this expedient, by which men cure their natural weakness, and lay themselves under the necessity of observing the laws of justice and equity, notwithstanding their violent propension to prefer contiguous to remote. It is evident such a remedy can never be effectual without correcting this propensity; and as it is impossible to change or correct any thing material in our nature, the utmost we can do is to change our circumstances and situation, and render the observance of the laws of justice our nearest interest, and their violation our most remote. But this being impracticable with respect to all mankind, it can only take place with respect to a few, whom we thus immediately interest in the execution of justice. These are the persons whom we call civil magistrates, kings and their ministers, our governors and rulers, who, being indifferent persons to the greatest part of the state, have no interest, or but a remote one, in any act of injustice; and, being satisfied with their present condition, and with their part in society, have an immediate interest in every execution of justice, which is so necessary to the upholding of society. Here, then, is the origin of civil government and society. Men are not able radically to cure, either in themselves or others, that narrowness of soul which makes them prefer the present to the remote. They cannot change their natures. All they can do is to change their situation, and render the observance of justice the immediate interest of some particular persons, and its violation their more remote. These persons, then, are not only induced to observe those rules in their own conduct, but also to constrain others to a like regularity, and enforce the dictates of equity through the whole society. And if it be necessary, they may also interest others more immediately in the execution of justice, and create a number of officers, civil and military, to assist them in their government.

But this execution of justice, though the principal, is not the only advantage of government. As violent passion hinders men from seeing distinctly the interest they have in an equitable behaviour towards others, so it hinders them from seeing that equity itself, and gives them a remarkable partiality in their own favours. This inconvenience is corrected in the same manner as that above mentioned. The same persons who execute the laws of justice, will also decide all controversies concerning them; and, being indifferent to the greatest part of the society, will decide them more equitably than every one would in his own case.

By means of these two advantages in the *execution* and *decision* of justice, men acquire a security against each other's weakness and passion, as well as against their own, and, under the shelter of their governors, begin to taste at ease the sweets of society and mutual assistance. But government extends further its beneficial influence; and, not contented to protect men in those conventions they make for their mutual interest, it often obliges them to make such conventions, and forces them to seek their own advantage, by a concurrence in some common end or purpose. There is no quality in human nature which causes more fatal errors in our conduct, than that which leads us to prefer whatever is present to the distant and remote, and makes us desire objects more according to their situation than their intrinsic value. Two neighbours may agree to drain a meadow, which they possess in common: because it is easy for them to know each other's mind; and each must perceive, that the immediate consequence of his failing in his part, is the abandoning the whole project. But it is very difficult, and indeed impossible, that a thousand persons should agree in any such action; it being difficult for them to concert so complicated a design, and still more difficult for them to execute it; while each seeks a pretext to free himself of the trouble and expence, and would lay the whole burden on others. Political society easily remedies both these inconveniences. Magistrates find an immediate interest in the interest of any considerable part of their subjects. They need consult nobody but themselves to form any scheme for the promoting of that interest. And as the failure of any one piece in the execution is connected, though not immediately, with the failure of the whole, they prevent that failure, because they find no interest in it, either immediate or remote. Thus, bridges are built, harbors opened, ramparts raised, canals formed, fleets equipped, and armies disciplined, every where, by the care of government, which, though composed of men subject to all human infirmities, becomes, by one of the finest and most subtile inventions imaginable, a composition which is in some measure exempted from all these infirmities.

Section VIII: *Of the Source of Allegiance*

Though government be an invention very advantageous, and even in some circumstances absolutely necessary to mankind, it is not necessary in all circumstances; nor is it impossible for men to preserve society for some time, without having recourse to such an invention. Men, it is true, are always much inclined to prefer present interest to distant and remote; nor is it easy for them to resist the temptation of any advantage that they may immediately enjoy, in apprehension of an evil that lies at a distance from them; but still this weakness is less conspicuous where the possessions and the pleasures of life are few and of little value, as they always are in the infancy of society. An Indian is but little tempted to dispossess another of his hut, or to steal his bow, as being already provided of the same advantages; and as to any superior fortune which may attend one above another in hunting and fishing, it is only casual and temporary, and will have but small tendency to disturb society. And so far am I from thinking with some philosophers, that men are utterly incapable of society without government, that I assert the first rudiments of government to arise from quarrels, not among men of the same society, but among those of different societies. A less degree of riches will suffice to this latter effect, than is requisite for the former. Men fear nothing from public war and violence but the resistance they meet with, which, because they share it in common, seems less terrible, and, because it comes from strangers, seems less pernicious in its consequences, than when they are exposed singly against one whose commerce is advantageous to them, and without whose society it is impossible they can subsist. Now foreign war, to a society without government, necessarily produces civil war. Throw any considerable goods among men, they instantly fall a quarreling, while each strives to get possession of what pleases him, without regard to the consequences. In a foreign war, the most considerable of all goods, life and limbs, are at stake; and as every one shuns dangerous ports, seizes the best arms, seeks excuse for the slightest wounds, the laws, which may be well enough observed while men were calm, can now no longer take place, when they are in such commotion.

This we find verified in the American tribes, where men live in concord and amity among themselves, without any established government, and never pay submission to any of their fellows, except in time of war, when their captain enjoys a shadow of authority, which he loses after their return from the field and the establishment of peace with the neighbouring tribes. This authority, however, instructs them in the advantages of government, and teaches them to have recourse to it, when, either by the pillage of war, by commerce, or by any fortuitous inventions, their riches and possessions have become so considerable as to make them forget, on every emergence, the interest they have in the preservation of peace and justice. Hence we may give a plausible reason, among others, why all governments are at first monarchical, without any mixture and variety; and why republics arise only from the abuses of monarchy and despotic power. Camps are the true mothers of cities; and as war cannot be administered, by reason of the suddenness of every exigency, without some authority in a single person, the same kind of authority naturally takes place in that civil government which succeeds the military. And this reason I take to be more natural than the common one derived from patriarchal government, or the authority of a father, which is said first to take place in one family, and to accustom the members of it to the government of a single person. The state of society without government is one of the most natural states of men, and must subsist with the conjunction of many families, and long after the first generation. Nothing but an encrease of riches and possessions could oblige men to quit it; and so barbarous and uninstructed are all societies on their first formation, that many years must elapse before these can encrease to such a degree as to disturb men in the enjoyment of peace and concord.

But though it be possible for men to maintain a small uncultivated society without government, it is impossible they should maintain a society of any kind without justice, and the observance of those three fundamental laws concerning the stability of possession, its translation by consent, and the performance of promises. These are therefore antecedent to government, and are supposed to impose an obligation, before the duty of allegiance to civil magistrates has once been thought of. Nay, I shall go further, and assert, that government, *upon its first establishment,* would naturally be supposed to derive its obligation from those laws of nature, and, in particular, from that concerning the performance of promises. When men have once perceived the necessity of government to maintain peace and execute justice, they would naturally assemble together, would choose magistrates, determine their power, and *promise* them obedience. As a promise is supposed to be a bond or security already in use, and attended with a moral obligation, it is to be considered as the original sanction of government, and as the source of the first obligation to obedience. This reasoning appears so natural, that it has become the foundation of our fashionable system of politics, and is in a manner the creed of a party amongst us, who pride themselves, with reason, on the soundness of their philosophy and their liberty of thought. "All men," say they, "are born free and equal: government and superiority can only be established by consent: the consent of men, in establishing government, imposes on them a new obligation, unknown to the laws of nature. Men, therefore, are bound to obey their magistrates, only because they promise it; and if they had not given their word, either expressly or tacitly, to preserve allegiance, it would never have become a part of their moral duty."[15] This conclusion, however, when carried so far as to comprehend government in all its ages and situations, is entirely erroneous; and I maintain, that though the duty of allegiance be at first grafted on the obligation of promises, and be for some time supported by that obligation, yet it quickly takes root of itself, and has an original obligation and authority, independent of all contracts. This is a principle of moment, which we must examine with care and attention, before we proceed any further.

It is reasonable for those philosophers who assert justice to be a natural virtue, and antecedent to human conventions, to resolve all civil allegiance into the obligation of a promise, and assert that it is our own consent alone which binds us to any submission to magistracy. For as all government is plainly an invention of men, and the origin of most governments is known in history, it is necessary to mount higher, in order to find the source of our political duties, if we would assert them to have any *natural* obligation of morality. These philosophers, therefore, quickly observe, that society is as ancient as the human species, and those three fundamental laws of nature as ancient as society; so that, taking advantage of the antiquity and obscure origin

15. [Hume is pointing to an essential tenet of Locke's political philosophy. See Locke's *Two Treatises of Government*, ed. by P. Laslett, student edition (Cambridge: Cambridge University Press, 1988), pp. 269–76 and 330–33.]

of these laws, they first deny them to be artificial and voluntary inventions of men, and then seek to ingraft on them those other duties which are more plainly artificial. But being once undeceived in this particular, and having found that *natural* as well as civil justice derives its origin from human conventions, we shall quickly perceive how fruitless it is to resolve the one into the other, and seek, in the laws of nature, a stronger foundation for our political duties than interest and human conventions; while these laws themselves are built on the very same foundation. On whichever side we turn this subject, we shall find that these two kinds of duty are exactly on the same footing, and have the same source both of their *first invention* and *moral obligation.* They are contrived to remedy like inconveniences, and acquire their moral sanction in the same manner, from their remedying those inconveniences. These are two points which we shall endeavour to prove as distinctly as possible.

We have already shewn, that men *invented* the three fundamental laws of nature, when they observed the necessity of society to their mutual subsistence, and found that it was impossible to maintain any correspondence together, without some restraint on their natural appetites. The same self-love, therefore, which renders men so incommodious to each other, taking a new and more convenient direction, produces the rules of justice, and is the *first* motive of their observance. But when men have observed, that though the rules of justice be sufficient to maintain any society, yet it is impossible for them, of themselves, to observe those rules in large and polished societies; they establish government as a new invention to attain their ends, and preserve the old, or procure new advantages, by a more strict execution of justice. So far, therefore, our *civil* duties are connected with our *natural,* that the former are invented chiefly for the sake of the latter; and that the principal object of government is to constrain men to observe the laws of nature. In this respect, however, that law of nature, concerning the performance of promises, is only comprised along with the rest; and its exact observance is to be considered as an effect of the institution of government, and not the obedience to government as an effect of the obligation of a promise. Though the object of our civil duties be the enforcing of our natural, yet the *first*[16] motive of the invention, as well as performance of both, is nothing but self-interest; and since

16. First in time, not in dignity or force.

there is a separate interest in the obedience to government, from that in the performance of promises, we must also allow of a separate obligation. To obey the civil magistrate is requisite to preserve order and concord in society. To perform promises is requisite to beget mutual trust and confidence in the common offices of life. The ends, as well as the means, are perfectly distinct; nor is the one subordinate to the other.

To make this more evident, let us consider that men will often bind themselves by promises to the performance of what it would have been their interest to perform, independent of these promises; as when they would give others a fuller security, by superadding a new obligation of interest to that which they formerly lay under. The interest in the performance of promises, besides its moral obligation, is general, avowed, and of the last consequence in life. Other interests may be more particular and doubtful; and we are apt to entertain a greater suspicion, that men may indulge their humour or passion in acting contrary to them. Here, therefore, promises come naturally in play, and are often required for fuller satisfaction and security. But supposing those other interests to be as general and avowed as the interest in the performance of a promise, they will be regarded as on the same footing, and men will begin to repose the same confidence in them. Now this is exactly the case with regard to our civil duties, or obedience to the magistrate; without which no government could subsist, nor any peace or order be maintained in large societies, where there are so many possessions on the one hand, and so many wants, real or imaginary, on the other. Our civil duties, therefore, must soon detach themselves from our promises, and acquire a separate force and influence. The interest in both is of the very same kind: it is general, avowed, and prevails in all times and places. There is, then, no pretext of reason for founding the one upon the other, while each of them has a foundation peculiar to itself. We might as well resolve the obligation to abstain from the possessions of others, into the obligation of a promise, as that of allegiance. The interests are not more distinct in the one case than the other. A regard to property is not more necessary to natural society, than obedience is to civil society or government; nor is the former society more necessary to the being of mankind, than the latter to their well-being and happiness. In short, if the performance of promises be advantageous, so is obedience to government; if the former interest be general, so is the latter; if the one interest be obvious and avowed, so is the other. And as these two rules are founded on like obligations of interest, each of them must have a peculiar authority, independent of the other.

But it is not only the *natural* obligations of interest, which are distinct in promises and allegiance; but also the *moral* obligations of honour and conscience: nor does the merit or demerit of the one depend in the least upon that of the other. And, indeed, if we consider the close connexion there is betwixt the natural and moral obligations, we shall find this conclusion to be entirely unavoidable. Our interest is always engaged on the side of obedience to magistracy; and there is nothing but a great present advantage that can lead us to rebellion, by making us overlook the remote interest which we have in the preserving of peace and order in society. But though a present interest may thus blind us with regard to our own actions, it takes not place with regard to those of others; nor hinders them from appearing in their true colours, as highly prejudicial to public interest, and to our own in particular. This naturally gives us an uneasiness, in considering such seditious and disloyal actions, and makes us attach to them the idea of vice and moral deformity. It is the same principle which causes us to disapprove of all kinds of private injustice, and, in particular, of the breach of promises. We blame all treachery and breach of faith; because we consider that the freedom and extent of human commerce depend entirely on a fidelity with regard to promises. We blame all disloyalty to magistrates; because we perceive that the execution of justice, in the stability of possession, its translation by consent, and the performance of promises, is impossible, without submission to government. As there are here two interests entirely distinct from each other, they must give rise to two moral obligations, equally separate and independent. Though there was no such thing as a promise in the world, government would still be necessary in all large and civilized societies; and if promises had only their own proper obligation, without the separate sanction of government, they would have but little efficacy in such societies. This separates the boundaries of our public and private duties, and shews that the latter are more dependent on the former, than the former on the latter. *Education,* and *the artifice of politicians* concur to bestow a further morality on loyalty, and to brand all rebellion with a greater degree of guilt and infamy. Nor is it a wonder that politicians should be very industrious in inculcating such notions, where their interest is so particularly concerned.

Lest those arguments should not appear entirely conclusive (as I think they are), I shall have recourse to authority, and shall prove, from the universal consent of mankind, that the obligation of submission to government is not derived from any promise of the subjects. Nor need any one wonder, that though I have all along endeavoured to establish my system on pure reason, and have scarce ever cited the judgment even of philosophers or historians on any article, I should now appeal to popular authority, and oppose the sentiments of the rabble to any philosophical reasoning. For it must be observed, that the opinions of men, in this case, carry with them a peculiar authority, and are, in a great measure, infallible.[17] The distinction of moral good and evil is founded on the pleasure or pain which results from the view of any sentiment or character; and, as that pleasure or pain cannot be unknown to the person who feels it, it follows,[18] that there is just so much vice or virtue in any character as every one places in it, and that it is impossible in this particular we can ever be mistaken. And, though our judgments concerning the *origin* of any vice or virtue, be not so certain as those concerning their *degrees*, yet, since the question in this case regards not any philosophical origin of an obligation, but a plain matter of fact, it is not easily conceived how we can fall into an error. A man who acknowledges himself to be bound to another for a certain sum, must certainly know whether it be by his own bond, or that of his father; whether it be of his mere good-will, or for money lent him; and under what conditions, and for what purposes, he has bound himself. In like manner, it being certain that there is a moral obligation to submit to government, because every one thinks so; it must be as certain that this obligation arises not from a promise; since no one, whose judgment has not been led astray by too strict adherence to a system of philosophy, has ever yet dreamt of ascribing it to that origin. Neither magistrates nor subjects have formed this idea of our civil duties.

We find that magistrates are so far from deriving their authority, and the obligation to obedience in their subjects, from the foundation

17. [Hume makes the same arresting claim concerning the infallibility of opinion in two other places. See this edition, pp. 61 and 180.]

18. This proposition must hold strictly true with regard to every quality that is determined merely by sentiment. In what sense we can talk either of a *right* or a *wrong* taste in morals, eloquence, or beauty, shall be considered afterwards. In the meantime it may be observed, that there is such an uniformity in the *general* sentiments of mankind, as to render such questions of but small importance.

of a promise or original contract, that they conceal, as far as possible, from their people, especially from the vulgar, that they have their origin from thence. Were this the sanction of government, our rulers would never receive it tacitly, which is the utmost that can be pretended; since what is given tacitly and insensibly, can never have such influence on mankind as what is performed expressly and openly. A tacit promise is, where the will is signified by other more diffuse signs than those of speech; but a will there must certainly be in the case, and that can never escape the person's notice who exerted it, however silent or tacit. But were you to ask the far greatest part of the nation, whether they had ever consented to the authority of their rulers, or promised to obey them, they would be inclined to think very strangely of you: and would certainly reply, that the affair depended not on their consent, but that they were born to such an obedience. In consequence of this opinion, we frequently see them imagine such persons to be their natural rulers, as are at that time deprived of all power and authority, and whom no man, however foolish, would voluntarily choose; and this merely because they are in that line which ruled before, and in that degree of it which used to succeed: though perhaps in so distant a period, that scarce any man alive could ever have given any promise of obedience. Has a government, then, no authority over such as these, because they never consented to it, and would esteem the very attempt of such a free choice a piece of arrogance and impiety? We find by experience, that it punishes them very freely for what it calls treason and rebellion, which, it seems, according to this system, reduces itself to common injustice. If you say, that by dwelling in its dominions, they in effect consented to the established government, I answer, that this can only be where they think the affair depends on their choice, which few or none beside those philosophers have ever yet imagined. It never was pleaded as an excuse for a rebel, that the first act he performed, after he came to years of discretion, was to levy war against the sovereign of the state; and that, while he was a child he could not bind himself by his own consent, and having become a man, showed plainly, by the first act he performed, that he had no design to impose on himself any obligation to obedience. We find, on the contrary, that civil laws punish this crime at the same age as any other which is criminal of itself, without our consent; that is, when the person is come to the full use of reason: whereas to this crime they ought in justice to allow some intermediate time, in which a tacit consent at least might be supposed. To which we may add, that a man living under an absolute government would owe it no allegiance; since, by its very nature, it depends not on consent. But as that is as *natural* and *common* a government as any, it must certainly occasion some obligation; and it is plain from experience, that men who are subjected to it do always think so. This is a clear proof that we do not commonly esteem our allegiance to be derived from our consent or promise; and a further proof is, that when our promise is upon any account expressly engaged, we always distinguish exactly betwixt the two obligations, and believe the one to add more force to the other, than in a repetition of the same promise. Where no promise is given, a man looks not on his faith as broken in private matters, upon account of rebellion; but keeps those two duties of honour and allegiance perfectly distinct and separate. As the uniting of them was thought by these philosophers a very subtile invention, this is a convincing proof that it is not a true one; since no man can either give a promise, or be restrained by its sanction and obligation, unknown to himself.

Section IX: *Of the Measures of Allegiance*

Those political writers who have had recourse to a promise, or original contract, as the source of our allegiance to government, intended to establish a principle which is perfectly just and reasonable; though the reasoning upon which they endeavoured to establish it was fallacious and sophistical. They would prove, that our submission to government admits of exceptions, and that an egregious tyranny in the rulers is sufficient to free the subjects from all ties of allegiance. Since men enter into society, say they, and submit themselves to government by their free and voluntary consent, they must have in view certain advantages which they propose to reap from it, and for which they are contented to resign their native liberty. There is therefore something mutual engaged on the part of the magistrate, viz. protection and security; and it is only by the hopes he affords of these advantages, that he can ever persuade men to submit to him. But when, instead of protection and security, they meet with tyranny and oppression, they are freed from their promises, (as happens in all conditional contracts) and return to that state of liberty which preceded the institution of government. Men would never be so foolish as to enter into such engagements as should turn entirely to the advantage of others, without any view of bettering their own condition. Whoever proposes to draw any profit from our submission, must engage himself, either expressly or tacitly, to make us reap some advantage from his authority; nor ought he to expect, that, without the performance of his part, we will ever continue in obedience.

I repeat it: This conclusion is just, though the principles be erroneous; and I flatter myself that I can establish the same conclusion on more reasonable principles. I shall not take such a compass, in establishing our political duties, as to assert that men perceive the advantages of government; that they institute government with a view to those advantages; that this institution requires a promise of obedience, which imposes a moral obligation to a certain degree, but, being conditional, ceases to be binding whenever the other contracting party performs not his part of the engagement. I perceive that a promise itself arises entirely from human conventions, and is invented with a view to a certain interest. I seek, therefore, some such interest more immediately connected with government, and which may be at once the original motive to its institution, and the source of our obedience to it. This interest I find to consist in the security and protection which we enjoy in political society, and which we can never attain when perfectly free and independent. As interest, therefore, is the immediate sanction of government, the one can have no longer being than the other; and whenever the civil magistrate carries his oppression so far as to render his authority perfectly intolerable, we are no longer bound to submit to it. The cause ceases; the effect must cease also.

So far the conclusion is immediate and direct, concerning the *natural* obligation which we have to allegiance. As to the *moral* obligation, we may observe that the maxim would here be false, that *when the cause ceases the effect must cease also.* For there is a principle of human nature, which we have frequently taken notice of, that men are mightily addicted to *general rules,* and that we often carry our maxims beyond those reasons which first induced us to establish them. Where cases are similar in many circumstances, we are apt to put them on the same footing, without considering that they differ in the most material circumstances, and that the resemblance is more apparent than real. It may therefore be thought that, in the case of allegiance, our moral obligation of duty will not cease, even though the natural obligation of interest, which is its cause, has ceased, and that men may be bound by *conscience* to submit to a tyrannical government, against their own and the public interest. And indeed, to the force of this argument I so far submit, as to acknowledge, that general rules commonly extend beyond the principles on which they are founded; and that we seldom make any exception to them, unless that exception have the qualities of a general rule, and be founded on very numerous and common instances. Now this I assert to be entirely the present case. When men submit to the authority of others, it is to procure themselves some security against the wickedness and injustice of men, who are perpetually carried, by their unruly passions, and by their present and immediate interest, to the violation of all the laws of society. But as this imperfection is inherent in human nature, we know that it must attend men in all their states and conditions, and that those whom we choose for rulers, do not immediately become of a superior nature to the rest of mankind, upon account of their superior power and authority. What we expect from them depends not on a change of their nature, but of their situation, when they acquire a more immediate interest in the preservation of order and the execution of justice. But besides that this interest is only more immediate in the execution of justice among their subjects; besides this, I say, we may often expect, from the irregularity of human nature, that they will neglect even this immediate interest, and be transported by their passions into all the excesses of cruelty and ambition. Our general knowledge of human nature, our observation of the past history of mankind, our experience of present times; all these causes must induce us to open the door to exceptions, and must make us conclude, that we may resist the more violent effects of supreme power without any crime or injustice.

Accordingly we may observe, that this is both the general practice and principle of mankind, and that no nation that could find any remedy ever yet suffered the cruel ravages of a tyrant, or were blamed for their resistance. Those who took up arms against Dionysius or Nero, or Philip the Second,[19] have the favour of every reader in the perusal of their history; and nothing but the most violent perversion of common sense can ever lead us to condemn them. It is certain, therefore, that in all our notions of morals, we never entertain such an absurdity as that of passive obedience, but make allowances for resistance in the more flagrant instances of tyranny and oppression. The general opinion of mankind has some authority in all cases; but in this of morals it is perfectly infallible. Nor is it less infallible, because men cannot distinctly

19. [Dionysius was a tyrant of Syracuse from 405 to 367 B.C. Nero (A.D. 37–68) was Emperor of Rome from A.D. 54 to 68. Philip the Second was King of Macedon from 359 to 336 B.C.]

explain the principles on which it is founded. Few persons can carry on this train of reasoning: "Government is a mere human invention for the interest of society. Where the tyranny of the governor removes this interest, it also removes the natural obligation to obedience. The moral obligation is founded on the natural, and therefore must cease where that ceases; especially where the subject is such as makes us foresee very many occasions wherein the natural obligation may cease, and causes us to form a kind of general rule for the regulation of our conduct in such occurrences." But though this train of reasoning be too subtile for the vulgar, it is certain that all men have an implicit notion of it, and are sensible that they owe obedience to government merely on account of the public interest; and, at the same time, that human nature is so subject to frailties and passions, as may easily pervert this institution, and change their governors into tyrants and public enemies. If the sense of public interest were not our original motive to obedience, I would fain ask, what other principle is there in human nature capable of subduing the natural ambition of men, and forcing them to such a submission? Imitation and custom are not sufficient. For the question still recurs, what motive first produces those instances of submission which we imitate, and that train of actions which produces the custom? There evidently is no other principle than public interest; and if interest first produces obedience to government the obligation to obedience must cease whenever the interest ceases in any great degree, and in a considerable number of instances.

Section X: *Of the Objects of Allegiance*

But though, on some occasions, it may be justifiable, both in sound politics and morality, to resist supreme power, it is certain that, in the ordinary course of human affairs, nothing can be more pernicious and criminal; and that, besides the convulsions which always attend revolutions, such a practice tends directly to the subversion of all government, and the causing an universal anarchy and confusion among mankind. As numerous and civilized societies cannot subsist without government, so government is entirely useless without an exact obedience. We ought always to weigh the advantages which we reap from authority, against the disadvantages: and by this means we shall become more scrupulous of putting in practice the doctrine of resistance. The common rule requires submission; and it is only in cases of grievous tyranny and oppression, that the exception can take place.

Since, then, such a blind submission is commonly due to magistracy, the next question is, *to whom it is due, and whom we are to regard as our lawful magistrates?* In order to answer this question, let us recollect what we have already established concerning the origin of government and political society. When men have once experienced the impossibility of preserving any steady order in society, while every one is his own master, and violates or observes the laws of society, according to his present interest or pleasure, they naturally run into the invention of government, and put it out of their own power, as far as possible, to transgress the laws of society. Government, therefore, arises from the voluntary convention of men; and it is evident, that the same convention which establishes government, will also determine the persons who are to govern, and will remove all doubt and ambiguity in this particular. And the voluntary consent of men must here have the greater efficacy, that the authority of the magistrate does *at first* stand upon the foundation of a promise of the subjects, by which they bind themselves to obedience, as in every other contract or engagement. The same promise, then, which binds them to obedience, ties them down to a particular person, and makes him the object of their allegiance.

But when government has been established on this footing for some considerable time, and the separate interest which we have in submission has produced a separate sentiment of morality, the case is entirely altered, and a promise is no longer able to determine the particular magistrate; since it is no longer considered as the foundation of government. We naturally suppose ourselves born to submission; and imagine that such particular persons have a right to command, as we on our part are bound to obey. These notions of right and obligation are derived from nothing but the *advantage* we reap from government, which gives us a repugnance to practise resistance ourselves, and makes us displeased with any instance of it in others. But here it is remarkable, that in this new state of affairs, the original sanction of government, which is *interest,* is not admitted to determine the persons whom we are to obey, as the original sanction did at first, when affairs were on the footing of a *promise.* A *promise* fixes and determines the persons, without any uncertainty: but it is evident, that if men were to regulate their conduct in this particular, by the view of a peculiar interest, either public or private, they would involve themselves in endless confusion, and would render all government, in a great measure, ineffectual. The private interest of every one is different; and, though the public interest in itself be always one and the same, yet it becomes the source of as great dissensions, by reason of the different opinions of particular persons concerning it. The same interest, therefore, which causes us to submit to magistracy, makes us renounce itself in the choice of our magistrates, and binds us down to a certain form of government, and to particular persons, without allowing us to aspire to the utmost perfection in either. The case is here the same as in that law of nature concerning the stability of possession. It is highly advantageous, and even absolutely necessary to society, that possession should be stable; and this leads us to the establishment of such a rule: but we find, that were we to follow the same advantage, in assigning particular possessions to particular persons, we should disappoint our end, and perpetuate the confusion which that rule is intended to prevent. We must therefore proceed by general rules, and regulate ourselves by general interests, in modifying the law of nature concerning the stability of possession. Nor need we fear, that our attachment to this law will diminish upon account of the seeming frivolousness of those interests by which it is determined. The impulse of the mind is derived from a very strong interest; and those other more minute interests serve only to direct the motion, without adding any thing to it, or diminishing from it. It is the same case with government. Nothing is more advantageous to society than such an invention; and this interest is sufficient to make us embrace it with ardour and alacrity; though we are obliged afterwards to regulate and direct our devotion to government by several considerations which are not of the same importance, and to choose our magistrates without having in view any particular advantage from the choice.

The *first* of those principles I shall take notice of, as a foundation of the right of magistracy, is that which gives authority to all the most established governments of the world, without exception: I mean, *long possession* in any one form of government, or succession of princes. It is certain, that if we remount to the first origin of every nation, we shall find that there scarce is any race of kings, or form of a commonwealth, that is not primarily founded on usurpation and rebellion, and whose title is not at first worse than doubtful and uncertain. Time alone gives solidity to their right; and, operating gradually on the minds of men, reconciles them to any authority, and makes it seem just and reasonable. Nothing causes any sentiment to have a greater influence upon us than custom, or turns our imagination more strongly to any object. When we have been long accustomed to obey any set of men, that general instinct or tendency which we have to suppose a moral obligation attending loyalty, takes easily this direction, and chooses that set of men for its objects. It is interest which gives the general instinct; but it is custom which gives the particular direction.

And here it is observable, that the same length of time has a different influence on our sentiments of morality, according to its different influence on the mind. We naturally judge of every thing by comparison; and since, in considering the fate of kingdoms and republics, we embrace a long extent of time, a small duration has not, in this case, a like influence on our sentiments, as when we consider any other object. One thinks he acquires a right to a horse, or a suit of cloaths, in a very short time; but a century is scarce sufficient to establish any new government, or remove all scruples in the minds of the subjects concerning it. Add to this, that a shorter period of time will suffice to give a prince a title to any additional power he may usurp, than will serve to fix his right, where the whole is an usurpation. The kings of France have not been possessed of absolute power for above two reigns; and yet nothing will appear more extravagant to Frenchmen than to talk of their liberties. If we consider what has been said concerning *accession,* we shall easily account for this phenomenon.

When there is no form of government established by long possession, the *present* possession is sufficient to supply its place, and may be regarded as the *second* source of all public authority. Right to authority is nothing but the constant possession of authority, maintained by the laws of society and the interests of mankind; and nothing can be more natural than to join this constant possession to the present one, according to the principles above mentioned. If the same principles did not take place with regard to the property of private persons, it was because these principles were counterbalanced by very strong considerations of interest; when we observed that all restitution would by that means be prevented, and every violence be authorized and protected. And, though the same motives may seem to have force with regard to public authority, yet they are opposed by a contrary interest; which consists in the preservation of peace, and the avoiding of all changes, which, however they may be easily produced in private affairs, are unavoidably attended with bloodshed and confusion where the public is interested.

Any one who, finding the impossibility of accounting for the right of the present possessor, by any received system of ethics, should resolve to deny absolutely that right, and assert that it is not authorized by morality, would be justly thought to maintain a very extravagant paradox, and to shock the common sense and judgment of mankind. No maxim is more conformable, both to prudence and morals, than to submit quietly to the government which we find established in the country where we happen to live, without enquiring too curiously into its origin and first establishment. Few governments will bear being examined so rigorously. How many kingdoms are there at present in the world, and how many more do we find in history, whose governors have no better foundation for their authority than that of present possession? To confine ourselves to the Roman and Grecian empire; is it not evident, that the long succession of emperors, from the dissolution of the Roman liberty, to the final extinction of that empire by the Turks,[20] could not so much as pretend to any other title to the empire? The election of the senate was a mere form, which always followed the choice of the legions; and these were almost always divided in the different provinces, and nothing but the sword was able to terminate the difference. It was by the sword, therefore, that every emperor acquired, as well as defended, his right; and we must either say, that all the known world, for so many ages, had no government, and owed no allegiance to any one, or must allow, that the right of the stronger, in public affairs, is to be received as legitimate, and authorized by morality, when not opposed by any other title.

The right of *conquest* may be considered as a *third* source of the title of sovereigns. This right resembles very much that of present possession, but has rather a superior force, being seconded by the notions of glory and honour which we ascribe to *conquerors,* instead of the sentiments of hatred and detestation which attend *usurpers.* Men naturally favour those they love; and therefore are more apt to ascribe a right to successful violence, betwixt one sovereign and another, than to the successful rebellion of a subject against his sovereign.[21]

20. [The Roman Empire began in 28 B.C. with Octavian (formally named Emperor Augustus in 27 B.C.) and ended in the East in 1453 with the fall of Constantinople.]

21. It is not here asserted, that *present possession* or *conquest* are sufficient to give a title against *long possession* and *positive laws:* but only that they have some force, and will be able to cast the balance where the titles are otherwise equal, and will even be sufficient *sometimes* to sanctify the weaker title. What degree of force they have is difficult to determine. I believe all moderate men will allow, that they have great force in all disputes concerning the rights of princes.

When neither long possession, nor present possession, nor conquest take place, as when the first sovereign who founded any monarchy dies; in that case, the right of *succession* naturally prevails in their stead, and men are commonly induced to place the son of their late monarch on the throne, and suppose him to inherit his father's authority. The presumed consent of the father, the imitation of the succession to private families, the interest which the state has in choosing the person who is most powerful and has the most numerous followers; all these reasons lead men to prefer the son of their late monarch to any other person.[22]

These reasons have some weight; but I am persuaded, that, to one who considers impartially of the matter, it will appear that there concur some principles of the imagination along with those views of interest. The royal authority seems to be connected with the young prince even in his father's lifetime, by the natural transition of the thought, and still more after his death; so that nothing is more natural than to complete this union by a new relation, and by putting him actually in possession of what seems so naturally to belong to him.

To confirm this, we may weigh the following phenomena, which are pretty curious in their kind. In elective monarchies, the right of succession has no place by the laws and settled custom; and yet its influence is so natural, that it is impossible entirely to exclude it from the imagination, and render the subjects indifferent to the son of their deceased monarch. Hence, in some governments of this kind, the choice commonly falls on one or other of the royal family; and in some governments they are all excluded. Those contrary phenomena proceed from the same principle. Where the royal family is excluded, it is from a refinement in politics, which makes people sensible of their propensity to choose a sovereign in that family, and gives them a jealousy of their liberty, lest their new monarch, aided by this propensity, should establish his family, and destroy the freedom of elections for the future.

The history of Artaxerxes and the younger Cyrus,[23] may furnish us with some reflections to the same purpose. Cyrus pretended a right to the throne above his elder brother, because he was born after his

22. To prevent mistakes I must observe, that this case of succession is not the same with that of hereditary monarchies, where custom has fixed the right of succession. These depend upon the principle of long possession above explained.

23. [The younger Cyrus's older brother, Arsaces, ascended to the throne of Persia as Artaxerxes II in 404 B.C. Cyrus died in 401 B.C. attempting to overthrow him.]

father's accession. I do not pretend that this reason was valid. I would only infer from it, that he would never have made use of such a pretext, were it not for the qualities of the imagination above mentioned, by which we are naturally inclined to unite by a new relation whatever objects we find already united. Artaxerxes had an advantage above his brother, as being the eldest son, and the first in succession; but Cyrus was more closely related to the royal authority, as being begot after his father was invested with it.

Should it here be pretended, that the view of convenience may be the source of all the right of succession, and that men gladly take advantage of any rule by which they can fix the successor of their late sovereign, and prevent that anarchy and confusion which attends all new elections; to this I would answer, that I readily allow that this motive may contribute something to the effect; but at the same time I assert, that, without another principle, it is impossible such a motive should take place. The interest of a nation requires that the succession to the crown should be fixed one way or other; but it is the same thing to its interest in what way it be fixed; so that if the relation of blood had not an effect independent of public interest, it would never have been regarded without a positive law; and it would have been impossible that so many positive laws of different nations could ever have concurred precisely in the same views and intentions.

This leads us to consider the *fifth* source of authority, viz. *positive laws,* when the legislature establishes a certain form of government and succession of princes. At first sight, it may be thought that this must resolve into some of the preceding titles of authority. The legislative power, whence the positive law is derived, must either be established by original contract, long possession, present possession, conquest, or succession; and consequently the positive law must derive its force from some of those principles. But here it is remarkable, that though a positive law can only derive its force from these principles, yet it acquires not all the force of the principle from whence it is derived, but loses considerably in the transition, as it is natural to imagine. For instance, a government is established for many centuries on a certain system of laws, forms, and methods of succession. The legislative power established by this long succession, changes, all on a sudden, the whole system of government, and introduces a new constitution in its stead. I believe few of the subjects will think themselves bound to comply with this alteration, unless it have an evident tendency to the public good, but will think themselves still at liberty to return to the ancient government. Hence the notion of *fundamental laws,* which are supposed to be unalterable by the will of the sovereign; and of this nature the Salic law is understood to be in France. How far these fundamental laws extend, is not determined in any government, nor is it possible it ever should. There is such an insensible gradation from the most material laws to the most trivial, and from the most ancient laws to the most modern, that it will be impossible to set bounds to the legislative power, and determine how far it may innovate in the principles of government. That is the work more of imagination and passion than of reason.

Whoever considers the history of the several nations of the world, their revolutions, conquests, encrease, and diminution, the manner in which their particular governments are established, and the successive right transmitted from one person to another, will soon learn to treat very lightly all disputes concerning the rights of princes, and will be convinced that a strict adherence to any general rules, and the rigid loyalty to particular persons and families, on which some people set so high a value, are virtues that hold less of reason than of bigotry and superstition. In this particular, the study of history confirms the reasonings of true philosophy, which, shewing us the original qualities of human nature, teaches us to regard the controversies in politics as incapable of any decision in most cases, and as entirely subordinate to the interests of peace and liberty. Where the public good does not evidently demand a change, it is certain that the concurrence of all those titles, *original contract, long possession, present possession, succession,* and *positive laws,* forms the strongest title to sovereignty, and is justly regarded as sacred and inviolable. But when these titles are mingled and opposed in different degrees, they often occasion perplexity, and are less capable of solution from the arguments of lawyers and philosophers, than from the swords of the soldiery. Who shall tell me, for instance, whether Germanicus or Drusus ought to have succeeded Tiberius,[24] had he died while they were both alive, without naming any of them for his successor? Ought the right of adoption to be received as equivalent to that of blood, in a nation where it had the same effect in private families, and had already, in two instances, taken place in the public? Ought Germanicus to be esteemed the eldest son,

24. [Tiberius was Emperor of Rome from A.D. 14 to 37. Germanicus, born in 24 B.C., was adopted by his uncle Tiberius in A.D. 4. Drusus, the biological son of Tiberius, was born in 13 B.C.]

because he was born before Drusus; or the younger, because he was adopted after the birth of his brother? Ought the right of the elder to be regarded in a nation, where the eldest brother had no advantage in the succession to private families? Ought the Roman empire at that time to be esteemed hereditary, because of two examples; or ought it, even so early, to be regarded as belonging to the stronger, or the present possessor, as being founded on so recent an usurpation? Upon whatever principles we may pretend to answer these and such like questions, I am afraid we shall never be able to satisfy an impartial enquirer, who adopts no party in political controversies, and will be satisfied with nothing but sound reason and philosophy.

But here an *English* reader will be apt to enquire concerning that famous *revolution* which has had such a happy influence on our constitution, and has been attended with such mighty consequences.[25] We have already remarked, that, in the case of enormous tyranny and oppression, it is lawful to take arms even against supreme power; and that, as government is a mere human invention, for mutual advantage and security, it no longer imposes any obligation, either natural or moral, when once it ceases to have that tendency. But though this *general* principle be authorized by common sense, and the practice of all ages, it is certainly impossible for the laws, or even for philosophy, to establish any *particular* rules by which we may know when resistance is lawful, and decide all controversies which may arise on that subject. This may not only happen with regard to supreme power, but it is possible, even in some constitutions, where the legislative authority is not lodged in one person, that there may be a magistrate so eminent and powerful as to oblige the laws to keep silence in this particular. Nor would this silence be an effect only of their *respect*, but also of their *prudence;* since it is certain that, in the vast variety of circumstances which occur in all governments, an exercise of power, in so great a magistrate, may at one time be beneficial to the public, which at another time would be pernicious and tyrannical. But notwithstanding this silence of the laws in limited monarchies, it is certain that the people still retain the right of resistance; since it is impossible, even in the

25. [Hume is referring to the Revolution of 1688, a revolution that he discusses in volume VI of *The History of England.* In that volume, Hume argues that English liberty, in its most pronounced sense, begins in the seventeenth century. This places him starkly at odds with a Whig understanding that would trace English liberty back to at least the Magna Charta in 1215. See n. 133.]

most despotic governments, to deprive them of it. The same necessity of self-preservation, and the same motive of public good, give them the same liberty in the one case as in the other. And we may further observe, that in such mixed governments, the cases wherein resistance is lawful must occur much oftener, and greater indulgence be given to the subjects to defend themselves by force of arms, than in arbitrary governments. Not only where the chief magistrate enters into measures in themselves extremely pernicious to the public, but even when he would encroach on the other parts of the constitution, and extend his power beyond the legal bounds, it is allowable to resist and dethrone him; though such resistance and violence may, in the general tenor of the laws, be deemed unlawful and rebellious. For, besides that nothing is more essential to public interest than the preservation of public liberty, it is evident, that if such a mixed government be once supposed to be established, every part or member of the constitution must have a right of self-defence, and of maintaining its ancient bounds against the encroachment of every other authority. As matter would have been created in vain, were it deprived of a power of resistance, without which no part of it could preserve a distinct existence, and the whole might be crowded up into a single point; so it is a gross absurdity to suppose, in any government, a right without a remedy, or allow that the supreme power is shared with the people, without allowing that it is lawful for them to defend their share against every invader. Those, therefore, who would seem to respect our free government, and yet deny the right of resistance, have renounced all pretensions to common sense, and do not merit a serious answer.

It does not belong to my present purpose to shew that these general principles are applicable to the late *revolution;* and that all the rights and privileges which ought to be sacred to a free nation, were at that time threatened with the utmost danger. I am better pleased to leave this controverted subject, if it really admits of controversy, and to indulge myself in some philosophical reflections which naturally arise from that important event.

First, We may observe, that should the *lords* and *commons* in our constitution, without any reason from public interest, either depose the king in being, or, after his death, exclude the prince, who, by laws and settled custom, ought to succeed, no one would esteem their proceedings legal, or think themselves bound to comply with them. But should the king, by his unjust practices, or his attempts for a tyrannical and despotic power, justly forfeit his legal, it then not only becomes morally lawful and suitable to the nature of political society to dethrone him; but, what is more, we are apt likewise to think that the remaining members of the constitution acquire a right of excluding his next heir, and of choosing whom they please for his successor. This is founded on a very singular quality of our thought and imagination. When a king forfeits his authority, his heir ought naturally to remain in the same situation as if the king were removed by death; unless by mixing himself in the tyranny, he forfeit it for himself. But though this may seem reasonable, we easily comply with the contrary opinion. The deposition of a king, in such a government as ours, is certainly an act beyond all common authority; and an illegal assuming a power for public good, which, in the ordinary course of government, can belong to no member of the constitution. When the public good is so great and so evident as to justify the action, the commendable use of this licence causes us naturally to attribute to the *parliament* a right of using further licences; and the ancient bounds of the laws being once transgressed with approbation, we are not apt to be so strict in confining ourselves precisely within their limits. The mind naturally runs on with any train of action which it has begun; nor do we commonly make any scruple concerning our duty, after the first action of any kind which we perform. Thus at the *revolution,* no one who thought the deposition of the father justifiable, esteemed themselves to be confined to his infant son; though, had that unhappy monarch died innocent at that time, and had his son, by any accident, been conveyed beyond seas, there is no doubt but a regency would have been appointed till he should come to age, and could be restored to his dominions. As the slightest properties of the imagination have an effect on the judgments of the people, it shews the wisdom of the laws and of the parliament to take advantage of such properties, and to choose the magistrates either in or out of a line, according as the vulgar will most naturally attribute authority and right to them.

Secondly, Though the accession of the Prince of Orange[26] to the throne might at first give occasion to many disputes, and his title be contested, it ought not now to appear doubtful, but must have acquired a sufficient authority from those three princes who have succeeded him upon the same title. Nothing is more usual, though nothing may,

26. [William of Orange became William III, King of England, in 1689, jointly ruling with his wife, Mary II, until her death in 1694, and then alone until his death in 1702. See n. 135.]

at first sight, appear more unreasonable, than this way of thinking. Princes often *seem* to acquire a right from their successors, as well as from their ancestors; and a king who, during his lifetime, might justly be deemed an usurper, will be regarded by posterity as a lawful prince, because he has had the good fortune to settle his family on the throne, and entirely change the ancient form of government. Julius Caesar[27] is regarded as the first Roman emperor; while Sylla and Marius,[28] whose titles were really the same as his, are treated as tyrants and usurpers. Time and custom give authority to all forms of government, and all successions of princes; and that power, which at first was founded only on injustice and violence, becomes in time legal and obligatory. Nor does the mind rest there; but, returning back upon its footsteps, transfers to their predecessors and ancestors that right which it naturally ascribes to the posterity, as being related together, and united in the imagination. The present King of France makes Hugh Capet a more lawful prince than Cromwell; as the established liberty of the Dutch is no inconsiderable apology for their obstinate resistance to Philip the Second.

Section XI: *Of the Laws of Nations*

When civil government has been established over the greatest part of mankind, and different societies have been formed contiguous to each other, there arises a new set of duties among the neighbouring states, suitable to the nature of that commerce which they carry on with each other. Political writers tell us, that in every kind of intercourse, a body

27. [Julius Caesar (100–44 B.C.) joined with Pompey and Crassus to form the First Triumvirate of Rome in 60 B.C., heading the government of Rome. Caesar broke with Pompey, his chief rival for power, in 49 B.C., eventually becoming "Dictator" of Rome from 46 B.C. until his death in March of 44 B.C. Caesar was perhaps the greatest military genius of ancient Rome, and there was a time when his *Gallic War* was required reading for every educated person.]

28. [Although Sylla was Consul (supreme civil and military magistrate of Rome during the Republic) of Rome in 88 B.C., he quickly lost his power which he immediately attempted to regain by violence. Four years later he reverted to great acts of violence again, leading to his being elected "Dictator" in 83 B.C. Marius was Consul of Rome from 107 to 101 B.C. He attempted to gain power again in 88 B.C. but was rebuffed by Sylla's violence. After some maneuvering, he managed to capture Rome in 86 B.C., leading to his being elected Consul, but he died before he could take office.]

politic is to be considered as one person; and, indeed, this assertion is so far just, that different nations, as well as private persons, require mutual assistance; at the same time that their selfishness and ambition are perpetual sources of war and discord. But though nations in this particular resemble individuals, yet as they are very different in other respects, no wonder they regulate themselves by different maxims, and give rise to a new set of rules, which we call the *laws of nations.*[29] Under this head we may comprise the sacredness of the persons of ambassadors, the declaration of war, the abstaining from poisoned arms, with other duties of that kind, which are evidently calculated for the commerce that is peculiar to different societies.

But though these rules be superadded to the laws of nature, the former do not entirely abolish the latter; and one may safely affirm, that the three fundamental rules of justice, the stability of possession, its transference by consent, and the performance of promises, are duties of princes as well as of subjects. The same interest produces the same effect in both cases. Where possession has no stability, there must be perpetual war. Where property is not transferred by consent, there can be no commerce. Where promises are not observed, there can be no leagues nor alliances. The advantages, therefore, of peace, commerce, and mutual succour, make us extend to different kingdoms the same notions of justice which take place among individuals.

There is a maxim very current in the world, which few politicians are willing to avow, but which has been authorized by the practice of all ages, *that there is a system of morals calculated for princes, much more free than that which ought to govern private persons.* It is evident this is not to be understood of the lesser *extent* of public duties and obligations; nor will any one be so extravagant as to assert, that the most solemn treaties ought to have no force among princes. For as princes do actually form treaties among themselves, they must propose some advantage from the execution of them; and the prospect of such advantage for the future must engage them to perform their part, and must establish that law of nature. The meaning, therefore, of this political

29. [Hugo Grotius (1583–1645) was the most influential political thinker in early modern Europe calling attention to the importance of the laws of nations. See his *On the Law of War and Peace*, trans. by Francis W. Kelsey, (Oxford: Oxford University Press, 1925). In his *An Enquiry Concerning the Principles of Morals*, Hume remarks that his theory of the origin of justice "is in the main" the same as that "hinted at and adopted by Grotius" (p. 95, n. 63).]

maxim is, that though the morality of princes has the same *extent,* yet it has not the same *force* as that of private persons, and may lawfully be transgressed from a more trivial motive. However shocking such a proposition may appear to certain philosophers, it will be easy to defend it upon those principles, by which we have accounted for the origin of justice and equity.

When men have found by experience that it is impossible to subsist without society, and that it is impossible to maintain society, while they give free course to their appetites; so urgent an interest quickly restrains their actions, and imposes an obligation to observe those rules which we call the *laws of justice.* This obligation of interest rests not here; but, by the necessary course of the passions and sentiments, gives rise to the moral obligation of duty; while we approve of such actions as tend to the peace of society, and disapprove of such as tend to its disturbance. The same *natural* obligation of interest takes place among independent kingdoms, and gives rise to the same *morality;* so that no one of ever so corrupt morals will approve of a prince who voluntarily, and of his own accord, breaks his word, or violates any treaty. But here we may observe, that though the intercourse of different states be advantageous, and even sometimes necessary, yet it is not so necessary nor advantageous as that among individuals, without which it is utterly impossible for human nature ever to subsist. Since, therefore, the *natural* obligation to justice, among different states, is not so strong as among individuals, the *moral* obligation which arises from it must partake of its weakness; and we must necessarily give a greater indulgence to a prince or minister who deceives another, than to a private gentleman who breaks his word of honour.

Should it be asked, *what proportion these two species of morality bear to each other?* I would answer, that this is a question to which we can never give any precise answer; nor is it possible to reduce to numbers the proportion which we ought to fix betwixt them. One may safely affirm, that this proportion finds itself without any art or study of men; as we may observe on many other occasions. The practice of the world goes further in teaching us the degrees of our duty, than the most subtile philosophy which was ever yet invented. And this may serve as a convincing proof, that all men have an implicit notion of the foundation of those moral rules concerning natural and civil justice, and are sensible that they arise merely from human conventions, and from the interest which we have in the preservation of peace and order. For otherwise the diminution of the interest would never produce a relaxation of the morality, and reconcile us more easily to any transgression of justice among princes and republics, than in the private commerce of one subject with another.

Section XII:
Of Chastity and Modesty

If any difficulty attend this system concerning the laws of nature and nations, it will be with regard to the universal approbation or blame which follows their observance or transgression, and which some may not think sufficiently explained from the general interests of society. To remove, as far as possible, all scruples of this kind, I shall here consider another set of duties, viz. the *modesty* and *chastity* which belong to the fair sex: and I doubt not but these virtues will be found to be still more conspicuous instances of the operation of those principles which I have insisted on.[30]

There are some philosophers who attack the female virtues with great vehemence, and fancy they have gone very far in detecting popular errors, when they can shew that there is no foundation in nature for all that exterior modesty which we require in the expressions, and dress, and behaviour of the fair sex. I believe I may spare myself the trouble of insisting on so obvious a subject, and may proceed, without further preparation, to examine after what manner such notions arise from education, from the voluntary conventions of men, and from the interest of society.

Whoever considers the length and feebleness of human infancy, with the concern which both sexes naturally have for their offspring, will easily perceive that there must be a union of male and female for the education of the young, and that this union must be of considerable duration. But in order to induce the men to impose on themselves this restraint, and undergo cheerfully all the fatigues and expences to which it subjects them, they must believe that the children are their own, and that their natural instinct is not directed to a wrong object, when they give a loose to love and tenderness. Now, if we examine the structure of the human body, we shall find, that this security is very difficult to be attained on our part; and that since, in the copulation of the sexes,

30. [See Hume's essays on "Of Imprudence and Modesty" and "Of Love and Marriage," in *Essays, Moral, Political, and Literary* for further discussion on some of the points in this section.]

the principle of generation goes from the man to the woman, an error may easily take place on the side of the former, though it be utterly impossible with regard to the latter. From this trivial and anatomical observation is derived that vast difference betwixt the education and duties of the two sexes.

Were a philosopher to examine the matter *a priori,* he would reason after the following manner. Men are induced to labour for the maintenance and education of their children, by the persuasion that they are really their own; and therefore it is reasonable, and even necessary, to give them some security in this particular. This security cannot consist entirely in the imposing of severe punishments on any transgressions of conjugal fidelity on the part of the wife; since these public punishments cannot be inflicted without legal proof, which it is difficult to meet with in this subject. What restraint, therefore, shall we impose on women, in order to counterbalance so strong a temptation as they have to infidelity? There seems to be no restraint possible, but in the punishment of bad fame or reputation; a punishment which has a mighty influence on the human mind, and at the same time is inflicted by the world upon surmises and conjectures, and proofs that would never be received in any court of judicature. In order, therefore, to impose a due restraint on the female sex, we must attach a peculiar degree of shame to their infidelity, above what arises merely from its injustice, and must bestow proportionable praises on their chastity.

But though this be a very strong motive to fidelity, our philosopher would quickly discover that it would not alone be sufficient to that purpose. All human creatures, especially of the female sex, are apt to overlook remote motives in favour of any present temptation: the temptation is here the strongest imaginable; its approaches are insensible and seducing; and a woman easily finds, or flatters herself she shall find, certain means of securing her reputation, and preventing all the pernicious consequences of her pleasures. It is necessary, therefore, that beside the infamy attending such licences, there should be some preceding backwardness or dread, which may prevent their first approaches, and may give the female sex a repugnance to all expressions, and postures, and liberties, that have an immediate relation to that enjoyment.

Such would be the reasonings of our speculative philosopher; but I am persuaded that, if he had not a perfect knowledge of human nature, he would be apt to regard them as mere chimerical speculations, and would consider the infamy attending infidelity, and backwardness to all its approaches, as principles that were rather to be wished than hoped for in the world. For what means, would he say, of persuading mankind that the transgressions of conjugal duty are more infamous than any other kind of injustice, when it is evident they are more excusable, upon account of the greatness of the temptation? And what possibility of giving a backwardness to the approaches of a pleasure to which nature has inspired so strong a propensity, and a propensity that it is absolutely necessary in the end to comply with, for the support of the species?

But speculative reasonings, which cost so much pains to philosophers,[31] are often formed by the world naturally, and without reflection; as difficulties which seem unsurmountable in theory, are easily got over in practice. Those who have an interest in the fidelity of women, naturally disapprove of their infidelity, and all the approaches to it. Those who have no interest are carried along with the stream. Education takes possession of the ductile minds of the fair sex in their infancy. And when a general rule of this kind is once established, men are apt to extend it beyond those principles from which it first arose. Thus bachelors, however debauched, cannot choose but be shocked with any instance of lewdness or impudence in women. And though all these maxims have a plain reference to generation, yet women past child-bearing have no more privilege in this respect than those who are in the flower of their youth and beauty. Men have undoubtedly an implicit notion, that all those ideas of modesty and decency have a regard to generation; since they impose not the same laws, *with the same force,* on the male sex, where that reason takes not place. The exception is there obvious and extensive, and founded on a remarkable difference, which produces a clear separation and disjunction of ideas. But as the case is not the same with regard to the different ages of women, for this reason, though men know that these notions are founded on the public interest, yet the general rule carries us beyond the original principle, and makes us extend the notions of modesty over the whole sex, from their earliest infancy to their extremest old age and infirmity.

Courage, which is the point of honour among men, derives its merit in a great measure from artifice, as well as the chastity of women; though it has also some foundation in nature, as we shall see afterwards.

31. [The pain of philosophical reflection is a frequent theme of sec. 1 of Hume's *An Enquiry Concerning Human Understanding* and Bk. I, Pt. IV of the *Treatise*.]

As to the obligations which the male sex lie under with regard to chastity, we may observe that, according to the general notions of the world, they bear nearly the same proportion to the obligations of women, as the obligations of the law of nations do to those of the law of nature. It is contrary to the interest of civil society, that men should have an *entire* liberty of indulging their appetites in venereal enjoyment; but as this interest is weaker than in the case of the female sex, the moral obligation arising from it must be proportionably weaker. And to prove this we need only appeal to the practice and sentiments of all nations and ages.

From *An Enquiry concerning the Principles of Morals*

Section III: *Of Justice*

PART I

That Justice is useful to society, and consequently that *part* of its merit, at least, must arise from that consideration, it would be a superfluous undertaking to prove. That public utility is the *sole* origin of justice, and that reflections on the beneficial consequences of this virtue are the *sole* foundation of its merit; this proposition, being more curious and important, will better deserve our examination and enquiry.

Let us suppose, that nature has bestowed on the human race such profuse *abundance* of all *external* conveniences, that, without any uncertainty in the event, without any care or industry on our part, every individual finds himself fully provided with whatever his most voracious appetites can want, or luxurious imagination wish or desire. His natural beauty, we shall suppose, surpasses all acquired ornaments: The perpetual clemency of the seasons renders useless all cloaths or covering: The raw herbage affords him the most delicious fare; the clear fountain, the richest beverage. No laborious occupation required: No tillage: No navigation. Music, poetry, and contemplation form his sole business: Conversation, mirth, and friendship his sole amusement.

It seems evident, that, in such a happy state, every other social virtue would flourish, and receive tenfold encrease; but the cautious, jealous virtue of justice would never once have been dreamed of. For what purpose make a partition of goods, where every one has already more than enough? Why give rise to property, where there cannot possibly be any injury? Why call this object *mine*, when, upon the seizing of it by another, I need but stretch out my hand to possess myself of what is equally valuable? Justice, in that case, being totally USELESS, would be an idle ceremonial, and could never possibly have place in the catalogue of virtues.

We see, even in the present necessitous condition of mankind, that, wherever any benefit is bestowed by nature in an unlimited abundance, we leave it always in common among the whole human race, and make no subdivisions of right and property. Water and air, though the most necessary of all objects, are not challenged as the property of individuals; nor can any man commit injustice by the most lavish use and enjoyment of these blessings. In fertile extensive countries, with few inhabitants, land is regarded on the same footing. And no topic is so much insisted on by those, who defend the liberty of the seas, as the unexhausted use of them in navigation. Were the advantages, procured by navigation, as inexhaustible, these reasoners had never had any adversaries to refute; nor had any claims ever been advanced of a separate, exclusive dominion over the ocean.

It may happen, in some countries, at some periods, that there be established a property in water, none in land;[32] if the latter be in greater abundance than can be used by the inhabitants, and the former be found, with difficulty, and in very small quantities.

Again; suppose, that, though the necessities of human race continue the same as at present, yet the mind is so enlarged, and so replete with friendship and generosity, that every man has the utmost tenderness for every man, and feels no more concern for his own interest than for that of his fellows: It seems evident, that the USE of justice would, in this case, be suspended by such an extensive benevolence, nor would the divisions and barriers of property and obligation have ever been thought of. Why should I bind another, by a deed or promise, to do me any good office, when I know that he is already prompted, by the strongest inclination, to seek my happiness, and would, of himself, perform the desired service; except the hurt, he thereby receives, be greater than the benefit accruing to me? in which case, he knows, that, from my innate humanity and friendship, I should be the first to oppose myself to his imprudent generosity. Why raise land-marks between my neighbour's field and mine, when my heart has made no division between our interests; but shares all his joys and sorrows with the same force and vivacity as if originally my own? Every man, upon this supposition, being a second self to another, would trust all his interests to the discretion of every man; without jealousy, without partition, without distinction. And the whole human race would form only one family; where all would lie in common, and be used freely, without regard to property; but cautiously too, with as entire regard to the necessities of each individual, as if our own interests were most intimately concerned.

In the present disposition of the human heart, it would, perhaps, be difficult to find compleat instances of such enlarged affections; but still we may observe, that the case of families approaches towards it;

32. Genesis, chap. xiii. and xxi.

and the stronger the mutual benevolence is among the individuals, the nearer it approaches; till all distinction of property be, in a great measure, lost and confounded among them. Between married persons, the cement of friendship is by the laws supposed so strong as to abolish all division of possessions; and has often, in reality, the force ascribed to it. And it is observable, that, during the ardour of new enthusiasms, when every principle is inflamed into extravagance, the community of goods has frequently been attempted; and nothing but experience of its inconveniencies, from the returning or disguised selfishness of men, could make the imprudent fanatics adopt anew the ideas of justice and of separate property. So true is it, that this virtue derives its existence entirely from its necessary *use* to the intercourse and social state of mankind.

To make this truth more evident, let us reverse the foregoing suppositions; and carrying every thing to the opposite extreme, consider what would be the effect of these new situations. Suppose a society to fall into such want of all common necessaries, that the utmost frugality and industry cannot preserve the greater number from perishing, and the whole from extreme misery: It will readily, I believe, be admitted, that the strict laws of justice are suspended, in such a pressing emergence, and give place to the stronger motives of necessity and self-preservation. Is it any crime, after a shipwreck, to seize whatever means or instrument of safety one can lay hold of, without regard to former limitations of property? Or if a city besieged were perishing with hunger; can we imagine, that men will see any means of preservation before them, and lose their lives, from a scrupulous regard to what, in other situations, would be the rules of equity and justice? The USE and TENDENCY of that virtue is to procure happiness and security, by preserving order in society: But where the society is ready to perish from extreme necessity, no greater evil can be dreaded from violence and injustice; and every man may now provide for himself by all the means, which prudence can dictate, or humanity permit. The public, even in less urgent necessities, opens granaries, without the consent of proprietors; as justly supposing, that the authority of magistracy may, consistent with equity, extend so far: But were any number of men to assemble, without the tye of laws or civil jurisdiction; would an equal partition of bread in a famine, though effected by power and even violence, be regarded as criminal or injurious?

Suppose likewise, that it should be a virtuous man's fate to fall into the society of ruffians, remote from the protection of laws and government; what conduct must he embrace in that melancholy situation? He sees such a desperate rapaciousness prevail; such a disregard to equity, such contempt of order, such stupid blindness to future consequences, as must immediately have the most tragical conclusion, and must terminate in destruction to the greater number, and in a total dissolution of society to the rest. He, mean while, can have no other expedient than to arm himself, to whomever the sword he seizes, or the buckler, may belong: To make provision of all means of defence and security: And his particular regard to justice being no longer of USE to his own safety or that of others, he must consult the dictates of self-preservation alone, without concern for those who no longer merit his care and attention.

When any man, even in political society, renders himself, by his crimes, obnoxious to the public, he is punished by the laws in his goods and person; that is, the ordinary rules of justice are, with regard to him, suspended for a moment, and it becomes equitable to inflict on him, for the *benefit* of society, what, otherwise, he could not suffer without wrong or injury.

The rage and violence of public war; what is it but a suspension of justice among the warring parties, who perceive, that this virtue is now no longer of any *use* or advantage to them? The laws of war, which then succeed to those of equity and justice, are rules calculated for the *advantage* and *utility* of that particular state, in which men are now placed. And were a civilized nation engaged with barbarians, who observed no rules even of war, the former must also suspend their observance of them, where they no longer serve to any purpose; and must render every action or rencounter as bloody and pernicious as possible to the first aggressors.

Thus, the rules of equity or justice depend entirely on the particular state and condition, in which men are placed, and owe their origin and existence to that UTILITY, which results to the public from their strict and regular observance. Reverse, in any considerable circumstance, the condition of men: Produce extreme abundance or extreme necessity: Implant in the human breast perfect moderation and humanity, or perfect rapaciousness and malice: By rendering justice totally *useless*, you thereby totally destroy its essence, and suspend its obligation upon mankind.

The common situation of society is a medium amidst all these extremes. We are naturally partial to ourselves, and to our friends; but are capable of learning the advantage resulting from a more equitable conduct. Few enjoyments are given us from the open and liberal hand of nature; but by art, labour, and industry, we can extract them in great abundance. Hence the ideas of property become necessary in all civil society: Hence justice derives its usefulness to the public: And hence alone arises its merit and moral obligation.

These conclusions are so natural and obvious, that they have not escaped even the poets, in their descriptions of the felicity, attending the golden age or the reign of Saturn. The seasons, in that first period of nature, were so temperate, if we credit these agreeable fictions, that there was no necessity for men to provide themselves with cloaths and houses, as a security against the violence of heat and cold: The rivers flowed with wine and milk: The oaks yielded honey; and nature spontaneously produced her greatest delicacies. Nor were these the chief advantages of that happy age. Tempests were not alone removed from nature; but those more furious tempests were unknown to human breasts, which now cause such uproar, and engender such confusion. Avarice, ambition, cruelty, selfishness, were never heard of: Cordial affection, compassion, sympathy, were the only movements with which the mind was yet acquainted. Even the punctilious distinction of *mine* and *thine* was banished from among that happy race of mortals, and carried with it the very notion of property and obligation, justice and injustice.

This *poetical* fiction of the *golden age* is, in some respects, of a piece with the *philosophical* fiction of the *state of nature;* only that the former is represented as the most charming and most peaceable condition, which can possibly be imagined; whereas the latter is painted out as a state of mutual war and violence, attended with the most extreme necessity. On the first origin of mankind, we are told, their ignorance and savage nature were so prevalent, that they could give no mutual trust, but must each depend upon himself, and his own force or cunning for protection and security. No law was heard of: No rule of justice known: No distinction of property regarded: Power was the only measure of right; and a perpetual war of all against all was the result of men's untamed selfishness and barbarity.[33]

33. This fiction of a state of nature, as a state of war, was not first started by Mr. Hobbes, as is commonly imagined. [Thomas Hobbes (1588–1679) weaves together the idea of a state of nature with that of a state of war in *Leviathan*, ed. by E. Curley (Indianapolis: Hackett Publishing, 1994), ch. XIII.] Plato endeavours to refute an hypothesis very like it in the 2d, 3d, and 4th books de republica. [Plato (428–348 B.C.), *The Republic*, bks. II–IV. There Plato constructs a city "in speech," one that postulates neither

Whether such a condition of human nature could ever exist, or if it did, could continue so long as to merit the appellation of a *state*, may justly be doubted. Men are necessarily born in a family-society, at least; and are trained up by their parents to some rule of conduct and behaviour. But this must be admitted, that, if such a state of mutual war and violence was ever real, the suspension of all laws of justice, from their absolute inutility, is a necessary and infallible consequence.

The more we vary our views of human life, and the newer and more unusual the lights are, in which we survey it, the more shall we be convinced, that the origin here assigned for the virtue of justice is real and satisfactory.

---

human gregariousness nor a state of war among human beings. Hume is probably attributing the idea that the state of nature is a state of war to Thrasymachus.] CICERO, on the contrary, supposes it certain and universally acknowledged in the following passage.

'Quis enim vestrum, judices, ignorat, ita naturam rerum tulisse, ut quodam tempore homines, nondum neque naturali, neque civili jure descripto, fusi per agros, ac dispersi vagarentur, tantumque haberent quantum manu ac viribus, per caedem ac vulnera, aut eripere, aut retinere potuissent? Qui igitur primi virtute et consilio praestanti extiterunt, ii perspecto genere humanae docilitatis atque ingenii, dissipatos, unum in locum congregarunt, eosque ex feritate illa ad justitiam ac mansuetudinem transduxerunt. Tum res ad communem utilitatem, quas publicas appellamus, tum conventicula hominum, quae postea civitates nominatae sunt, tum domicilia conjuncta, quas urbes dicamus, invento et divino et humano jure, moenibus sepserunt. Atque inter hanc vitam, perpolitam humanitate, et illam immanem, nihil tam interest quam JUS atque VIS. Horum utro uti nolimus, altero est utendum. Vim volumus extingui? Jus valeat necesse est, id est, judicia, quibus omne jus continetur. Judicia displicent, aut nulla sunt? Vis dominetur necesse est? Haec vident omnes.'—*Pro Sext.* l. 42. [Cicero (106–43 B.C.), *Pro Sestio*, 42.91–2: "For which of us, gentlemen does not know the natural course of human history—how there was once a time, before either natural or civil law had been formulated, when men roamed, scattered and dispersed over the country, and had no other possessions than just so much as they had been able either to seize by strength and violence, or keep at the cost of slaughter and wounds? So then those who at first showed themselves to be most eminent for merit and wisdom, having perceived the essential teachableness of human nature, gathered together into one place those who had been scattered abroad, and brought them from that state of savagery to one of justice and humanity. Then things serving for common use, which we call public, associations of men, which were afterwards called states, then continuous series of dwelling-places which we call cities, they enclosed with walls, after divine and human law had been introduced. Now, between life thus refined and humanized, and that life of savagery, nothing marks the difference so clearly as law and violence. Whichever of the two we are unwilling to use, we must use the other. If we would have violence abolished, law must prevail, that is the administration of justice, on which law wholly depends; if we dislike the administration of justice, or if there is none, force must rule. All are aware of this" (trans. by R. Gardner).]

Were there a species of creatures, intermingled with men, which, though rational, were possessed of such inferior strength, both of body and mind, that they were incapable of all resistance, and could never, upon the highest provocation, make us feel the effects of their resentment; the necessary consequence, I think, is, that we should be bound, by the laws of humanity, to give gentle usage to these creatures, but should not, properly speaking, lie under any restraint of justice with regard to them, nor could they possess any right or property, exclusive of such arbitrary lords. Our intercourse with them could not be called society, which supposes a degree of equality; but absolute command on the one side, and servile obedience on the other. Whatever we covet, they must instantly resign: Our permission is the only tenure, by which they hold their possessions: Our compassion and kindness the only check, by which they curb our lawless will: And as no inconvenience ever results from the exercise of a power, so firmly established in nature, the restraints of justice and property, being totally *useless*, would never have place in so unequal a confederacy.

This is plainly the situation of men, with regard to animals; and how far these may be said to possess reason, I leave it to others to determine.[34] The great superiority of civilized EUROPEANS above barbarous INDIANS,[35] tempted us to imagine ourselves on the same footing with regard to them, and made us throw off all restraints of justice, and even of humanity, in our treatment of them. In many nations, the female sex are reduced to like slavery, and are rendered incapable of all property, in opposition to their lordly masters. But though the males, when united, have, in all countries, bodily force sufficient to maintain this severe tyranny, yet such are the insinuation, address, and charms

34. [Hume discusses the power of reason in animals in the *Treatise*, pp. 176–79, and also in *An Enquiry Concerning Human Understanding*, 69–72.]

35. [The distinction between those who are civilized and barbarians ultimately goes back to Greece and the distinction between Greeks and barbarians (those who are not Greek and thus do not speak Greek). In the eighteenth century, it became quite commonplace to distinguish between the civilized and the barbarous. Under the influence of Jean-Jacques Rousseau (1712–78), many thinkers came to believe that those who were civilized were not superior, but inferior, in important ways, to those who were uncivilized or barbarian. It is worth contrasting, in this regard, Hume's essays on "Of the Rise and Progress of the Arts and Sciences," "Of Commerce," and "Of Refinement in the Arts" (all in this edition) with Rousseau's *Discourse on the Sciences and the Arts* and *Discourse on the Origins of Inequality*. The latter works can be found in Rousseau, *Basic Political Writings*, trans. by D. Cress (Indianapolis: Hackett Publishing, 1987).]

of their fair companions, that women are commonly able to break the confederacy, and share with the other sex in all the rights and privileges of society.

Were the human species so framed by nature as that each individual possessed within himself every faculty, requisite both for his own preservation and for the propagation of his kind: Were all society and intercourse cut off between man and man, by the primary intention of the supreme Creator: It seems evident, that so solitary a being would be as much incapable of justice, as of social discourse and conversation. Where mutual regards and forbearance serve to no manner of purpose, they would never direct the conduct of any reasonable man. The headlong course of the passions would be checked by no reflection on future consequences. And as each man is here supposed to love himself alone, and to depend only on himself and his own activity for safety and happiness, he would, on every occasion, to the utmost of his power, challenge the preference above every other being, to none of which he is bound by any ties, either of nature or of interest.

But suppose the conjunction of the sexes to be established in nature, a family immediately arises; and particular rules being found requisite for its subsistence, these are immediately embraced; though without comprehending the rest of mankind within their prescriptions. Suppose, that several families unite together into one society, which is totally disjoined from all others, the rules, which preserve peace and order, enlarge themselves to the utmost extent of that society; but becoming then entirely useless, lose their force when carried one step farther. But again suppose, that several distinct societies maintain a kind of intercourse for mutual convenience and advantage, the boundaries of justice still grow larger, in proportion to the largeness of men's views, and the force of their mutual connexions. History, experience, reason sufficiently instruct us in this natural progress of human sentiments, and in the gradual enlargement of our regards to justice, in proportion as we become acquainted with the extensive utility of that virtue.

PART II

If we examine the *particular* laws, by which justice is directed, and property determined; we shall still be presented with the same conclusion. The good of mankind is the only object of all these laws and regulations. Not only it is requisite, for the peace and interest of society, that men's possessions should be separated; but the rules, which we follow, in making the separation, are such as can best be contrived to serve farther the interests of society.

We shall suppose, that a creature, possessed of reason, but unacquainted with human nature, deliberates with himself what RULES of justice or property would best promote public interest, and establish peace and security among mankind: His most obvious thought would be, to assign the largest possessions to the most extensive virtue, and give every one the power of doing good, proportioned to his inclination. In a perfect theocracy, where a being, infinitely intelligent, governs by particular volitions, this rule would certainly have place, and might serve to the wisest purposes: But were mankind to execute such a law; so great is the uncertainty of merit, both from its natural obscurity, and from the self-conceit of each individual, that no determinate rule of conduct would ever result from it; and the total dissolution of society must be the immediate consequence. Fanatics may suppose, *that dominion is founded on grace,* and *that saints alone inherit the earth;* but the civil magistrate very justly puts these sublime theorists on the same footing with common robbers, and teaches them by the severest discipline, that a rule, which, in speculation, may seem the most advantageous to society, may yet be found, in practice, totally pernicious and destructive.

That there were *religious* fanatics of this kind in ENGLAND, during the civil wars, we learn from history; though it is probable, that the obvious *tendency* of these principles excited such horror in mankind, as soon obliged the dangerous enthusiasts to renounce, or at least conceal their tenets. Perhaps, the *levellers,*[36] who claimed an equal distribution of property, were a kind of *political* fanatics, which arose from the religious species, and more openly avowed their pretensions; as carrying a more plausible appearance, of being practicable in themselves, as well as useful to human society.

It must, indeed, be confessed, that nature is so liberal to mankind, that, were all her presents equally divided among the species, and improved by art and industry, every individual would enjoy all the necessaries, and even most of the comforts of life; nor would ever be liable to any ills, but such as might accidentally arise from the sickly frame and constitution of his body. It must also be confessed, that, wherever we depart from this equality, we rob the poor of more satisfac-

36. [See n. 185.]

tion than we add to the rich, and that the slight gratification of a frivolous vanity, in one individual, frequently costs more than bread to many families, and even provinces. It may appear withal, that the rule of equality, as it would be highly *useful,* is not altogether *impracticable;* but has taken place, at least in an imperfect degree, in some republics; particularly that of SPARTA; where it was attended, it is said, with the most beneficial consequences. Not to mention, that the AGRARIAN laws, so frequently claimed in ROME, and carried into execution in many GREEK cities, proceeded, all of them, from a general idea of the utility of this principle.

But historians, and even common sense, may inform us, that, however specious these ideas of *perfect* equality may seem, they are really, at bottom, *impracticable;* and were they not so, would be extremely *pernicious* to human society. Render possessions ever so equal, men's different degrees of art, care, and industry will immediately break that equality. Or if you check these virtues, you reduce society to the most extreme indigence; and instead of preventing want and beggary in a few, render it unavoidable to the whole community. The most rigorous inquisition too is requisite to watch every inequality on its first appearance; and the most severe jurisdiction, to punish and redress it. But besides, that so much authority must soon degenerate into tyranny, and be exerted with great partialities; who can possibly be possessed of it, in such a situation as is here supposed? Perfect equality of possessions, destroying all subordination, weakens extremely the authority of magistracy, and must reduce all power nearly to a level, as well as property.

We may conclude, therefore, that, in order to establish laws for the regulation of property, we must be acquainted with the nature and situation of man; must reject appearances which may be false, though specious; and must search for those rules, which are, on the whole, most *useful* and *beneficial.* Vulgar sense and slight experience are sufficient for this purpose; where men give not way to too selfish avidity, or too extensive enthusiasm.

Who sees not, for instance, that whatever is produced or improved by a man's art or industry ought, for ever, to be secured to him, in order to give encouragement to such *useful* habits and accomplishments? That the property ought also to descend to children and relations, for the same *useful* purpose? That it may be alienated by consent, in order to beget that commerce and intercourse, which is so *beneficial* to human society? And that all contracts and promises ought carefully to be fulfilled, in order to secure mutual trust and confidence, by which the general *interest* of mankind is so much promoted?

Examine the writers on the laws of nature; and you will always find, that, whatever principles they set out with, they are sure to terminate here at last, and to assign, as the ultimate reason for every rule which they establish, the convenience and necessities of mankind. A concession thus extorted, in opposition to systems, has more authority than if it had been made in prosecution of them.

What other reason, indeed, could writers ever give, why this must be *mine* and that *yours*, since uninstructed nature, surely, never made any such distinction? The objects, which receive those appellations, are, of themselves, foreign to us; they are totally disjoined and separated from us; and nothing but the general interests of society can form the connexion.

Sometimes, the interests of society may require a rule of justice in a particular case; but may not determine any particular rule, among several, which are all equally beneficial. In that case, the slightest *analogies* are laid hold of, in order to prevent that indifference and ambiguity, which would be the source of perpetual dissention. Thus possession alone, and first possession, is supposed to convey property, where no body else has any preceding claim and pretension. Many of the reasonings of lawyers are of this analogical nature, and depend on very slight connexions of the imagination.

Does any one scruple, in extraordinary cases, to violate all regard to the private property of individuals, and sacrifice to public interest a distinction, which had been established for the sake of that interest? The safety of the people is the supreme law: All other particular laws are subordinate to it, and dependant on it: And if, in the *common* course of things, they be followed and regarded; it is only because the public safety and interest *commonly* demand so equal and impartial an administration.

Sometimes both *utility* and *analogy* fail, and leave the laws of justice in total uncertainty. Thus, it is highly requisite, that prescription or long possession should convey property; but what number of days or months or years should be sufficient for that purpose, it is impossible for reason alone to determine. *Civil laws* here supply the place of the natural *code*, and assign different terms for prescription, according to the different *utilities*, proposed by the legislator. Bills of exchange and promissory notes, by the laws of most countries, prescribe sooner than bonds, and mortgages, and contracts of a more formal nature.

In general, we may observe, that all questions of property are subordinate to the authority of civil laws, which extend, restrain, modify, and alter the rules of natural justice, according to the particular *convenience* of each community. The laws have, or ought to have, a constant reference to the constitution of government, the manners, the climate, the religion, the commerce, the situation of each society. A late author of genius, as well as learning, has prosecuted this subject at large, and has established, from these principles, a system of political knowledge, which abounds in ingenious and brilliant thoughts, and is not wanting in solidity.[37]

37. The author of *L'Esprit des Loix.* [Montesquieu (1689–1755), *The Spirit of the Laws*, trans. by A. Cohler *et al.* (Cambridge: Cambridge University Press, 1989), pp. 3–7 (pt. I, bk. I, ch. 1–2). For Hume's arguments that morality cannot be founded on relations see the *Treatise*, pp. 13–15 and 456–70.] This illustrious writer, however, sets out with a different theory, and supposes all right to be founded on certain *rapports* or relations; which is a system, that, in my opinion, never will be reconciled with true philosophy. Father Malebranche, as far as I can learn, was the first that started this abstract theory of morals, which was afterwards adopted by Cudworth, Clarke, and others; [Hume is principally referring to Nicholas Malebranche's (1638–1715), *Traité de morale* (*Treatise of Morality*), Ralph Cudworth's (1617–88) *A Treatise concerning Eternal and Immutable Morality*, Samuel Clarke's (1675–1729) *A Discourse concerning the Unchangeable Obligations of Natural Religion*, and William Wollaston's (1659–1724) *The Religion of Nature Delineated.* For a selection from Malebranche's work, see *Moral Philosophy from Montaigne to Kant*, ed. by J. B. Schneewind, 2 vols. (Cambridge: Cambridge University Press, 1990), vol. I, pp. 258–73. For selections from the above works of Cudworth, Clark, and Wollaston, see *British Moralists: 1650–1800*, ed. by D. D. Raphael, 2 vols. (Indianapolis: Hackett Publishing, 1991).] and as it excludes all sentiment, and pretends to found every thing on reason, it has not wanted followers in this philosophic age. See *Section 1. and Appendix I.* With regard to justice, the virtue here treated of, the inference against this theory seems short and conclusive. Property is allowed to be dependent on civil laws; civil laws are allowed to have no other object, but the interest of society: This therefore must be allowed to be the sole foundation of property and justice. Not to mention, that our obligation itself to obey the magistrate and his laws is founded on nothing but the interests of society.

If the ideas of justice, sometimes, do not follow the dispositions of civil law: we shall find, that these cases, instead of objections, are confirmations of the theory delivered above. Where a civil law is so perverse as to cross all the interests of society, it loses all its authority, and men judge by the ideas of natural justice, which are conformable to those interests. Sometimes also civil laws, for useful purposes, require a ceremony or form to any deed; and where that is wanting, their decrees run contrary to the usual tenour of justice; but one who takes advantage of such chicanes, is not commonly regarded as an honest man. Thus, the interests of society require, that contracts be fulfilled; and there is not a more material article either of natural or civil justice: But the omission of a trifling circumstance will often, by law, invalidate a contract, *in foro humano,* [in the forum of humanity, that is, in the eyes of the world] but not *in foro*

What is a man's property? Any thing, which it is lawful for him, and for him alone, to use. *But what rule have we, by which we can distinguish these objects?* Here we must have recourse to statutes, customs, precedents, analogies, and a hundred other circumstances; some of which are constant and inflexible, some variable and arbitrary. But the ultimate point, in which they all professedly terminate, is, the interest and happiness of human society. Where this enters not into consideration, nothing can appear more whimsical, unnatural, and even superstitious, than all or most of the laws of justice and of property.

Those, who ridicule vulgar superstitions, and expose the folly of particular regards to meats, days, places, postures, apparel, have an easy task; while they consider all the qualities and relations of the objects, and discover no adequate cause for that affection or antipathy, veneration or horror, which have so mighty an influence over a considerable part of mankind. A SYRIAN would have starved rather than taste pigeon; an EGYPTIAN would not have approached bacon: But if these species of food be examined by the senses of sight, smell, or taste, or scrutinized by the sciences of chymistry, medicine, or physics; no difference is ever found between them and any other species, nor can that precise circumstance be pitched on, which may afford a just foundation for the religious passion. A fowl on Thursday is lawful food; on Friday abominable: Eggs, in this house, and in this diocese, are permitted during Lent; a hundred paces farther, to eat them is a damnable sin. This earth or building, yesterday was profane; to-day, by the muttering of certain words, it has become holy and sacred. Such reflections as these, in the mouth of a philosopher, one may safely say, are too obvious to have any influence; because they must always, to every man, occur at first sight; and where they prevail not, of themselves, they are surely obstructed by education, prejudice, and passion, not by ignorance or mistake.

It may appear to a careless view, or rather a too abstracted reflection, that there enters a like superstition into all the sentiments of justice; and that, if a man expose its object, or what we call property, to the

---

conscientiae, [in the forum of conscience, that is, through the eyes of one's own conscience] as divines express themselves. In these cases, the magistrate is supposed only to withdraw his power of enforcing the right, not to have altered the right. Where his intention extends to the right, and is conformable to the interests of society; it never fails to alter the right; a clear proof of the origin of justice and of property, as assigned above.

same scrutiny of sense and science, he will not, by the most accurate enquiry, find any foundation for the difference made by moral sentiment. I may lawfully nourish myself from this tree; but the fruit of another of the same species, ten paces off, it is criminal for me to touch. Had I worne this apparel an hour ago, I had merited the severest punishment; but a man, by pronouncing a few magical syllables, has now rendered it fit for my use and service. Were this house placed in the neighbouring territory, it had been immoral for me to dwell in it; but being built on this side the river, it is subject to a different municipal law, and, by its becoming mine, I incur no blame or censure. The same species of reasoning, it may be thought, which so successfully exposes superstition, is also applicable to justice; nor is it possible, in the one case more than in the other, to point out, in the object, that precise quality or circumstance, which is the foundation of the sentiment.

But there is this material difference between *superstition* and *justice*, that the former is frivolous, useless, and burdensome; the latter is absolutely requisite to the well-being of mankind and existence of society. When we abstract from this circumstance (for it is too apparent ever to be overlooked) it must be confessed, that all regards to right and property, seem entirely without foundation, as much as the grossest and most vulgar superstition. Were the interests of society no wise concerned, it is as unintelligible, why another's articulating certain sounds implying consent, should change the nature of my actions with regard to a particular object, as why the reciting of a liturgy by a priest, in a certain habit and posture, should dedicate a heap of brick and timber, and render it, thenceforth and for ever, sacred.[38]

38. It is evident that the will or consent alone never transfers property, nor causes the obligation of a promise (for the same reasoning extends to both) but the will must be expressed by words or signs, in order to impose a tye upon any man. The expression being once brought in as subservient to the will, soon becomes the principal part of the promise; nor will a man be less bound by his word, though he secretly give a different direction to his intention, and with-hold the assent of his mind. But though the expression makes, on most occasions, the whole of the promise, yet it does not always so; and one who should make use of any expression, of which he knows not the meaning, and which he uses without any sense of the consequences, would not certainly be bound by it. Nay, though he know its meaning, yet if he uses it in jest only, and with such signs as evidently show, that he has no serious intention of binding himself, he would not lie under any obligation of performance; but it is necessary, that the words be a perfect expression of the will, without any contrary signs. Nay, even this we must not carry so

These reflections are far from weakening the obligations of justice, or diminishing any thing from the most sacred attention to property. On the contrary, such sentiments must acquire new force from the present reasoning. For what stronger foundation can be desired or conceived for any duty, than to observe, that human society, or even human nature could not subsist, without the establishment of it; and will still arrive at greater degrees of happiness and perfection, the more inviolable the regard is, which is paid to that duty?

The dilemma seems obvious: As justice evidently tends to promote

---

far as to imagine, that one, whom, by our quickness of understanding, we conjecture, from certain signs, to have an intention of deceiving us, is not bound by his expression or verbal promise, if we accept of it; but must limit this conclusion to those cases where the signs are of a different nature from those of deceit. All these contradictions are easily accounted for, if justice arise entirely from its usefulness to society; but will never be explained on any other hypothesis.

It is remarkable, that the moral decisions of the *Jesuits* and other relaxed casuists, [*Casuistry* was, both in its origin and during Hume's lifetime, a derogatory term. It referred to a putative science of forming general rules of morality that would apply to particular circumstances—especially, when there appeared to be a conflict of duties—leading one to an understanding of what one's duty is in those circumstances.] were commonly formed in prosecution of some such subtilties of reasoning as are here pointed out, and proceed as much from the habit of scholastic refinement as from any corruption of the heart, if we may follow the authority of Mons. BAYLE. See his Dictionary, article LOYOLA. [Pierre Bayle's (1647–1706) most celebrated work is the *Historical and Critical Dictionary* (1697).] And why has the indignation of mankind risen so high against these casuists; but because every one perceived, that human society could not subsist were such practices authorized, and that morals must always be handled with a view to public interest, more than philosophical regularity? If the secret direction of the intention, said every man of sense, could invalidate a contract; where is our security? And yet a metaphysical schoolman might think, that where an intention was supposed to be requisite, if that intention really had not place, no consequence ought to follow, and no obligation be imposed. The casuistical subtilties may not be greater than the subtilties of lawyers, hinted at above; but as the former are *pernicious,* and the latter *innocent* and even *necessary,* this is the reason of the very different reception they meet with from the world.

It is a doctrine of the church of Rome, that the priest, by a secret direction of his intention, can invalidate any sacrament. This position is derived from a strict and regular prosecution of the obvious truth, that empty words alone, without any meaning or intention in the speaker, can never be attended with any effect. If the same conclusion be not admitted in reasonings concerning civil contracts, where the affair is allowed to be of so much less consequence than the eternal salvation of thousands, it proceeds entirely from men's sense of the danger and inconvenience of the doctrine in the former case: And we may thence observe, that however positive, arrogant, and dogmatical any superstition may appear, it never can convey any thorough persuasion of the reality of its objects, or put them, in any degree, on a balance with the common incidents of life, which we learn from daily observation and experimental reasoning.

public utility and to support civil society, the sentiment of justice is either derived from our reflecting on that tendency, or like hunger, thirst, and other appetites, resentment, love of life, attachment to offspring, and other passions, arises from a simple original instinct in the human breast, which nature has implanted for like salutary purposes. If the latter be the case, it follows, that property, which is the object of justice, is also distinguished by a simple, original instinct, and is not ascertained by any argument or reflection. But who is there that ever heard of such an instinct? Or is this a subject, in which new discoveries can be made? We may as well expect to discover, in the body, new senses, which had before escaped the observation of all mankind.

But farther, though it seems a very simple proposition to say, that nature, by an instinctive sentiment, distinguishes property, yet in reality we shall find, that there are required for that purpose ten thousand different instincts, and these employed about objects of the greatest intricacy and nicest discernment. For when a definition of *property* is required, that relation is found to resolve itself into any possession acquired by occupation, by industry, by prescription, by inheritance, by contract, &c. Can we think, that nature, by an original instinct, instructs us in all these methods of acquisition?

These words too, inheritance and contract, stand for ideas infinitely complicated; and to define them exactly, a hundred volumes of laws, and a thousand volumes of commentators, have not been found sufficient. Does nature, whose instincts in men are all simple, embrace such complicated and artificial objects, and create a rational creature, without trusting any thing to the operation of his reason?

But even though all this were admitted, it would not be satisfactory. Positive laws can certainly transfer property. Is it by another original instinct, that we recognize the authority of kings and senates, and mark all the boundaries of their jurisdiction? Judges too, even though their sentence be erroneous and illegal, must be allowed, for the sake of peace and order, to have decisive authority, and ultimately to determine property. Have we original, innate ideas of praetors, and chancellors and juries? Who sees not, that all these institutions arise merely from the necessities of human society?

All birds of the same species, in every age and country, build their nests alike: In this we see the force of instinct. Men, in different times and places, frame their houses differently: Here we perceive the influence of reason and custom. A like inference may be drawn from comparing the instinct of generation and the institution of property.

How great soever the variety of municipal laws, it must be confessed, that their chief out-lines pretty regularly concur; because the purposes, to which they tend, are every where exactly similar. In like manner, all houses have a roof and walls, windows and chimneys; though diversified in their shape, figure, and materials. The purposes of the latter, directed to the conveniences of human life, discover not more plainly their origin from reason and reflection, than do those of the former, which point all to a like end.

I need not mention the variations, which all the rules of property receive from the finer turns and connexions of the imagination, and from the subtilties and abstractions of law-topics and reasonings. There is no possibility of reconciling this observation to the notion of original instincts.

What alone will beget a doubt concerning the theory, on which I insist, is the influence of education and acquired habits, by which we are so accustomed to blame injustice, that we are not, in every instance, conscious of any immediate reflection on the pernicious consequences of it. The views the most familiar to us are apt, for that very reason, to escape us; and what we have very frequently performed from certain motives, we are apt likewise to continue mechanically, without recalling, on every occasion, the reflections, which first determined us. The convenience, or rather necessity, which leads to justice, is so universal, and every where points so much to the same rules, that the habit takes place in all societies; and it is not without some scrutiny, that we are able to ascertain its true origin. The matter, however, is not so obscure, but that, even in common life, we have, every moment, recourse to the principle of public utility, and ask, *What must become of the world, if such practices prevail? How could society subsist under such disorders?* Were the distinction or separation of possessions entirely useless, can any one conceive, that it ever should have obtained in society?

Thus we seem, upon the whole, to have attained a knowledge of the force of that principle here insisted on, and can determine what degree of esteem or moral approbation may result from reflections on public interest and utility. The necessity of justice to the support of society is the SOLE foundation of that virtue; and since no moral excellence is more highly esteemed, we may conclude, that this circumstance of usefulness has, in general, the strongest energy, and most entire command over our sentiments. It must, therefore, be the source of a considerable part of the merit ascribed to humanity, benevolence, friendship, public spirit, and other social virtues of that stamp; as it is the SOLE source of the moral approbation paid to fidelity, justice, veracity, integrity, and those other estimable and useful qualities and principles. It is entirely agreeable to the rules of philosophy, and even of common reason; where any principle has been found to have a great force and energy in one instance, to ascribe to it a like energy in all similar instances. This indeed is NEWTON'S chief rule of philosophizing.[39]

39. Principia, lib. iii. [Sir Isaac Newton, *Mathematical Principles of Natural Philosophy*, ed. by F. Cajori, 2 vols. (Berkeley: University of California Press, 1934), vol. II, bk. III.]

Part II
Political Intimations

From *Essays, Moral, Political, and Literary*

Essay I: *Of the Liberty of the Press*

Nothing is more apt to surprize a foreigner, than the extreme liberty, which we enjoy in this country,[40] of communicating whatever we please to the public, and of openly censuring every measure, entered into by the king or his ministers. If the administration resolve upon war, it is affirmed, that, either wilfully or ignorantly, they mistake the interests of the nation, and that peace, in the present situation of affairs, is infinitely preferable. If the passion of the ministers lie towards peace, our political writers breathe nothing but war and devastation, and represent the pacific conduct of the government as mean and pusillanimous. As this liberty is not indulged in any other government, either republican or monarchical; in HOLLAND and VENICE, more than in FRANCE or SPAIN; it may very naturally give occasion to a question, *How it happens that* GREAT BRITAIN *alone enjoys this peculiar privilege?*

The reason, why the laws indulge us in such a liberty seems to be derived from our mixed form of government, which is neither wholly monarchical, nor wholly republican.[41] It will be found, if I mistake not, a true observation in politics, that the two extremes in government, liberty and slavery,[42] commonly approach nearest to each other; and

40. [See Hume's revealing letter of June 16, 1768 to Anne-Robert-Jacques Turgot in *The Letters of David Hume*, vol. II, pp. 179–81.]

41. [Although Hume often mentions several types of regimes, he does not offer a thematic discussion or a complete classification of them. Here Hume is distinguishing monarchical, republican, and mixed regimes on the basis of chosen representation. A pure monarchy, or what Hume calls an absolute monarchy, is a regime in which the monarch is not chosen to represent its citizens; a pure republic is one in which at least all of the major (and perhaps minor) offices are filled by chosen representatives; a mixed regime has both chosen and unchosen representatives.]

42. [As is clear from the discussion that follows, the distinction between liberty and slavery is not identical to that of republic and monarchy; however, there is some correspondence. Especially pertinent here is Hume's understanding of a "free government" as one in which there is a separation of powers, something lacking in an absolute monarchy. See the final paragraph of "Of the Origin of Government" (in this edition).]

that, as you depart from the extremes, and mix a little of monarchy with liberty, the government becomes always the more free; and on the other hand, when you mix a little of liberty with monarchy, the yoke becomes always the more grievous and intolerable. In a government, such as that of FRANCE, which is absolute, and where law, custom, and religion concur, all of them, to make the people fully satisfied with their condition, the monarch cannot entertain any *jealousy* against his subjects, and therefore is apt to indulge them in great *liberties* both of speech and action. In a government altogether republican, such as that of HOLLAND, where there is no magistrate so eminent as to give *jealousy* to the state, there is no danger in intrusting the magistrates with large discretionary powers; and though many advantages result from such powers, in preserving peace and order, yet they lay a considerable restraint on men's actions, and make every private citizen pay a great respect to the government. Thus it seems evident, that the two extremes of absolute monarchy and of a republic, approach near to each other in some material circumstances. In the *first,* the magistrate has no jealousy of the people: in the *second,* the people have none of the magistrate: Which want of jealousy begets a mutual confidence and trust in both cases, and produces a species of liberty in monarchies, and of arbitrary power in republics.

To justify the other part of the foregoing observation, that, in every government, the means are most wide of each other, and that the mixtures of monarchy and liberty render the yoke either more easy or more grievous; I must take notice of a remark in TACITUS with regard to the ROMANS under the emperors, that they neither could bear total slavery nor total liberty, *Nec totam servitutem, nec totam libertatem pati possunt.*[43] This remark a celebrated poet has translated and applied to the ENGLISH, in his lively description of queen ELIZABETH'S policy and government,

Et fit aimer son joug a l'Anglois indompté,
Qui ne peut ni servir, ni vivre en liberté,
HENRIADE, liv. I.[44]

According to these remarks, we are to consider the ROMAN government under the emperors as a mixture of despotism and liberty, where

43. [Tacitus (*c.* A.D. 56–120), *The Histories*, 1.16.]

44. [Voltaire (1694–1778), *La Henriade*: "And she made her yoke dear to the unconquered English, who can neither serve nor live in liberty."]

the despotism prevailed; and the ENGLISH government as a mixture of the same kind, where the liberty predominates. The consequences are conformable to the foregoing observation; and such as may be expected from those mixed forms of government, which beget a mutual watchfulness and jealousy. The ROMAN emperors were, many of them, the most frightful tyrants that ever disgraced human nature; and it is evident, that their cruelty was chiefly excited by their *jealousy,* and by their observing that all the great men of ROME bore with impatience the dominion of a family, which, but a little before, was no wise superior to their own. On the other hand, as the republican part of the government prevails in ENGLAND, though with a great mixture of monarchy, it is obliged, for its own preservation, to maintain a watchful *jealousy* over the magistrates, to remove all discretionary powers, and to secure every one's life and fortune by general and inflexible laws. No action must be deemed a crime but what the law has plainly determined to be such: No crime must be imputed to a man but from a legal proof before his judges; and even these judges must be his fellow-subjects, who are obliged, by their own interest, to have a watchful eye over the encroachments and violence of the ministers. From these causes it proceeds, that there is as much liberty, and even, perhaps, licentiousness in GREAT BRITAIN, as there were formerly slavery and tyranny in ROME.

These principles account for the great liberty of the press in these kingdoms, beyond what is indulged in any other government. It is apprehended, that arbitrary power would steal in upon us, were we not careful to prevent its progress, and were there not an easy method of conveying the alarm from one end of the kingdom to the other. The spirit of the people must frequently be rouzed, in order to curb the ambition of the court; and the dread of rouzing this spirit must be employed to prevent that ambition. Nothing so effectual to this purpose as the liberty of the press, by which all the learning, wit, and genius of the nation may be employed on the side of freedom, and every one be animated to its defence. As long, therefore, as the republican part of our government can maintain itself against the monarchical, it will naturally be careful to keep the press open, as of importance to its own preservation.

[a]It must however be allowed, that the unbounded liberty of the press, though it be difficult, perhaps impossible, to propose a suitable remedy for it, is one of the evils, attending those mixt forms of government.

Essay II: *That Politics May Be Reduced to a Science*

It is a question with several, whether there be any essential difference between one form of government and another? and, whether every form may not become good or bad, according as it is well or ill administered?[45] Were it once admitted, that all governments are alike, and that the only difference consists in the character and conduct of the governors, most political disputes would be at an end, and all *Zeal* for one constitution above another, must be esteemed mere bigotry and folly. But, though a friend to moderation, I cannot forbear condemning this sentiment, and should be sorry to think, that human affairs admit of no greater stability, than what they receive from the casual humours and characters of particular men.

It is true; those who maintain, that the goodness of all government consists in the goodness of the administration, may cite many particular instances in history, where the very same government, in different hands, has varied suddenly into the two opposite extremes of good and bad. Compare the FRENCH government under HENRY III.[46] and under HENRY IV.[47] Oppression, levity, artifice on the part of the rulers; faction, sedition, treachery, rebellion, disloyalty on the part of the subjects: These compose the character of the former miserable aera. But when the patriot and heroic prince, who succeeded, was once firmly seated on the throne, the government, the people, every thing seemed to be totally changed; and all from the difference of the temper and conduct of these two sovereigns. Instances of this kind may be multiplied, almost without number, from ancient as well as modern history, foreign as well as domestic.

But here it may be proper to make a distinction. All absolute governments[b] must very much depend on the administration; and this is one of the great inconveniences attending that form of government. But a republican and free government would be an obvious absurdity, if the particular checks and controuls, provided by the constitution, had really no influence, and made it not the interest, even of bad men, to act for

45. *For forms of government let fools contest,*
Whate'er is best administer'd is best. ESSAY on Man, Book 3. [The *Essay on Man* (1733–34) was written by Alexander Pope (1688–1744).]

46. [King of France from 1574 to 1589.]

47. [King of France from 1589 to 1610.]

the public good. Such is the intention of these forms of government, and such is their real effect, where they are wisely constituted: As on the other hand, they are the source of all disorder, and of the blackest crimes, where either skill or honesty has been wanting in their original frame and institution.

So great is the force of laws, and of particular forms of government, and so little dependence have they on the humours and tempers of men, that consequences almost as general and certain may sometimes be deduced from them, as any which the mathematical sciences afford us.

The constitution of the ROMAN republic gave the whole legislative power to the people, without allowing a negative voice either to the nobility or consuls. This unbounded power they possessed in a collective, not in a representative body. The consequences were: When the people, by success and conquest, had become very numerous, and had spread themselves to a great distance from the capital, the city-tribes, though the most contemptible, carried almost every vote: They were, therefore, most cajoled by every one that affected popularity: They were supported in idleness by the general distribution of corn, and by particular bribes, which they received from almost every candidate: By this means, they became every day more licentious, and the CAMPUS MARTIUS was a perpetual scene of tumult and sedition: Armed slaves were introduced among these rascally citizens; so that the whole government fell into anarchy, and the greatest happiness, which the ROMANS could look for, was the despotic power of the CAESARS. Such are the effects of democracy without a representative.

A Nobility may possess the whole, or any part of the legislative power of a state, in two different ways. Either every nobleman shares the power as part of the whole body, or the whole body enjoys the power as composed of parts, which have each a distinct power and authority. The VENETIAN aristocracy is an instance of the first kind of government: The POLISH of the second. In the VENETIAN government the whole body of nobility possesses the whole power, and no nobleman has any authority which he receives not from the whole. In the POLISH government every nobleman, by means of his fiefs, has a distinct hereditary authority over his vassals, and the whole body has no authority but what it receives from the concurrence of its parts. The different operations and tendencies of these two species of government might be made apparent even *a priori.* A VENETIAN nobility is preferable to a POLISH, let the humours and education of men be ever so much varied. A nobility, who possess their power in common, will preserve peace and order, both among themselves, and their subjects; and no member can have authority enough to controul the laws for a moment. The nobles will preserve their authority over the people, but without any grievous tyranny, or any breach of private property; because such a tyrannical government promotes not the interests of the whole body, however it may that of some individuals. There will be a distinction of rank between the nobility and people, but this will be the only distinction in the state. The whole nobility will form one body, and the whole people another, without any of those private feuds and animosities, which spread ruin and desolation every where. It is easy to see the disadvantages of a POLISH nobility in every one of these particulars.

It is possible so to constitute a free government, as that a single person, call him doge, prince, or king, shall possess a large share of power, and shall form a proper balance or counterpoise to the other parts of the legislature. This chief magistrate may be either *elective* or *hereditary;* and though the former institution may, to a superficial view, appear the most advantageous; yet a more accurate inspection will discover in it greater inconveniencies than in the latter, and such as are founded on causes and principles eternal and immutable. The filling of the throne, in such a government, is a point of too great and too general interest, not to divide the whole people into factions: Whence a civil war, the greatest of ills, may be apprehended, almost with certainty, upon every vacancy. The prince elected must be either a *Foreigner* or a *Native:* The former will be ignorant of the people whom he is to govern; suspicious of his new subjects, and suspected by them; giving his confidence entirely to strangers, who will have no other care but of enriching themselves in the quickest manner, while their master's favour and authority are able to support them. A native will carry into the throne all his private animosities and friendships, and will never be viewed in his elevation, without exciting the sentiment of envy in those, who formerly considered him as their equal. Not to mention that a crown is too high a reward ever to be given to merit alone, and will always induce the candidates to employ force, or money, or intrigue, to procure the votes of the electors: So that such an election will give no better chance for superior merit in the prince, than if the state had trusted to birth alone for determining their sovereign.

It may therefore be pronounced as an universal axiom in politics, *That an hereditary prince, a nobility without vassals, and a people voting by their representatives, form the best* MONARCHY, ARISTOCRACY *and* DEMOCRACY. But in order to prove more fully, that politics admit of general truths, which are invariable by the humour or education either of subject or sovereign, it may not be amiss to observe some other principles of this science, which may seem to deserve that character.

It may easily be observed, that, though free governments[48] have been commonly the most happy for those who partake of their freedom; yet are they the most ruinous and oppressive to their provinces: And this observation may, I believe, be fixed as a maxim of the kind we are here speaking of. When a monarch extends his dominions by conquest, he soon learns to consider his old and his new subjects as on the same footing; because, in reality, all his subjects are to him the same, except the few friends and favourites, with whom he is personally acquainted. He does not, therefore, make any distinction between them in his *general* laws; and, at the same time, is careful to prevent all *particular* acts of oppression on the one as well as on the other. But a free state necessarily makes a great distinction, and must always do so, till men learn to love their neighbours as well as themselves. The conquerors, in such a government, are all legislators, and will be sure to contrive matters, by restrictions on trade, and by taxes, so as to draw some private, as well as public, advantage from their conquests. Provincial governors have also a better chance, in a republic, to escape with their plunder, by means of bribery or intrigue; and their fellow-citizens, who find their own state to be enriched by the spoils of the subject provinces, will be the more inclined to tolerate such abuses. Not to mention, that it is a necessary precaution in a free state to change the governors frequently; which obliges these temporary tyrants to be more expeditious and rapacious, that they may accumulate sufficient wealth before they give place to their successors. What cruel tyrants were the ROMANS over the world during the time of their commonwealth! It is true, they had laws to prevent oppression in their provincial magistrates; but CICERO[49] informs us, that the Romans could not better consult

48. [For Hume's most explicit discussion of "free government," see the final paragraph of "Of the Origin of Government" (in this edition).]

49. [Cicero (106–43 B.C.) influenced certain elements of Hume's thought. In a letter to Francis Hutcheson (see n. 1) dated September 17, 1739, Hume reports that in writing Book III of the *Treatise* he had Cicero's *De Officiis* "in [his] Eye in all of [his] reasonings." See *The Letters of David Hume*, vol. I, p. 34.]

the interests of the provinces than by repealing these very laws. For, in that case, says he, our magistrates, having entire impunity, would plunder no more than would satisfy their own rapaciousness; whereas, at present, they must also satisfy that of their judges, and of all the great men in ROME, of whose protection they stand in need. Who can read of the cruelties and oppressions of VERRES[50] without horror and astonishment? And who is not touched with indignation to hear, that, after CICERO had exhausted on that abandoned criminal all the thunders of his eloquence, and had prevailed so far as to get him condemned to the utmost extent of the laws; yet that cruel tyrant lived peaceably to old age, in opulence and ease, and, thirty years afterwards, was put into the proscription by MARK ANTHONY,[51] on account of his exorbitant wealth, where he fell with CICERO himself, and all the most virtuous men of ROME? After the dissolution of the commonwealth, the ROMAN yoke became easier upon the provinces, as TACITUS informs us;[52] and it may be observed, that many of the worst emperors, DOMITIAN,[53] for instance, were careful to prevent all oppression on the provinces. In[54] TIBERIUS'S time,[55] GAUL was esteemed richer than ITALY itself: Nor, do I find, during the whole time of the ROMAN monarchy, that the empire became less rich or populous in any of its provinces; though indeed its valour and military discipline were always upon the decline. The oppression and tyranny

50. [As Proconsul of Sicily from 73 to 71 B.C., Verres flagrantly plundered and oppressed the province. Although Verres had his father's wealth and power on his side, Cicero pressed an indictment against him on behalf of the Sicilians that resulted in Verres' fleeing to Massilia. Cicero's arguments against Verres are collected in *The Verrine Orations*, and this work continues to provide great insight into some of the abuses of provincial administration during the later years of the Roman Republic.]

51. [Marcus Antonius (*c.* 83–30 B.C.)]

52. Ann. lib. 1. cap. 2. [Tacitus (*c.* A.D. 56–120), *The Annals*, 1.2.]

53. SUET. in vita DOMIT. c. 8. [Suetonius (A.D. 69?–after 122?), "The Life of Domitian," in *The Lives of the Caesars*. Domitian was emperor from A.D. 81–96.]

54. *Egregium resumendoe libertati tempus, si ipsi florentes, quam inops* ITALIA *quam imbellis urbana plebs, nihil validum in exercitibus, nisi quod externum cogitarent.* TACIT. Ann. lib. 3. 40. [Tacitus, *The Annals*, 1.40: "It was an unequaled opportunity for regaining their independence; they had only to look from their own resources to the poverty of Italy, the unwarlike city population, the feebleness of the armies except for the leavening of foreigners."]

55. [Tiberius was Emperor of Rome from A.D. 14 to 37.]

of the CARTHAGINIANS over their subject states in AFRICA went so far, as we learn from POLYBIUS,[56] that, not content with exacting the half of all the produce of the land, which of itself was a very high rent, they also loaded them with many other taxes. If we pass from ancient to modern times, we shall still find the observation to hold. The provinces of absolute monarchies are always better treated than those of free states. Compare the *Pais conquis*[57] of FRANCE with IRELAND, and you will be convinced of this truth; though this latter kingdom, being, in a good measure, peopled from ENGLAND, possesses so many rights and privileges as should naturally make it challenge better treatment than that of a conquered province. CORSICA is also an obvious instance to the same purpose.

There is an observation in MACHIAVEL,[58] with regard to the conquests of ALEXANDER the Great, which I think, may be regarded as one of those eternal political truths, which no time nor accidents can vary. It may seem strange, says that politician, that such sudden conquests, as those of ALEXANDER, should be possessed so peaceably by his successors, and that the PERSIANS, during all the confusions and civil wars among the GREEKS, never made the smallest effort towards the recovery of their former independent government. To satisfy us concerning the cause of this remarkable event, we may consider, that a monarch may govern his subjects in two different ways. He may either follow the maxims of the eastern princes, and stretch his authority so far as to leave no distinction of rank among his subjects, but what proceeds immediately from himself; no advantages of birth; no hereditary honours and possessions; and, in a word, no credit among the people, except from his commission alone. Or a monarch may exert his power after a milder manner, like other EUROPEAN princes; and leave other sources of honour, beside his smile and favour: Birth, titles, possessions, valour, integrity, knowledge, or great and fortunate atchievements. In the former species of government, after a conquest, it is impossible ever to shake off the yoke; since no one possesses, among the people, so much personal credit and authority as to begin

56. Lib. 1. cap. 72. [Polybius (*c.* 200–118 B.C.), *The Histories*, 1.72.]

57. [Conquered lands]

58. [See Niccoló Machiavelli (1469–1527), *The Prince*, trans. by H. Mansfield (Chicago: University of Chicago Press, 1985), pp. 16–19. Machiavelli's two other great works are *Florentine Histories* and *Discourses on Livy*. Alexander the Great (356–323 B.C.) established a vast Greek empire that extended into Asia, Persia, Egypt, and India.]

such an enterprize: Whereas, in the latter, the least misfortune, or discord among the victors, will encourage the vanquished to take arms, who have leaders ready to prompt and conduct them in every undertaking.[59]

Such is the reasoning of MACHIAVEL, which seems solid and

59. I have taken it for granted, according to the supposition of MACHIAVEL, that the ancient PERSIANS had no nobility; though there is reason to suspect, that the FLORENTINE secretary, who seems to have been better acquainted with the ROMAN than the GREEK authors, was mistaken in this particular. The more ancient PERSIANS, whose manners are described by XENOPHON, [Xenophon (*c.* 428/7–354 B.C.), *Cyropaidea*, 2.1.9.] were a free people, and had nobility. Their *ὁμότιμοι* were preserved even after the extending of their conquests and the consequent change of their government. ARRIAN mentions them in DARIUS'S time, *De exped.* Alex. lib. ii. 11. [Arrian (A.D. 96?–180?), *Anabasis of Alexander & Indica*, 2.11.] Historians also speak often of the persons in command as men of family. TYGRANES, who was general of the MEDES under XERXES, was of the race of ACHMAENES, HEROD. lib. vii. cap. 62. [Herodotus (*c.* mid to late fifth century B.C.), *The History*, trans. by D. Grene (Chicago: University of Chicago Press, 1987), p. 492 (7.62).] ARTACHAEAS, who directed the cutting of the canal about mount ATHOS, was of the same family. Id. cap. 117. [Herodotus, *The History*, p. 507 (7.117).] MEGABYZUS was one of the seven eminent PERSIANS who conspired against the MAGI. His son, ZOPYRUS, was in the highest command under DARIUS, and delivered BABYLON to him. His grandson, MEGABYZUS, commanded the army, defeated at MARATHON. His great-grandson, ZOPYRUS, was also eminent, and was banished PERSIA. HEROD. lib. iii. 160, THUC. lib. i. 109. [Herodotus, *The History*, p. 279 (3.160); Thucydides (*c.* 460–400 B.C.), *History of the Peloponnesian War*, 1.109.] ROSACES, who commanded an army in EGYPT under ARTAXERXES, was also descended from one of the seven conspirators, DIOD. SIC. lib. xvi. 47. [Diodorus Siculus (died after 22 B.C.), *Library of History*, 16.47.] AGESILAUS, in XENOPHON, Hist. GRAEC. lib. iv. 1, [Xenophon, *Hellenica*, 4.1.] being desirous of making a marriage betwixt king COTYS his ally, and the daughter of SPITHRIDATES, a PERSIAN of rank, who had deserted to him, first asks COTYS what family SPITHRIDATES is of. One of the most considerable in PERSIA, says COTYS. ARIAEUS, when offered the sovereignty by CLEARCHUS and the ten thousand GREEKS, refused it as of too low a rank, and said, that so many eminent PERSIANS would never endure his rule. *Id. de exped.* lib. ii. [Xenophon, *Anabasis*, 2.1–2.] Some of the families descended from the seven PERSIANS abovementioned remained during all ALEXANDER'S successors; and MITHRIDATES, in ANTIOCHUS'S time, is said by POLYBIUS to be descended from one of them, lib. v. cap. 43. [Polybius, *The Histories*, 5.43.] ARTABAZUS was esteemed, as ARRIAN says, *ἐν τοῖς πρώτοις Περσῶν.* lib. iii. 23. [Arrian, *Anabasis of Alexander & Indica*, 3.23.] And when ALEXANDER married in one day 80 of his captains to PERSIAN women, his intention plainly was to ally the MACEDONIANS with the most eminent PERSIAN families. Id. lib. vii. 4. [Arrian, *Anabasis of Alexander & Indica*, 7.4.] DIODORUS SICULUS says they were of the most noble birth in PERSIA, lib. xvii. 107. [Diodorus Siculus, *Library of History*, 17.107.] The government of PERSIA was despotic, and conducted in many respects, after the eastern manner, but was not carried so far as to extirpate all nobility, and confound all ranks and orders.

conclusive; though I wish he had not mixed falsehood with truth, in asserting, that monarchies, governed according to eastern policy, though more easily kept when once subdued, yet are the most difficult to subdue; since they cannot contain any powerful subject, whose discontent and faction may facilitate the enterprizes of an enemy. For besides, that such a tyrannical government enervates the courage of men, and renders them indifferent towards the fortunes of their sovereign; besides this, I say, we find by experience, that even the temporary and delegated authority of the generals and magistrates; being always, in such governments, as absolute within its sphere, as that of the prince himself; is able, with barbarians, accustomed to a blind submission, to produce the most dangerous and fatal revolutions. So that, in every respect, a gentle government is preferable, and gives the greatest security to the sovereign as well as to the subject.

Legislators, therefore, ought not to trust the future government of a state entirely to chance, but ought to provide a system of laws to regulate the administration of public affairs to the latest posterity. Effects will always correspond to causes; and wise regulations in any commonwealth are the most valuable legacy that can be left to future ages. In the smallest court or office, the stated forms and methods, by which business must be conducted, are found to be a considerable check on the natural depravity of mankind. Why should not the case be the same in public affairs? Can we ascribe the stability and wisdom of the VENETIAN government, through so many ages, to any thing but the form of government? And is it not easy to point out those defects in the original constitution, which produced the tumultuous governments of ATHENS and ROME, and ended at last in the ruin of these two famous republics? And so little dependance has this affair on the humours and education of particular men, that one part of the same republic may be wisely conducted, and another weakly, by the very same men, merely on account of the difference of the forms and institutions, by which these parts are regulated. Historians inform us that this was actually the case with GENOA. For while the state

---

It left men who were still great, by themselves and their family, independent of their office and commission. And the reason why the MACEDONIANS kept so easily dominion over them was owing to other causes easy to be found in the historians; though it must be owned that MACHIAVEL'S reasoning is, in itself, just, however doubtful its application to the present case.

was always full of sedition, and tumult, and disorder, the bank of St. GEORGE, which had become a considerable part of the people, was conducted, for several ages, with the utmost integrity and wisdom.[60]

The ages of greatest public spirit are not always most eminent for private virtue. Good laws may beget order and moderation in the government, where the manners and customs have instilled little humanity or justice into the tempers of men. The most illustrious period of the ROMAN history, considered in a political view, is that between the beginning of the first and end of the last PUNIC war;[61] the due balance between the nobility and the people being then fixed by the contests of the tribunes, and not being yet lost by the extent of conquests. Yet at this very time, the horrid practice of poisoning was so common, that, during part of a season, a Praetor punished capitally for this crime above three thousand[62] persons in a part of ITALY; and found informations of this nature still multiplying upon him. There is a similar, or rather a worse instance,[63] in the more early times of the commonwealth. So depraved in private life were that people, whom in their histories we so much admire. I doubt not but they were really more virtuous during the time of the two *Triumvirates;*[64] when they

60. *Essempio veramente raro, & da Filosofi intante loro imaginate & vedute Republiche mai non trovato, vedere dentro ad un medesimo cerchio, fra medesimi cittadini, la liberta, & la tirannide, la vita civile & la corotta, la giustitia, & la licenza; perche quello ordine solo mantiere quella citta piena di costumi antichi & venerabili. E s'egli auvenisse (che col tempo in ogni modo auverrà) que* SAN GIORGIO *tutta quel la città occupasse, sarrebbe quella una Republica piu dalla* VENETIANA *memorabile.* Della Hist. Florentinè, lib. 8. [Niccoló Machiavelli, *Florentine Histories*, trans. by L. Banfield and H. Mansfield (Princeton: Princeton University Press, 1988), p. 352 (8.29): "An example truly rare, never found by the philosophers in all republics that they have imagined and seen: to see within the same circle, among the same citizens, liberty and tyranny, civil life and corrupt life, justice and license, because that order alone keeps the city full of its ancient and venerable customs. And if it should happen—which in time it surely will—that San Giorgio should take over the whole city, that would be a republic more memorable than the Venetian."]

61. [The Punic Wars were three wars fought between Rome and Carthage. This first lasted from 264 to 241 B.C., the second from 218 to 201 B.C., and the third from 149 to 146 B.C., ending with the destruction of Carthage.]

62. T. Livii, lib. 40. cap. 43. [Titus Livius (59 B.C.–A.D. 17), *The History of Rome*, trans. by D. Spillan *et al.*, 4 vols. (London: G. Bell and Sons, Ltd., 1911), vol. iv, p. 1900 (40.43).]

63. *Id.* lib. 8. cap. 18. [Titus Livius, *The History of Rome*, vol. I, pp. 527–28 (8.18).]

64. [Julius Caesar, Pompey, and Crassus were members of the so-called First Triumvirate (board of three) that ruled Rome from 60 B.C. until Crassus's death in 53 B.C.;

were tearing their common country to pieces, and spreading slaughter and desolation over the face of the earth, merely for the choice of tyrants.[65]

Here, then, is a sufficient inducement to maintain, with the utmost ZEAL, in every free state, those forms and institutions, by which liberty is secured, the public good consulted, and the avarice or ambition of particular men restrained and punished. Nothing does more honour to human nature, than to see it susceptible of so noble a passion; as nothing can be a greater indication of meanness of heart in any man, than to see him destitute of it. A man who loves only himself, without regard to friendship and desert, merits the severest blame; and a man, who is only susceptible of friendship, without public spirit, or a regard to the community, is deficient in the most material part of virtue.

But this is a subject which needs not be longer insisted on at present. There are enow of zealots on both sides who kindle up the passions of their partizans, and under pretence of public good, pursue the interests and ends of their particular faction. For my part, I shall always be more fond of promoting moderation than zeal; though perhaps the surest way of producing moderation in every party is to increase our zeal for the public. Let us therefore try, if it be possible, from the foregoing doctrine, to draw a lesson of moderation with regard to the parties, into which our country is at present divided; at the same time, that we allow not this moderation to abate the industry and passion, with which every individual is bound to pursue the good of his country.

Those who either attack or defend a minister in such a government as ours,[66] where the utmost liberty is allowed, always carry matters to an extreme, and exaggerate his merit or demerit with regard to the

---

they were followed in 44 B.C., at the time of Caesar's assassination, by the Second Triumvirate of Mark Antony, Lepidus, and Octavian (who would become the first Emperor of Rome).]

65. *L'Aigle contre L'Aigle,* ROMAINS *contre* ROMAINS,
Combatans seulement pour le choix de tyrans.
[A loose adaptation from Pierre Corneille's (1606–84) *Cinna*: Eagle against Eagle, Romans against Romans/ Fighting only for the choice of tyrants.]
CORNEILLE.

66. [Hume is discussing here and in what follows attacks made against Sir Robert Walpole (1676–1745) for his use, as Lord of the Treasury from 1741 to 1742, of patronage at the disposal of the Crown to control certain interests in the House of Commons. See Hume's essays "A Character of Sir Robert Walpole" and "Of some Remarkable Customs," in *Essays, Moral, Political, and Literary*.]

public. His enemies are sure to charge him with the greatest enormities, both in domestic and foreign management; and there is no meanness or crime, of which, in their account, he is not capable. Unnecessary wars, scandalous treaties, profusion of public treasure, oppressive taxes, every kind of mal-administration is ascribed to him. To aggravate the charge, his pernicious conduct, it is said, will extend its baleful influence even to posterity, by undermining the best constitution in the world, and disordering that wise system of laws, institutions, and customs, by which our ancestors, during so many centuries, have been so happily governed. He is not only a wicked minister in himself, but has removed every security provided against wicked ministers for the future.

On the other hand, the partizans of the minister make his panegyric run as high as the accusation against him, and celebrate his wise, steady, and moderate conduct in every part of his administration. The honour and interest of the nation supported abroad, public credit maintained at home, persecution restrained, faction subdued; the merit of all these blessings is ascribed solely to the minister. At the same time, he crowns all his other merits by a religious care of the best constitution in the world, which he has preserved in all its parts, and has transmitted entire, to be the happiness and security of the latest posterity.

When this accusation and panegyric are received by the partizans of each party, no wonder they beget an extraordinary ferment on both sides, and fill the nation with violent animosities. But I would fain persuade these party-zealots, that there is a flat contradiction both in the accusation and panegyric, and that it were impossible for either of them to run so high, were it not for this contradiction. If our constitution be really *that noble fabric, the pride of* BRITAIN, *the envy of our neighbours, raised by the labour of so many centuries, repaired at the expence of so many millions, and cemented by such a profusion of blood;*[67] I say, if our constitu-

67. *Dissertation on parties,* Letter 10. [Lord Bolingbroke (1678–1751), *A Dissertation upon Parties,* in *The Works of Lord Bolingbroke* (London: F. Cass, 1967), vol. II. *A Dissertation upon Parties,* which is a fierce attack on Walpole, first appeared in the periodical *The Craftsmen.* Bolingbroke was a close friend of Alexander Pope (see n. 45), especially from 1725 to 1735. In Hume's preface to the first volume of his essays in 1741, he says that the essays were first conceived of by him as being "weekly-papers," like the *Spectator* and *The Craftsman.* After indicating that he quickly dropped the idea of producing such a large number of essays in the relatively short span that a "weekly-paper" would have required, Hume remarks that he hopes that the reader recognizes that in the essays, he treats political subjects in a moderate and impartial manner, one

tion does in any degree deserve these eulogies, it would never have suffered a wicked and weak minister to govern triumphantly for a course of twenty years, when opposed by the greatest geniuses in the nation, who exercised the utmost liberty of tongue and pen, in parliament, and in their frequent appeals to the people. But, if the minister be wicked and weak, to the degree so strenuously insisted on, the constitution must be faulty in its original principles, and he cannot consistently be charged with undermining the best form of government in the world. A constitution is only so far good, as it provides a remedy against mal-administration; and if the BRITISH, when in its greatest vigour, and repaired by two such remarkable events, as the *Revolution* and *Accession,*[68] by which our ancient royal family was sacrificed to it; if our constitution, I say, with so great advantages, does not, in fact, provide any such remedy, we are rather beholden to any minister who undermines it, and affords us an opportunity of erecting a better in its place.

I would employ the same topics to moderate the zeal of those who defend the minister. *Is our constitution so excellent?* Then a change of ministry can be no such dreadful event; since it is essential to such a constitution, in every ministry, both to preserve itself from violation, and to prevent all enormities in the administration. *Is our constitution very bad?* Then so extraordinary a jealousy and apprehension, on account of changes, is ill placed; and a man should no more be anxious in this case, than a husband, who had married a woman from the stews, should be watchful to prevent her infidelity. Public affairs, in such a government, must necessarily go to confusion, by whatever hands they are conducted; and the zeal of *patriots* is in that case much less requisite than the patience and submission of *philosophers.* The virtue and good intentions of CATO and BRUTUS[69] are highly laudable; but, to what purpose did their zeal serve? Only to hasten the fatal period of the ROMAN government, and render its convulsions and dying agonies more violent and painful.

I would not be understood to mean, that public affairs deserve no care and attention at all. Would men be moderate and consistent, their

---

that refrains from "party-rage." Moderation is perhaps *the* cardinal political virtue in Hume's *Essays*.]

68. [Hume is referring the Revolution of 1688 that removed James II from the throne, and led to the assumption of the throne by Mary, the daughter of James II, and William of Orange, her husband. See n. 25.]

69. [Both Cato (95–46 B.C.) and Brutus (85?–42 B.C.) conspired against Caesar.]

claims might be admitted; at least might be examined. The *country-party* might still assert, that our constitution, though excellent, will admit of mal-administration to a certain degree; and therefore, if the minister be bad, it is proper to oppose him with a *suitable* degree of zeal. And, on the other hand, the *court-party* may be allowed, upon the supposition that the minister were good, to defend, and with *some* zeal too, his administration. I would only persuade men not to contend, as if they were fighting *pro aris & focis,*[70] and change a good constitution into a bad one, by the violence of their factions.

I have not here considered any thing that is personal in the present controversy. In the best civil constitution, where every man is restrained by the most rigid laws, it is easy to discover either the good or bad intentions of a minister, and to judge, whether his personal character deserve love or hatred. But such questions are of little importance to the public, and lay those, who employ their pens upon them, under a just suspicion either of malevolence or of flattery.

Essay III: *Of the Independency of Parliament*[c]

Political writers have established it as a maxim, that, in contriving any system of government, and fixing the several checks and controuls of the constitution, every man ought to be supposed a *knave,* and to have no other end, in all his actions, than private interest. By this interest we must govern him, and, by means of it, make him, notwithstanding his insatiable avarice and ambition, co-operate to public good. Without this, say they, we shall in vain boast of the advantages of any constitution, and shall find, in the end, that we have no security for our liberties or possessions, except the good-will of our rulers; that is, we shall have no security at all.

It is, therefore, a just *political* maxim, *that every man must be supposed a knave:* Though at the same time, it appears somewhat strange, that a maxim should be true in *politics,* which is false in *fact.* But to satisfy us on this head, we may consider, that men are generally more honest in their private than in their public capacity, and will go greater lengths to serve a party, than when their own private interest is alone concerned. Honour is a great check upon mankind: But where a considerable body of men act together, this check is, in a great measure, removed; since a man is sure to be approved of by his own party, for what

70. [in defense of our altars and fires]

promotes the common interest; and he soon learns to despise the clamours of adversaries. To which we may add, that every court or senate is determined by the greater number of voices; so that, if self-interest influences only the majority, (as it will always do) the whole senate follows the allurements of this separate interest, and acts as if it contained not one member, who had any regard to public interest and liberty.

When there offers, therefore, to our censure and examination, any plan of government, real or imaginary, where the power is distributed among several courts, and several orders of men, we should always consider the separate interest of each court, and each order; and, if we find that, by the skilful division of power, this interest must necessarily, in its operation, concur with public, we may pronounce that government to be wise and happy. If, on the contrary, separate interest be not checked, and be not directed to the public, we ought to look for nothing but faction, disorder, and tyranny from such a government. In this opinion I am justified by experience, as well as by the authority of all philosophers and politicians, both antient and modern.

How much, therefore, would it have surprised such a genius as CICERO,[71] or TACITUS,[72] to have been told, that, in a future age, there should arise a very regular system of *mixed* government, where the authority was so distributed, that one rank, whenever it pleased, might swallow up all the rest, and engross the whole power of the constitution. Such a government, they would say, will not be a mixed government. For so great is the natural ambition of men, that they are never satisfied with power; and if one order of men, by pursuing its own interest, can usurp upon every other order, it will certainly do so, and render itself, as far as possible, absolute and uncontroulable.

But, in this opinion, experience shews they would have been mistaken. For this is actually the case with the BRITISH constitution. The share of power, allotted by our constitution to the house of commons, is so great, that it absolutely commands all the other parts of the government. The king's legislative power is plainly no proper check to it. For though the king has a negative in framing laws; yet this, in fact, is esteemed of so little moment, that whatever is voted by the two houses, is always sure to pass into a law, and the royal assent is little better

71. [See n. 49.]

72. [Tacitus (*c.* A.D. 56–120) is best known for two works that cover the history of the Roman Empire from A.D. 14 to 96, *The Histories* and *Annals*.]

than a form. The principal weight of the crown lies in the executive power. But besides that the executive power in every government is altogether subordinate to the legislative; besides this, I say, the exercise of this power requires an immense expence; and the commons have assumed to themselves the sole right of granting money. How easy, therefore, would it be for that house to wrest from the crown all these powers, one after another; by making every grant conditional, and choosing their time so well, that their refusal of supply should only distress the government, without giving foreign powers any advantage over us? Did the house of commons depend in the same manner on the king, and had none of the members any property but from his gift, would not he command all their resolutions, and be from that moment absolute? As to the house of lords, they are a very powerful support to the Crown, so long as they are, in their turn, supported by it; but both experience and reason shew, that they have no force or authority sufficient to maintain themselves alone, without such support.

How, therefore, shall we solve this paradox? And by what means is this member of our constitution confined within the proper limits; since, from our very constitution, it must necessarily have as much power as it demands, and can only be confined by itself? How is this consistent with our experience of human nature? I answer, that the interest of the body is here restrained by that of the individuals, and that the house of commons stretches not its power, because such an usurpation would be contrary to the interest of the majority of its members. The crown has so many offices at its disposal, that, when assisted by the honest and disinterested part of the house, it will always command the resolutions of the whole so far, at least, as to preserve the antient constitution from danger. We may, therefore, give to this influence what name we please; we may call it by the invidious appellations of *corruption* and *dependence;* but some degree and some kind of it are inseparable from the very nature of the constitution, and necessary to the preservation of our mixed government.

Instead then of asserting[73] absolutely, that the dependence of parliament, in every degree, is an infringement of BRITISH liberty, the country-party should have made some concessions to their adversaries, and have only examined what was the proper degree of this dependence, beyond which it became dangerous to liberty. But such a moderation

73. See *Dissertation on Parties,* throughout. [Lord Bolingbroke, *Dissertation upon Parties*. See n. 67.]

is not to be expected in party-men of any kind. After a concession of this nature, all declamation must be abandoned; and a calm enquiry into the proper degree of court-influence and parliamentary dependence would have been expected by the readers. And though the advantage, in such a controversy, might possibly remain to the *country-party;* yet the victory would not be so compleat as they wish for, nor would a true patriot have given an entire loose to his zeal, for fear of running matters into a contrary extreme, by diminishing too[74] far the influence of the crown. It was, therefore, thought best to deny, that this extreme could ever be dangerous to the constitution, or that the crown could ever have too little influence over members of parliament.

All questions concerning the proper medium between extremes are difficult to be decided; both because it is not easy to find *words* proper to fix this medium, and because the good and ill, in such cases, run so gradually into each other, as even to render our *sentiments* doubtful and uncertain. But there is a peculiar difficulty in the present case, which would embarrass the most knowing and most impartial examiner. The power of the crown is always lodged in a single person, either king or minister; and as this person may have either a greater or less degree of ambition, capacity, courage, popularity, or fortune, the power, which is too great in one hand, may become too little in another. In pure republics, where the authority is distributed among several assemblies or senates, the checks and controuls are more regular in their operation; because the members of such numerous assemblies may be presumed to be always nearly equal in capacity and virtue; and it is only their number, riches, or authority, which enter into consideration. But a limited monarchy admits not of any such stability; nor is it possible to assign to the crown such a determinate degree of power, as will, in every hand, form a proper counterbalance to the other parts of the constitution. This is an unavoidable disadvantage, among the many advantages, attending that species of government.

74. By that *influence of the crown,* which I would justify, I mean only that which arises from the offices and honours that are at the disposal of the crown. As to private *bribery,* it may be considered in the same light as the practice of employing spies, which is scarcely justifiable in a good minister, and is infamous in a bad one: But to be a spy, or to be corrupted, is always infamous under all ministers, and is to be regarded as a shameless prostitution. POLYBIUS justly esteems the pecuniary influence of the senate and censors to be one of the regular and constitutional weights, which preserved the balance of the ROMAN government. Lib. vi. cap. 15. [Polybius (*c.* 200–118 B.C.), *The Histories*, 6.15.]

Essay IV: *Whether the British Government inclines more to Absolute Monarchy, or to a Republic*

It affords a violent prejudice against almost every science, that no prudent man, however sure of his principles, dares prophesy concerning any event, or foretel the remote consequences of things. A physician will not venture to pronounce concerning the condition of his patient a fortnight or month after: And still less dares a politician foretel the situation of public affairs a few years hence. HARRINGTON thought himself so sure of his general principle, *that the balance of power depends on that of property*, that he ventured to pronounce it impossible ever to re-establish monarchy in ENGLAND:[75] but his book was scarcely published when the king was restored; and we see, that monarchy has ever since subsisted upon the same footing as before. Notwithstanding this unlucky example, I will venture to examine an important question, to wit, *Whether the* BRITISH *government inclines more to absolute monarchy, or to a republic; and in which of these two species of government it will most probably terminate?* As there seems not to be any great danger of a sudden revolution either way, I shall at least escape the shame attending my temerity, if I should be found to have been mistaken.

Those who assert, that the balance of our government inclines towards absolute monarchy, may support their opinion by the following reasons. That property has a great influence on power cannot possibly be denied; but yet the general maxim, *that the balance of one depends on the balance of the other*, must be received with several limitations. It is evident, that much less property in a single hand will be able to counterbalance a greater property in several; not only because it is difficult to make many persons combine in the same views and measures; but because property, when united, causes much greater dependence, than the same property, when dispersed. A hundred persons, of 1000*l.* a year a-piece, can consume all their income, and no body shall ever be the better for them, except their servants and tradesmen, who justly regard their profits as the product of their own labour. But

75. [James Harrington (1611–77). The general principle at issue is found in several of Harrington's writings, most especially in *The Commonwealth of Oceana* and *The Prerogative of Popular Government*. Harrington's "pronouncement" can be found in a very short piece titled "The Ways and Means." See *The Political Works of James Harrington*, ed. by J.G.A. Pocock (Cambridge: Cambridge University Press, 1977).]

a man possessed of 100,000*l.* a year, if he has either any generosity or any cunning, may create a great dependence by obligations, and still a greater by expectations. Hence we may observe, that, in all free governments, any subject exorbitantly rich has always created jealousy, even though his riches bore no proportion to those of the state. CRASSUS'S[76] fortune, if I remember well, amounted only to about two millions and a half of our money; yet we find, that, though his genius was nothing extraordinary, he was able, by means of his riches alone, to counterbalance, during his lifetime, the power of POMPEY[77] as well as that of CAESAR, who afterwards became master of the world. The wealth of the MEDICI[78] made them masters of FLORENCE; though, it is probable, it was not considerable, compared to the united property of that opulent republic.

These considerations are apt to make one entertain a magnificent idea of the BRITISH spirit and love of liberty; since we could maintain our free government, during so many centuries, against our sovereigns, who, besides the power and dignity and majesty of the crown, have always been possessed of much more property than any subject has ever enjoyed in any commonwealth. But it may be said, that this spirit, however great, will never be able to support itself against that immense property, which is now lodged in the king, and which is still encreasing. Upon a moderate computation, there are near three millions a year at the disposal of the crown. The civil list amounts to near a million; the collection of all taxes to another; and the employments in the army and navy, together with ecclesiastical preferments, to above a third million: An enormous sum, and what may fairly be computed to be more than a thirtieth part of the whole income and labour of the kingdom. When we add to this great property, the encreasing luxury of the nation, our proneness to corruption, together with the great power and prerogatives of the crown, and the command of military force, there is no one but must despair of being able, without extraordinary efforts, to support our free government much longer under these disadvantages.

On the other hand, those who maintain, that the byass of the BRIT-

76. [A member of the first Triumvirate (see n. 27), Crassus made his wealth through proscriptions, declaring certain Roman citizens outlaws and confiscating their wealth.]

77. [A member of the first Triumvirate.]

78. [The ruling family in Florence during most of the fifteenth and sixteenth centuries. During this period, two members of the family were elected Pope.]

ISH government leans towards a republic, may support their opinion by specious arguments. It may be said, that, though this immense property in the crown, be joined to the dignity of first magistrate, and to many other legal powers and prerogatives, which should naturally give it greater influence; yet it really becomes less dangerous to liberty upon that very account. Were ENGLAND a republic, and were any private man possessed of a revenue, a third, or even a tenth part as large as that of the crown, he would very justly excite jealousy; because he would infallibly have great authority, in the government: And such an irregular authority, not avowed by the laws, is always more dangerous than a much greater authority, derived from them. A man, possessed of usurped power, can set no bounds to his pretensions: His partizans have liberty to hope for every thing in his favour: His enemies provoke his ambition, with his fears, by the violence of their opposition: And the government being thrown into a ferment, every corrupted humour in the state naturally gathers to him. On the contrary, a legal authority, though great, has always some bounds, which terminate both the hopes and pretensions of the person possessed of it: The laws must have provided a remedy against its excesses: Such an eminent magistrate has much to fear, and little to hope from his usurpations: And as his legal authority is quietly submitted to, he has small temptation and small opportunity of extending it farther. Besides, it happens, with regard to ambitious aims and projects, what may be observed with regard to sects of philosophy and religion. A new sect excites such a ferment, and is both opposed and defended with such vehemence, that it always spreads faster, and multiplies its partizans with greater rapidity, than any old established opinion, recommended by the sanction of the laws and of antiquity. Such is the nature of novelty, that, where any thing pleases, it becomes doubly agreeable, if new; but if it displeases, it is doubly displeasing, upon that very account. And, in most cases, the violence of enemies is favourable to ambitious projects, as well as the zeal of partizans.

It may farther be said, that, though men be much governed by interest; yet even interest itself, and all human affairs, are entirely governed by *opinion*. Now, there has been a sudden and sensible change in the opinions of men within these last fifty years, by the progress of learning and of liberty. Most people, in this island, have divested themselves of all superstitious reverence to names and authority: The clergy have much lost their credit: Their pretensions and doctrines have been ridiculed; and even religion can scarcely support itself in the world. The mere name of *king* commands little respect; and to talk of a king as GOD's vicegerent on earth, or to give him any of those magnificent titles, which formerly dazzled mankind, would but excite laughter in every one. Though the crown, by means of its large revenue, may maintain its authority in times of tranquillity, upon private interest and influence; yet, as the least shock or convulsion must break all these interests to pieces, the royal power, being no longer supported by the settled principles and opinions of men, will immediately dissolve. Had men been in the same disposition at the *revolution,* as they are at present, monarchy would have run a great risque of being entirely lost in this island.

Durst I venture to deliver my own sentiments amidst these opposite arguments, I would assert, that, unless there happen some extraordinary convulsion, the power of the crown, by means of its large revenue, is rather upon the encrease; though, at the same time I own, that its progress seems very slow, and almost insensible. The tide has run long, and with some rapidity, to the side of popular government, and is just beginning to turn towards monarchy.

It is well known, that every government must come to a period, and that death is unavoidable to the political as well as to the animal body. But, as one kind of death may be preferable to another, it may be enquired, whether it be more desirable for the BRITISH constitution to terminate in a popular government, or in absolute monarchy? Here I would frankly declare, that, though liberty be preferable to slavery, in almost every case; yet I should rather wish to see an absolute monarch than a republic in this island. For, let us consider, what kind of republic we have reason to expect. The question is not concerning any fine imaginary republic, of which a man may form a plan in his closet. There is no doubt, but a popular government may be imagined more perfect than absolute monarchy, or even than our present constitution. But what reason have we to expect that any such government will ever be established in GREAT BRITAIN, upon the dissolution of our monarchy? If any single person acquire power enough to take our constitution to pieces, and put it up a-new, he is really an absolute monarch; and we have already had an instance of this kind, sufficient to convince us, that such a person will never resign his power, or establish any free government. Matters, therefore, must be trusted to their natural progress and operation; and the house of commons, according to its present constitution, must be the only legislature in such a popular government. The inconveniencies attending such a situation of affairs, present themselves by thousands. If the house of commons, in such a case, ever dissolve itself, which is not to be expected, we may look for a civil war every election. If it continue itself, we shall suffer all the tyranny of a faction, subdivided into new factions. And, as such a violent government cannot long subsist, we shall, at last, after many convulsions, and civil wars, find repose in absolute monarchy, which it would have been happier for us to have established peaceably from the beginning. Absolute monarchy, therefore, is the easiest death, the true *Euthanasia* of the BRITISH constitution.

Thus, if we have reason to be more jealous of monarchy, because the danger is more imminent from that quarter; we have also reason to be more jealous of popular government, because that danger is more terrible. This may teach us a lesson of moderation in all our political controversies.

Essay V: *Of the Parties of Great Britain*

Were the BRITISH government proposed as a subject of speculation, one would immediately perceive in it a source of division and party, which it would be almost impossible for it, under any administration, to avoid. The just balance between the republican and monarchical part of our constitution is really, in itself, so extremely delicate and uncertain, that, when joined to men's passions and prejudices, it is impossible but different opinions must arise concerning it, even among persons of the best understanding. Those of mild tempers, who love peace and order, and detest sedition and civil wars, will always entertain more favourable sentiments of monarchy, than men of bold and generous spirits, who are passionate lovers of liberty, and think no evil comparable to subjection and slavery. And though all reasonable men agree in general to preserve our mixed government; yet, when they come to particulars, some will incline to trust greater powers to the crown, to bestow on it more influence, and to guard against its encroachments with less caution, than others who are terrified at the most distant approaches of tyranny and despotic power. Thus are there parties of PRINCIPLE[79] involved in the very nature of our constitution,

79. [Hume divides political parties into personal and, more importantly for him, real. The later he divides into parties from interest, principle, and affection. Hume most fully elucidates the differences between these types of parties in "Of Parties in General" (in this edition).]

which may properly enough be denominated those of COURT and COUNTRY. The strength and violence of each of these parties will much depend upon the particular administration. An administration may be so bad, as to throw a great majority into the opposition; as a good administration will reconcile to the court many of the most passionate lovers of liberty. But however the nation may fluctuate between them, the parties themselves will always subsist, so long as we are governed by a limited monarchy.

But, besides this difference of *Principle*, those parties are very much fomented by a difference of INTEREST, without which they could scarcely ever be dangerous or violent. The crown will naturally bestow all trust and power upon those, whose principles, real or pretended, are most favourable to monarchical government; and this temptation will naturally engage them to go greater lengths than their principles would otherwise carry them. Their antagonists, who are disappointed in their ambitious aims, throw themselves into the party whose sentiments incline them to be most jealous of royal power, and naturally carry those sentiments to a greater height than sound politics will justify. Thus *Court* and *Country*, which are the genuine offspring of the BRITISH government, are a kind of mixed parties, and are influenced both by principle and by interest. The heads of the factions are commonly most governed by the latter motive; the inferior members of them by the former.[d]

As to ecclesiastical parties; we may observe, that, in all ages of the world, priests have been enemies to liberty; and it is certain, that this steady conduct of theirs must have been founded on fixed reasons of interest and ambition. Liberty of thinking, and of expressing our thoughts, is always fatal to priestly power, and to those pious frauds, on which it is commonly founded; and, by an infallible connexion, which prevails among all kinds of liberty, this privilege can never be enjoyed, at least has never yet been enjoyed, but in a free government. Hence it must happen, in such a constitution as that of GREAT BRITAIN, that the established clergy, while things are in their natural situation, will always be of the *Court*-party; as, on the contrary, dissenters of all kinds will be of the *Country*-party; since they can never hope for that toleration, which they stand in need of, but by means of our free government. All princes, that have aimed at despotic power, have known of what importance it was to gain the established clergy: As the clergy, on their part, have shewn a great facility in entering into the views of such princes.[80] GUSTAVUS VAZA[81] was, perhaps, the only ambitious monarch, that ever depressed the church, at the same time that he discouraged liberty. But the exorbitant power of the bishops in SWEDEN, who, at that time, overtopped the crown itself, together with their attachment to a foreign family, was the reason of his embracing such an unusual system of politics.

This observation, concerning the propensity of priests to the government of a single person, is not true with regard to one sect only. The *Presbyterian* and *Calvinistic* clergy in HOLLAND were professed friends to the family of ORANGE; as the *Arminians*, who were esteemed heretics, were of the LOUVESTEIN faction, and zealous for liberty. But if a prince have the choice of both, it is easy to see, that he will prefer the episcopal to the presbyterian form of government, both because of the greater affinity between monarchy and episcopacy, and because of the facility, which he will find, in such a government, of ruling the clergy, by means of their ecclesiastical superiors.[82]

If we consider the first rise of parties in ENGLAND, during the great rebellion,[83] we shall observe, that it was conformable to this general theory, and that the species of government gave birth to them, by a regular and infallible operation. The ENGLISH constitution, before that period, had lain in a kind of confusion; yet so, as that the subjects possessed many noble privileges, which, though not exactly bounded and secured by law, were universally deemed, from long

80. Judaei sibi ipsi reges imposuere; qui mobilitate vulgi expulsi, resumpta per arma dominatione; fugas civium, urbium eversiones, fratrum, conjugam, parentum neces, aliaque solita regibus ausi, superstitionem fovebant; quia honor sacerdotii firmamentum potentiae assumebatur. TACIT. *hist. lib.* v. 8. [Tacitus (*c.* A.D. 56–120), *The Histories*, 5.8: "The Jews selected their own kings. These in turn were expelled by the fickle mob; but recovering their throne by force of arms, they banished citizens, destroyed towns, killed brothers, wives, and parents, and dared essay every other kind of royal crime without hesitation; but they fostered the national superstition, for they had assumed the priesthood to support their civil authority" (trans. by C.H. Moore).]

81. [King of Sweden from 1523 to his death in 1560.]

82. Populi imperium juxta libertatem: paucorum dominatio regiae libidini proprior est. TACIT. *Ann. lib.* vi. 41. [Tacitus, *Annals*, 6.41: "Supremacy of the people is akin to freedom; between the domination of a minority and the whim of a monarch the distance is small" (trans. by J. Jackson).]

83. [The "Great Rebellion" is the name for the Civil Wars of England and Scotland that began in 1642 and can be said to have ended in 1652. Hume discusses the rebellion at length in volumes V and VI of *The History of England*.]

possession, to belong to them as their birth-right. An ambitious, or rather a misguided, prince arose, who deemed all these privileges to be concessions of his predecessors, revokeable at pleasure; and, in prosecution of this principle, he openly acted in violation of liberty, during the course of several years. Necessity, at last, constrained him to call a parliament: The spirit of liberty arose and spread itself: The prince,[84] being without any support, was obliged to grant every thing required of him: And his enemies, jealous and implacable, set no bounds to their pretensions. Here then began those contests, in which it was no wonder, that men of that age were divided into different parties; since, even at this day, the impartial are at a loss to decide concerning the justice of the quarrel. The pretensions of the parliament, if yielded to, broke the balance of the constitution, by rendering the government almost entirely republican. If not yielded to, the nation was, perhaps, still in danger of absolute power, from the settled principles and inveterate habits of the king, which had plainly appeared in every concession that he had been constrained to make to his people. In this question, so delicate and uncertain, men naturally fell to the side which was most conformable to their usual principles; and the more passionate favourers of monarchy declared for the king, as the zealous friends of liberty sided with the parliament. The hopes of success being nearly equal on both sides, *interest* had no general influence in this contest: So that ROUND-HEAD and CAVALIER[85] were merely parties of principle; neither of which disowned either monarchy or liberty; but the former party inclined most to the republican part of our government, the latter to the monarchical. In this respect, they may be considered as court and country-party, enflamed into a civil war, by an unhappy concurrence of circumstances, and by the turbulent spirit of the age. The commonwealth's men, and the partizans of absolute power, lay concealed in both parties, and formed but an inconsiderable part of them.

The clergy had concurred with the king's arbitrary designs; and, in

84. [Charles I, who became King of England in 1625, was eventually beheaded in 1649, ending monarchical rule in England until the restoration of the Monarchy in 1660 with Charles II. Hume was often criticized for the sympathetic way in which he treated Charles I in *The History of England* (volume V). This accounts for his remark in "My Own Life" that he was assailed for having "shed a generous Tear for the Fate of Charles I" (p. 4).]

85. [Beginning in 1641, these two names denoted the adherents of the parliamentary party and the Royalists, respectively.]

return, were allowed to persecute their adversaries, whom they called heretics and schismatics. The established clergy were episcopal; the non-conformists presbyterian: So that all things concurred to throw the former, without reserve, into the king's party; and the latter into that of the parliament.

Every one knows the event of this quarrel; fatal to the king first, to the parliament afterwards. After many confusions and revolutions, the royal family was at last restored, and the ancient government re-established. CHARLES II. was not made wiser by the example of his father; but prosecuted the same measures, though at first, with more secrecy and caution. New parties arose, under the appellation of *Whig* and *Tory*,[86] which have continued ever since to confound and distract our government. To determine the nature of these parties is, perhaps, one of the most difficult problems, that can be met with, and is a proof that history may contain questions, as uncertain as any to be found in the most abstract sciences. We have seen the conduct of the two parties, during the course of seventy years, in a vast variety of circumstances, possessed of power, and deprived of it, during peace, and during war: Persons, who profess themselves of one side or other, we meet with every hour, in company, in our pleasures, in our serious occupations: We ourselves are constrained, in a manner, to take party; and living in a country of the highest liberty, every one may openly declare all his sentiments and opinions: Yet are we at a loss to tell the nature, pretensions, and principles of the different factions.

When we compare the parties of WHIG and TORY with those of ROUND-HEAD and CAVALIER, the most obvious difference, that appears between them, consists in the principles of *passive obedience,* and *indefeasible right,* which were but little heard of among the CAVALIERS, but became the universal doctrine, and were esteemed the true characteristic of a TORY. Were these principles pushed into their most obvious consequences, they imply a formal renunciation of all our liberties, and an avowal of absolute monarchy; since nothing can be a greater absurdity than a limited power, which must not be resisted, even when it exceeds its limitations. But as the most rational principles

86. [These two names became current around 1679, at the time of the Exclusion Crisis in England. The Whigs were exclusionists, attempting in Parliament to exclude the possibility of Charles II's Roman Catholic brother's (James) succeeding him. The Tories were strong supporters of hereditary succession and the powers of prerogative of the Crown.]

are often but a weak counterpoise to passion; it is no wonder that these absurd principles were found too weak for that effect. The TORIES, as men, were enemies to oppression; and also as ENGLISHMEN, they were enemies to arbitrary power. Their zeal for liberty, was, perhaps, less fervent than that of their antagonists; but was sufficient to make them forget all their general principles, when they saw themselves openly threatened with a subversion of the ancient government. From these sentiments arose the *revolution;*[87] an event of mighty consequence, and the firmest foundation of BRITISH liberty. The conduct of the TORIES during that event, and after it, will afford us a true insight into the nature of that party.

In the *first* place, they appear to have had the genuine sentiments of BRITONS in their affection for liberty, and in their determined resolution not to sacrifice it to any abstract principle whatsoever, or to any imaginary rights of princes. This part of their character might justly have been doubted of before the *revolution,* from the obvious tendency of their avowed principles, and from their compliances with a court, which seemed to make little secret of its arbitrary designs. The *revolution* shewed them to have been, in this respect, nothing, but a genuine *court-party,* such as might be expected in a BRITISH government: That is, *Lovers of liberty, but greater lovers of monarchy.* It must, however, be confessed, that they carried their monarchical principles farther, even in practice, but more so in theory, than was, in any degree, consistent with a limited government.

Secondly, Neither their principles nor affections concurred, entirely or heartily, with the settlement made at the *revolution,* or with that which has since taken place. This part of their character may seem opposite to the former; since any other settlement, in those circumstances of the nation, must probably have been dangerous, if not fatal to liberty. But the heart of man is made to reconcile contradictions; and this contradiction is not greater than that between *passive obedience,* and the *resistance* employed at the *revolution.* A TORY, therefore, since the *revolution,* may be defined in a few words, to be *a lover of monarchy, though without abandoning liberty; and a partizan of the family of* STUART.[88] As a WHIG may be defined to be *a lover of liberty though without*

87. [Hume is referring to the Revolution of 1688. Beginning around 1710, this revolution starts to be called the Glorious Revolution. Hume never refers to it by this name, however.]

88. [The ruling family of England from 1603 to 1649 and from 1660 to 1714.]

renouncing monarchy; and a friend to the settlement in the PROTESTANT *line.*

These different views, with regard to the settlement of the crown, were accidental, but natural additions to the principles of the *court* and *country* parties, which are the genuine divisions in the BRITISH government. A passionate lover of monarchy is apt to be displeased at any change of the succession; as savouring too much of a commonwealth: A passionate lover of liberty is apt to think that every part of the government ought to be subordinate to the interests of liberty.

Some, who will not venture to assert, that the *real* difference between WHIG and TORY was lost at the *revolution,* seem inclined to think, that the difference is now abolished, and that affairs are so far returned to their natural state, that there are at present no other parties among us but *court* and *country;* that is, men, who, by interest or principle, are attached either to monarchy or liberty. The TORIES have been so long obliged to talk in the republican stile, that they seem to have made converts of themselves by their hypocrisy, and to have embraced the sentiments, as well as language of their adversaries. There are, however, very considerable remains of that party in ENGLAND, with all their old prejudices; and a proof that *court* and *country* are not our only parties, is, that almost all the dissenters side with the court, and the lower clergy, at least, of the church of ENGLAND, with the opposition. This may convince us, that some biass still hangs upon our constitution, some extrinsic weight, which turns it from its natural course, and causes a confusion in our parties.[89, e]

Essay VI: Of Civil Liberty[f]

Those who employ their pens on political subjects, free from party-rage, and party-prejudices, cultivate a science, which, of all others, contributes most to public utility, and even to the private satisfaction of those who addict themselves to the study of it. I am apt, however, to entertain a suspicion, that the world is still too young to fix many general truths in politics, which will remain true to the latest posterity.

89. Some of the opinions delivered in these Essays, with regard to the public transactions in the last century, the Author, on more accurate examination, found reason to retract in his *History* of GREAT BRITAIN. And as he would not enslave himself to the systems of either party, neither would he fetter his judgment by his own preconceived opinions and principles; nor is he ashamed to acknowledge his mistakes. These mistakes were indeed, at that time, almost universal in this kingdom.

We have not as yet had experience of three thousand years; so that not only the art of reasoning is still imperfect in this science, as in all others, but we even want sufficient materials upon which we can reason. It is not fully known, what degree of refinement, either in virtue or vice, human nature is susceptible of; nor what may be expected of mankind from any great revolution in their education, customs, or principles. MACHIAVEL was certainly a great genius; but having confined his study to the furious and tyrannical governments of ancient times, or to the little disorderly principalities of ITALY, his reasonings especially upon monarchical government, have been found extremely defective; and there scarcely is any maxim in his *prince,* which subsequent experience has not entirely refuted. *A weak prince,* says he, *is incapable of receiving good counsel; for if he consult with several, he will not be able to choose among their different counsels. If he abandon himself to one, that minister may, perhaps, have capacity, but he will not long be a minister: He will be sure to dispossess his master, and place himself and his family upon the throne.*[90] I mention this, among many instances of the errors of that politician, proceeding, in a great measure, from his having lived in too early an age of the world, to be a good judge of political truth. Almost all the princes of EUROPE are at present governed by their ministers; and have been so for near two centuries; and yet no such event has ever happened, or can possibly happen. SEJANUS might project dethroning the CAESARS; but FLEURY, though ever so vicious, could not, while in his senses, entertain the least hopes of dispossessing the BOURBONS.[91]

Trade was never esteemed an affair of state till the last century; and there scarcely is any ancient writer on politics, who has made mention of it.[92] Even the ITALIANS have kept a profound silence with regard

90. [*The Prince,* trans. by H. Mansfield (Chicago: University of Chicago Press, 1985), pp. 93–95.]

91. [Sejanus (died A.D. 31) was sole commander of the Praetorian Guard under Tiberius. He was consul of Rome for a time following Tiberius's retirement in A.D. 27. Tiberius found out about Sejanus's plot to acquire unlimited power and wrote a letter to the Senate, leading to Sejanus's arrest and execution. Andre Hercule cardinal de Fleury, Bishop of Frejus, (died 1743) was the tutor and then de facto *premier ministre* (for some seventeen years) of Louis XV of France. The family Bourbon (which included Louis XV) gave rise to many notable Kings, Dukes, Counts, and Princes of France (beginning in the late sixteenth century) and Spain and Italy (beginning in the early eighteenth century).]

92. XENOPHON mentions it; but with a doubt if it be of any advantage to a state. *Εἰ δὲ καὶ ἐμπορία ὠφελεῖ τι πόλιν,* &c. XEN. HIERO. 9.9. [Xenophon (*c.* 428/7–

to it, though it has now engaged the chief attention, as well of ministers of state, as of speculative reasoners. The great opulence, grandeur, and military atchievements of the two maritime powers seem first to have instructed mankind in the importance of an extensive commerce.

Having, therefore, intended in this essay to make a full comparison of civil liberty and absolute government, and to show the great advantages of the former above the latter; I began to entertain a suspicion, that no man in this age was sufficiently qualified for such an undertaking; and that whatever any one should advance on that head would, in all probability, be refuted by further experience, and be rejected by posterity. Such mighty revolutions have happened in human affairs, and so many events have arisen contrary to the expectation of the ancients, that they are sufficient to beget the suspicion of still further changes.

It had been observed by the ancients, that all the arts and sciences arose among free nations; and, that the PERSIANS and EGYPTIANS, notwithstanding their ease, opulence, and luxury, made but faint efforts towards a relish in those finer pleasures, which were carried to such perfection by the GREEKS, amidst continual wars, attended with poverty, and the greatest simplicity of life and manners. It had also been observed, that, when the GREEKS lost their liberty, though they increased mightily in riches, by means of the conquests of ALEXANDER; yet the arts, from that moment, declined among them, and have never since been able to raise their head in that climate. Learning was transplanted to ROME, the only free nation at that time in the universe; and having met with so favourable a soil, it made prodigious shoots for above a century; till the decay of liberty produced also the decay of letters, and spread a total barbarism over the world. From these two experiments, of which each was double in its kind, and shewed the fall of learning in absolute governments, as well as its rise in popular ones, LONGINUS[93] thought himself sufficiently justified, in asserting, that the arts and sciences could never flourish, but in a free government:

---

354 B.C.), *Hiero*: "If imports are of any benefit to a city . . ." in Leo Strauss, *On Tyranny*, rev. ed., ed. by V. Gourevitch and M. Roth, *Hiero* trans. by M. Kendrick and rev. by S. Bernardete (New York: The Free Press, 1991), p. 18 (9.9).] PLATO totally excludes it from his imaginary republic De legibus, lib. iv. [Plato (428–348 B.C.), *The Laws*, bk. 4.]

93. [Longinus (A.D. 213?–273), *On the Sublime*, sec. 44. Through the nineteenth century, *On the Sublime* was attributed to Longinus; however, internal evidence suggests that it was written sometime in the first century A.D.]

And in this opinion, he has been followed by several eminent writers[94] in our own country, who either confined their view merely to ancient facts, or entertained too great a partiality in favour of that form of government, established amongst us.

But what would these writers have said, to the instances of modern ROME and of FLORENCE? Of which the former carried to perfection all the finer arts of sculpture, painting, and music, as well as poetry, though it groaned under tyranny, and under the tyranny of priests: While the latter made its chief progress in the arts and sciences, after it began to lose its liberty by the usurpation of the family of MEDICI.[95] ARIOSTO, TASSO, GALILEO, more than RAPHAEL, and MICHAEL ANGELO, were not born in republics.[96] And though the LOMBARD school was famous as well as the ROMAN, yet the VENETIANS have had the smallest share in its honours, and seem rather inferior to the other ITALIANS, in their genius for the arts and sciences. RUBENS[97] established his school at ANTWERP, not at AMSTERDAM: DRESDEN, not HAMBURGH, is the centre of politeness in GERMANY.

But the most eminent instance of the flourishing of learning in absolute governments, is that of FRANCE, which scarcely ever enjoyed any established liberty, and yet has carried the arts and sciences as near perfection as any other nation. The ENGLISH are, perhaps, greater philosophers; the ITALIANS better painters and musicians; the ROMANS were greater orators: But the FRENCH are the only people, except the GREEKS, who have been at once philosophers, poets, orators, historians, painters, architects, sculptors, and musicians. With regard to the stage, they have excelled even the GREEKS, who far excelled the ENGLISH. And, in common life, they have, in a great measure, perfected that art, the most useful and agreeable of any, *l'Art de Vivre*, the art of society and conversation.

94. Mr. ADDISON and LORD SHAFTESBURY. [See Joseph Addison (1672–1719), *The Tatler*, no. 161; and Anthony Ashley Cooper, Third Earl of Shaftesbury (1671–1713), *Characteristics*, 2 vols., ed. by. J. M. Robertson (London: Grant Richards, 1900), vol. I, p. 155 (Treatise III; "Soliloquy or Advice to an Author").]

95. [The ruling family in Florence during most of the fifteenth and sixteenth centuries. During this period, two members of the family were elected Pope.]

96. [Ariosto (1474–1533; Lombardy), Tasso (1544–95; Sorrento), Galileo (1564–1642; Pisa), Raphael (1483–1520; Urbino), and Michelangelo (1575–1664; Florence) were all born in Italy.]

97. [Peter Paul Rubens (1577–1640).]

If we consider the state of the sciences and polite arts in our own country, HORACE'S observation, with regard to the ROMANS, may, in a great measure, be applied to the BRITISH.

> —*Sed in longum tamen aevum*
> *Manserunt, hodieque manent* vestigia ruris.[98]

The elegance and propriety of style have been very much neglected among us. We have no dictionary of our language, and scarcely a tolerable grammar. The first polite prose we have, was writ by a man who is still alive.[99] As to SPRAT, LOCKE and, even TEMPLE, they knew too little of the rules of art to be esteemed elegant writers. The prose of BACON, HARRINGTON, and MILTON, is altogether stiff and pedantic;[100] though their sense be excellent. Men, in this country, have been so much occupied in the great disputes of *Religion, Politics,* and *Philosophy,* that they had no relish for the seemingly minute observations of grammar and criticism. And though this turn of thinking must have considerably improved our sense and our talent of reasoning; it must be confessed, that, even in those sciences above-mentioned, we have not any standard-book, which we can transmit to posterity: And the utmost we have to boast of, are a few essays towards a more just philosophy; which, indeed, promise well, but have not, as yet, reached any degree of perfection.

It has become an established opinion, that commerce can never flourish but in a free government; and this opinion seems to be founded

98. [Horace (65–8 B.C.), *Epistles*, 2.1.160: "... yet for many a year lived on, and still live on, traces of our rustic past" (trans. by H. R. Fairclough).]

99. Dr. SWIFT. [Jonathan Swift (1667–1745), most famous for *Gulliver's Travels*.]

100. [Thomas Sprat (1665–1713), John Locke (1632–1704;), Sir William Temple (1628–99), Sir Francis Bacon (1561–1626), James Harrington (1611–77), and John Milton (1608–74) were all English writers. In *The History of England*, Hume presents sketches of modern English literary figures (vol. V, pp. 149–55, and vol. VI, pp. 150–54). In a letter to William Strahan, his friend and printer, Hume inveighs against the then current state of English letters: "Considering the Treatment I have met with, it would have been very silly for me at my Years to continue writing any more; and still more blameable to warp my Principles and Sentiments in conformity to the Prejudices of a stupid, factious Nation, with whom I am heartily disgusted. ... [England] is so sunk in stupidity and Barbarism and Faction that you may as well think of Lapland for an author. The best Book, that has been writ by any Englishman these thirty years (for Dr. Franklin is an American) is Tristram Shandy, bad as it is" (*The Letters of David Hume*, vol. II, p. 269).]

on a longer and larger experience than the foregoing, with regard to the arts and sciences. If we trace commerce in its progress through TYRE, ATHENS, SYRACUSE, CARTHAGE, VENICE, FLORENCE, GENOA, ANTWERP, HOLLAND, ENGLAND, &c. we shall always find it to have fixed its seat in free governments. The three greatest trading towns now in Europe, are LONDON, AMSTERDAM, and HAMBURGH; all free cities, and protestant cities; that is, enjoying a double liberty. It must, however, be observed, that the great jealousy entertained of late, with regard to the commerce of FRANCE, seems to prove, that this maxim is no more certain and infallible than the foregoing, and that the subjects of an absolute prince may become our rivals in commerce, as well as in learning.

Durst I deliver my opinion in an affair of so much uncertainty, I would assert, that, notwithstanding the efforts of the FRENCH, there is something hurtful to commerce inherent in the very nature of absolute government, and inseparable from it: Though the reason I should assign for this opinion, is somewhat different from that which is commonly insisted on. Private property seems to me almost as secure in a civilized EUROPEAN monarchy, as in a republic; nor is danger much apprehended in such a government, from the violence of the sovereign; more than we commonly dread harm from thunder, or earthquakes, or any accident the most unusual and extraordinary. Avarice, the spur of industry, is so obstinate a passion, and works its way through so many real dangers and difficulties, that it is not likely to be scared by an imaginary danger, which is so small, that it scarcely admits of calculation. Commerce, therefore, in my opinion, is apt to decay in absolute governments, not because it is there less *secure,* but because it is less *honourable.* A subordination of ranks is absolutely necessary to the support of monarchy. Birth, titles, and place, must be honoured above industry and riches. And while these notions prevail, all the considerable traders will be tempted to throw up their commerce, in order to purchase some of those employments, to which privileges and honours are annexed.

Since I am upon this head, of the alterations which time has produced, or may produce in politics, I must observe, that all kinds of government, free and absolute, seem to have undergone, in modern times, a great change for the better, with regard both to foreign and domestic management. The *balance of power* is a secret in politics, fully known only to the present age; and I must add, that the internal POLICE of states has also received great improvements within the last century. We are informed by SALLUST,[101] that CATILINE'S army was much augmented by the accession of the highwaymen about ROME; though I believe, that all of that profession, who are at present dispersed over EUROPE, would not amount to a regiment. In CICERO'S pleadings for MILO,[102] I find this argument, among others, made use of to prove, that his client had not assassinated CLODIUS. Had MILO, said he, intended to have killed CLODIUS, he had not attacked him in the daytime, and at such a distance from the city: He had way-laid him at night, near the suburbs, where it might have been pretended, that he was killed by robbers; and the frequency of the accident would have favoured the deceit. This is a surprizing proof of the loose police of ROME, and of the number and force of these robbers; since CLODIUS[103] was at that time attended by thirty slaves, who were compleatly armed, and sufficiently accustomed to blood and danger in the frequent tumults excited by that seditious tribune.

But though all kinds of government be improved in modern times, yet monarchical government seems to have made the greatest advances towards perfection. It may now be affirmed of civilized monarchies, what was formerly said in praise of republics alone, *that they are a government of Laws, not of Men.* They are found susceptible of order, method, and constancy, to a surprizing degree. Property is there secure; industry encouraged; the arts flourish; and the prince lives secure among his subjects, like a father among his children. There are perhaps, and have been for two centuries, near two hundred absolute princes, great and small, in EUROPE; and allowing twenty years to each reign, we may suppose, that there have been in the whole two thousand monarchs or tyrants, as the GREEKS would have called them: Yet of these there has not been one, not even PHILIP II. of SPAIN, so bad as TIBERIUS, CALIGULA, NERO, or DOMITIAN,[104] who were four in twelve amongst the ROMAN emperors. It must, however, be confessed, that, though monarchical governments have approached nearer to popular ones, in gentleness and stability; they are still inferior. Our modern education and customs instil more humanity and modera-

101. [Sallust (probably 86–35 B.C.), *The War with Catiline*, 14.1 and 24.1.]

102. [Cicero (106–43 B.C.), *Pro Milone*.]

103. *Vide Asc. Ped. in Orat. pro Milone.* [The Speech on Behalf of Milo]

104. [Philip II was King of Spain from 1556 to 1598. Tiberius was Emperor of Rome from A.D. 14 to 37, Caligua from 37 to 41, Nero from 54 to 68, and Domitian from 81 to 96.]

tion than the ancient; but have not as yet been able to overcome entirely the disadvantages of that form of government.

But here I must beg leave to advance a conjecture, which seems probable, but which posterity alone can fully judge of. I am apt to think, that, in monarchical governments there is a source of improvement, and in popular governments a source of degeneracy, which in time will bring these species of civil polity still nearer an equality. The greatest abuses, which arise in FRANCE, the most perfect model of pure monarchy, proceed not from the number or weight of the taxes, beyond what are to be met with in free countries; but from the expensive, unequal, arbitrary, and intricate method of levying them, by which the industry of the poor, especially of the peasants and farmers, is, in a great measure, discouraged, and agriculture rendered a beggarly and slavish employment. But to whose advantage do these abuses tend? If to that of the nobility, they might be esteemed inherent in that form of government; since the nobility are the true supports of monarchy; and it is natural their interest should be more consulted, in such a constitution, than that of the people. But the nobility are, in reality, the chief losers by this oppression; since it ruins their estates, and beggars their tenants. The only gainers by it are the *Finançiers*, a race of men rather odious to the nobility and the whole kingdom. If a prince or minister, therefore, should arise, endowed with sufficient discernment to know his own and the public interest, and with sufficient force of mind to break through ancient customs, we might expect to see these abuses remedied; in which case, the difference between that absolute government and our free one, would not appear so considerable as at present.

The source of degeneracy, which may be remarked in free governments, consists in the practice of contracting debt, and mortgaging the public revenues, by which taxes may, in time, become altogether intolerable, and all the property of the state be brought into the hands of the public. This practice is of modern date. The ATHENIANS, though governed by a republic, paid near two hundred *per Cent.* for those sums of money, which any emergence made it necessary for them to borrow; as we learn from XENOPHON.[105] Among the moderns, the

105. *Κτῆσιν δὲ ἀπ' οὐδενὸς ἂν οὕτω καλὴν κτήσαιντο, ὥσπερ ἀφ οὗ ἂν προτελέσωσιν εἰς τὴν ἀφορμήν—οἱ δέ γε πλεῖστοι 'Αθηναίων πλείονα λήψονται κατ̓ ἐνιαυτόν ἢ ὅσα ἂν εἰσενέγκωσιν̓ οἱ γὰρ μνᾶν προτελέσαντες, ἐγγὺς δυοῖν μναῖν πρόσοδον ἕξουσι—ὃ δοκεῖ τῶν ἀνθρωπίνων ἀσφαλέστατόν τε καὶ πόλυχρονιώτατον εἶναι.* ΞΕΝ. ΠΟΡΟΙ. III. 9. 10. [Xenophon, *Ways and Means*, 3.9–

DUTCH first introduced the practice of borrowing great sums at low interest, and have well nigh ruined themselves by it. Absolute princes have also contracted debt; but as an absolute prince may make a bankruptcy when he pleases, his people can never be oppressed by his debts. In popular governments, the people, and chiefly those who have the highest offices, being commonly the public creditors, it is difficult for the state to make use of this remedy, which, however it may sometimes be necessary, is always cruel and barbarous. This, therefore seems to be an inconvenience, which nearly threatens all free governments; especially our own, at the present juncture of affairs. And what a strong motive is this, to encrease our frugality of public money; lest for want of it, we be reduced, by the multiplicity of taxes, or what is worse, by our public impotence and inability for defence, to curse our very liberty, and wish ourselves in the same state of servitude with all the nations that surround us?

Essay VII: Of the Balance of Power

It is a question whether the *idea* of the balance of power be owing entirely to modern policy, or whether the *phrase* only has been invented in these later ages? It is certain, that XENOPHON,[106] in his Institution of CYRUS, represents the combination of the ASIATIC powers to have arisen from a jealousy of the encreasing force of the MEDES and PERSIANS; and though that elegant composition should be supposed altogether a romance, this sentiment, ascribed by the author to the eastern princes, is at least a proof of the prevailing notion of ancient times.

In all the politics of GREECE, the anxiety, with regard to the balance of power, is apparent, and is expressly pointed out to us, even by the ancient historians. THUCYDIDES[107] represents the league, which was formed against ATHENS, and which produced the PELOPONNESIAN war, as entirely owing to this principle. And after the decline

---

10: "But no investment can yield them so fine a return as the money advanced by them to form the capital fund. . . . But most of the Athenians will get over a hundred per cent. in a year, for those who advance one *mina* will draw an income of nearly two *minae*, guaranteed by the state, which is to all appearances the safest and most durable of human institutions" (trans. by E. C. Marchant).]

106. Lib. i. 5, 3. [Xenophon (*c.* 428/7–354 B.C.), *Cyropaidea*, 1.5.2–3.)]

107. Lib. i. 23. [Thucydides (*c.* 460–400 B.C.), *History of the Peloponnesian War*, 1.23.]

of ATHENS, when the THEBANS and LACEDEMONIANS disputed for sovereignty, we find, that the ATHENIANS (as well as many other republics) always threw themselves into the lighter scale, and endeavoured to preserve the balance. They supported THEBES against SPARTA, till the great victory gained by EPAMINONDAS at LEUCTRA; after which they immediately went over to the conquered, from generosity, as they pretended, but in reality from their jealousy of the conquerors.[108]

Whoever will read DEMOSTHENES'S oration for the MEGALOPOLITANS, may see the utmost refinements on this principle, that ever entered into the head of a VENETIAN or ENGLISH speculatist. And upon the first rise of the MACEDONIAN power, this orator immediately discovered the danger, sounded the alarm throughout all GREECE, and at last assembled that confederacy under the banners of ATHENS, which fought the great and decisive battle of CHAERONEA.

It is true, the GRECIAN wars are regarded by historians as wars of emulation rather than of politics; and each state seems to have had more in view the honour of leading the rest, than any well-grounded hopes of authority and dominion. If we consider, indeed, the small number of inhabitants in any one republic, compared to the whole, the great difficulty of forming sieges in those times, and the extraordinary bravery and discipline of every freeman among that noble people; we shall conclude, that the balance of power was, of itself, sufficiently secured in GREECE, and needed not to have been guarded with that caution which may be requisite in other ages. But whether we ascribe the shifting of sides in all the GRECIAN republics to *jealous emulation* or *cautious politics*, the effects were alike, and every prevailing power was sure to meet with a confederacy against it, and that often composed of its former friends and allies.

The same principle, call it envy or prudence, which produced the *Ostracism* of ATHENS, and *Petalism* of SYRACUSE, and expelled every citizen whose fame or power overtopped the rest; the same principle, I say, naturally discovered itself in foreign politics, and soon raised enemies to the leading state, however moderate in the exercise of its authority.

The PERSIAN monarch was really, in his force, a petty prince, compared to the GRECIAN republics; and therefore it behoved him,

108. XENOPH. Hist. GRAEC. lib. vi. and vii. [Xenophon, *Hellenica*, 6 and 7.]

from views of safety more than from emulation, to interest himself in their quarrels, and to support the weaker side in every contest. This was the advice given by ALCIBIADES to TISSAPHERNES,[109] and it prolonged near a century the date of the PERSIAN empire; till the neglect of it for a moment, after the first appearance of the aspiring genius of PHILIP, brought that lofty and frail edifice to the ground, with a rapidity of which there are few instances in the history of mankind.

The successors of ALEXANDER[110] showed great jealousy of the balance of power; a jealousy founded on true politics and prudence, and which preserved distinct for several ages the partition made after the death of that famous conqueror. The fortune and ambition of ANTIGONUS[111] threatened them anew with a universal monarchy; but their combination, and their victory at IPSUS saved them. And in subsequent times, we find, that, as the Eastern princes considered the GREEKS and MACEDONIANS as the only real military force, with whom they had any intercourse, they kept always a watchful eye over that part of the world. The PTOLEMIES, in particular, supported first ARATUS and the ACHAEANS, and then CLEOMENES king of SPARTA, from no other view than as a counterbalance to the MACEDONIAN monarchs. For this is the account which POLYBIUS gives of the EGYPTIAN politics.[112]

The reason, why it is supposed, that the ancients were entirely ignorant of the *balance of power*, seems to be drawn from the ROMAN history more than the GRECIAN; and as the transactions of the former are generally more familiar to us, we have thence formed all our conclusions. It must be owned, that the Romans never met with any such general combination or confederacy against them, as might naturally have been expected from the rapid conquests and declared ambition; but were allowed peaceably to subdue their neighbours, one after another, till they extended their dominion over the whole known world. Not to mention the fabulous history of their ITALIC wars; there was,

109. THUCYD. lib. viii. 46. [Thucydides, *History of the Peloponnesian War*, 8.46.]

110. [Alexander the Great of Macedon (356–323 B.C.) established a vast Greek empire that extended into Asia, Persia, Egypt, and India.]

111. DIOD. SIC. lib. xx. 106. [Diodorus Siculus (died after 22 B.C.), *Library of History*, 20.106. Antigonus was one of Alexander's generals who was defeated in 301 B.C. in his attempt to restore the empire.]

112. Lib. ii. cap. 51. [Polybius (*c.* 200–118 B.C.), *The Histories*, 2.51.]

upon HANNIBAL'S invasion of the ROMAN state,[113] a remarkable crisis, which ought to have called up the attention of all civilized nations. It appeared afterwards (nor was it difficult to be observed at the time)[114] that this was a contest for universal empire; yet no prince or state seems to have been in the least alarmed about the event or issue of the quarrel. PHILIP of MACEDON remained neuter, till he saw the victories of Hannibal; and then most imprudently formed an alliance with the conqueror, upon terms still more imprudent. He stipulated, that he was to assist the CARTHAGINIAN state in their conquest of Italy; after which they engaged to send over forces into GREECE, to assist him in subduing the GRECIAN commonwealths.[115]

The RHODIAN and ACHAEAN republics are much celebrated by ancient historians for their wisdom and sound policy; yet both of them assisted the ROMANS in their wars against PHILIP and ANTIOCHUS.[116] And what may be esteemed still a stronger proof, that this maxim was not generally known in those ages; no ancient author has remarked the imprudence of these measures, nor has even blamed that absurd treaty above-mentioned, made by PHILIP with the CARTHAGINIANS. Princes and statesmen, in all ages, may, before-hand, be blinded in their reasonings with regard to events: But it is somewhat extraordinary, that historians, afterwards, should not form a sounder judgment of them. MASSINISSA, ATTALUS, PRUSIAS,[117] in gratifying their private passions, were, all of them,

113. [Hannibal (247–183/82 B.C.) was the great Carthaginian general who led Carthage during the second Punic War with Rome.]

114. It was observed by some, as appears by the speech of AGELAUS of NAUPACTUM, in the general congress of GREECE. See POLYB. lib. v. cap. 104. [Polybius, *The Histories*, 5.104]

115. TITI LIVII. lib. xxiii. cap. 33. [Titus Livius (59 B.C.-A.D. 17), *The History of Rome*, trans. by D. Spillan *et al.*, 4 vols. (London: G. Bell and Sons, Ltd., 1911), vol. II, pp. 875–76 (23.33).]

116. [Philip V (238–179 B.C.) was King of Macedon and sided with Hannibal against Rome in the time of the second Punic War. Antiochus III (*c.* 242–187), King of the Seleucid Empire, was defeated in battles in Greece by Roman forces around 190 B.C.]

117. [The Numidian Massinissa (*c.* 240–148 B.C.) fought with Carthage against Rome from 212 to 206 B.C., but was then embraced by the Romans, leading to his becoming King of all of Numidia around 200 B.C. Massinissa gradually extended his empire at Carthage's expense, finally impelling Carthage to break her treaty with Rome. Massinissa then fought against Carthage, defeating her in 150 B.C. By this point the Romans feared his ambition and treated him coldly. Attalus I (269–197 B.C.), King of Pergamum, first joined forces with the Aetolians and then enlisted Roman aid to fight

the instruments of the ROMAN greatness; and never seem to have suspected, that they were forging their own chains, while they advanced the conquests of their ally. A simple treaty and agreement between MASSINISSA and the CARTHAGINIANS, so much required by mutual interest, barred the ROMANS from all entrance into AFRICA, and preserved liberty to mankind.

The only prince we meet with in the ROMAN history, who seems to have understood the balance of power, is HIERO king of SYRACUSE.[118] Though the ally of ROME, he sent assistance to the CARTHAGINIANS, during the war of the auxiliaries; "Esteeming it requisite," says POLYBIUS,[119] "both in order to retain his dominions in SICILY, and to preserve the ROMAN friendship, that CARTHAGE should be safe; lest by its fall the remaining power should be able, without contrast or opposition, to execute every purpose and undertaking. And here he acted with great wisdom and prudence. For that is never, on any account, to be overlooked; nor ought such a force ever to be thrown into one hand, as to incapacitate the neighbouring states from defending their rights against it." Here is the aim of modern politics pointed out in express terms.

In short, the maxim of preserving the balance of power is founded so much on common sense and obvious reasoning, that it is impossible it could altogether have escaped antiquity, where we find, in other particulars, so many marks of deep penetration and discernment. If it was not so generally known and acknowledged as at present, it had, at least, an influence on all the wiser and more experienced princes and politicians. And indeed, even at present, however generally known and acknowledged among speculative reasoners, it has not, in practice, an authority much more extensive among those who govern the world.

After the fall of the ROMAN empire, the form of government, established by the northern conquerors, incapacitated them, in a great measure, for farther conquests, and long maintained each state in its proper boundaries. But when vassalage and the feudal militia were abolished, mankind were anew alarmed by the danger of universal

---

against the ambitious Philip V of Macedon. Prusias I (*c.* 230–182 B.C.), King of Bithynia, remained neutral in the war between Antiochus III and Roman forces because of assurances Rome had given him that he could keep certain lands, assurances that were later withdrawn.]

118. [Hiero II (*c.* 306–215 B.C.) was King of Syracuse from 269 to 215 B.C.]

119. Lib. i. cap. 83. [Polybius, *The Histories*, 1.83.]

monarchy, from the union of so many kingdoms and principalities in the person of the emperor CHARLES.[120] But the power of the house of AUSTRIA, founded on extensive but divided dominions, and their riches, derived chiefly from mines of gold and silver, were more likely to decay, of themselves, from internal defects, than to overthrow all the bulwarks raised against them. In less than a century, the force of that violent and haughty race was shattered, their opulence dissipated, their splendor eclipsed. A new power succeeded, more formidable to the liberties of EUROPE, possessing all the advantages of the former, and labouring under none of its defects; except a share of that spirit of bigotry and persecution, with which the house of AUSTRIA was so long, and still is so much infatuated.

In the general wars, maintained against this ambitious power, GREAT BRITAIN has stood foremost; and she still maintains her station. Beside her advantages of riches and situation, her people are animated with such a national spirit, and are so fully sensible of the blessings of their government, that we may hope their vigour never will languish in so necessary and so just a cause. On the contrary, if we may judge by the past, their passionate ardour seems rather to require some moderation; and they have oftener erred from a laudable excess than from a blameable deficiency.

In the *first* place, we seem to have been more possessed with the ancient GREEK spirit of jealous emulation, than actuated by the prudent views of modern politics. Our wars with FRANCE have been begun with justice, and even, perhaps, from necessity; but have always been too far pushed from obstinacy and passion. The same peace, which was afterwards made at RYSWICK in 1697, was offered so early as the year ninety-two; that concluded at UTRECHT in 1712 might have been finished on as good conditions at GERTRUYTENBERG in the year eight; and we might have given at FRANKFORT, in 1743, the same terms, which we were glad to accept of at AIX-LA-CHAPELLE in the year forty-eight. Here then we see, that above half of our wars with FRANCE, and all our public debts, are owing more to our own imprudent vehemence, than to the ambition of our neighbours.

In the *second* place, we are so declared in our opposition to FRENCH power, and so alert in defence of our allies, that they always reckon upon our force as upon their own; and expecting to carry on war at

120. [Charles V became King of Spain in 1516 and was Holy Roman Emperor from 1519 to 1556.]

our expence, refuse all reasonable terms of accommodation. *Habent subjectos, tanquam suos: viles, ut alienos.*[121] All the world knows, that the factious vote of the House of Commons, in the beginning of the last parliament, with the professed humour of the nation, made the queen of HUNGARY inflexible in her terms, and prevented that agreement with PRUSSIA, which would immediately have restored the general tranquillity of EUROPE.

In the *third* place, we are such true combatants, that, when once engaged, we lose all concern for ourselves and our posterity, and consider only how we may best annoy the enemy. To mortgage our revenues at so deep a rate, in wars, where we were only accessories, was surely the most fatal delusion, that a nation, which had any pretension to politics and prudence, has ever yet been guilty of. That remedy of funding, if it be a remedy, and not rather a poison, ought, in all reason, to be reserved to the last extremity; and no evil, but the greatest and most urgent, should ever induce us to embrace so dangerous an expedient.

These excesses, to which we have been carried, are prejudicial; and may, perhaps, in time, become still more prejudicial another way, by begetting, as is usual, the opposite extreme, and rendering us totally careless and supine with regard to the fate of EUROPE. The ATHENIANS, from the most bustling, intriguing, warlike people of GREECE, finding their error in thrusting themselves into every quarrel, abandoned all attention to foreign affairs; and in no contest ever took part on either side, except by their flatteries and complaisance to the victor.

Enormous monarchies are, probably, destructive to human nature; in their progress, in their continuance,[122] and even in their downfal, which never can be very distant from their establishment. The military genius, which aggrandized the monarchy, soon leaves the court, the capital, and the center of such a government; while the wars are carried on at a great distance, and interest so small a part of the state. The ancient nobility, whose affections attach them to their sovereign, live all at court; and never will accept of military employments, which would

121. [This is a paraphrase of Tacitus's remark in *The Histories* (1.37) that, "They treat us like slaves, as though we belonged to them, but they regard us as worthless, as though we belonged to someone else."]

122. If the ROMAN empire was of advantage, it could only proceed from this, that mankind were generally in a very disorderly, uncivilized condition, before its establishment.

carry them to remote and barbarous frontiers, where they are distant both from their pleasures and their fortune. The arms of the state, must, therefore, be entrusted to mercenary strangers, without zeal, without attachment, without honour; ready on every occasion to turn them against the prince, and join each desperate malcontent, who offers pay and plunder. This is the necessary progress of human affairs: Thus human nature checks itself in its airy elevation: Thus ambition blindly labours for the destruction of the conqueror, of his family, and of every thing near and dear to him. The BOURBONS, trusting to the support of their brave, faithful, and affectionate nobility, would push their advantage, without reserve or limitation. These, while fired with glory and emulation, can bear the fatigues and dangers of war; but never would submit to languish in the garrisons of HUNGARY or LITHUANIA, forgot at court, and sacrificed to the intrigues of every minion or mistress, who approaches the prince. The troops are filled with CRAVATES and TARTARS, HUSSARS and COSSACS; intermingled, perhaps, with a few soldiers of fortune from the better provinces: And the melancholy fate of the ROMAN emperors, from the same cause, is renewed over and over again, till the final dissolution of the monarchy.

Essay VIII: Of the Coalition of Parties

To abolish all distinctions of party may not be practicable, perhaps not desirable, in a free government.[123] The only dangerous parties are such as entertain opposite views with regard to the essentials of government, the succession of the crown, or the more considerable privileges belonging to the several members of the constitution; where there is no room for any compromise or accommodation, and where the controversy may appear so momentous as to justify even an opposition by arms to the pretensions of antagonists. Of this nature was the animosity, continued for above a century past, between the parties in ENGLAND; an animosity which broke out sometimes into civil war,[124] which occasioned violent revolutions, and which continually endangered the peace and tranquillity of the nation. But as there have appeared of late the strongest symptoms of an universal desire to abolish these party distinctions; this tendency to a coalition affords the most agreeable prospect of

123. [See n. 42.]
124. [See n. 83.]

future happiness, and ought to be carefully cherished and promoted by every lover of his country.

There is not a more effectual method of promoting so good an end, than to prevent all unreasonable insult and triumph of the one party over the other, to encourage moderate opinions, to find the proper medium in all disputes, to persuade each that its antagonist may possibly be sometimes in the right, and to keep a balance in the praise and blame, which we bestow on either side. The two former Essays, concerning the *original contract* and *passive obedience*,[125] are calculated for this purpose with regard to the *philosophical* and *practical* controversies between the parties, and tend to show that neither side are in these respects so fully supported by reason as they endeavour to flatter themselves. We shall proceed to exercise the same moderation with regard to the *historical* disputes between the parties, by proving that each of them was justified by plausible topics; that there were on both sides wise men, who meant well to their country; and that the past animosity between the factions had no better foundation than narrow prejudice or interested passion.

The popular party, who afterwards acquired the name of whigs, might justify, by very specious arguments, that opposition to the crown, from which our present free constitution is derived. Though obliged to acknowledge, that precedents in favour of prerogative had uniformly taken place during many reigns before CHARLES the First,[126] they thought, that there was no reason for submitting any longer to so dangerous an authority. Such might have been their reasoning: As the rights of mankind[127] are for ever to be deemed sacred, no prescription of tyranny or arbitrary power can have authority sufficient to abolish them. Liberty is a blessing so inestimable, that, wherever there appears any probability of recovering it, a nation may willingly run many hazards, and ought not even to repine at the greatest effusion of blood or dissipation of treasure. All human institutions, and none more than government, are in continual fluctuation. Kings are sure to embrace every opportunity of extending their prerogatives: And if favourable incidents be not also laid hold of for extending and securing the privileges of the people, an universal despotism must for ever prevail amongst mankind. The example of all the neighbouring nations proves,

125. ["Of the Original Contract" and "Of Passive Obedience" (in this edition).]

126. [See n. 84.]

127. [This is one of only a handful of times that Hume invokes the idiom of rights.]

that it is no longer safe to entrust with the crown the same high prerogatives, which had formerly been exercised during rude and simple ages. And though the example of many late reigns may be pleaded in favour of a power in the prince somewhat arbitrary, more remote reigns afford instances of stricter limitations imposed on the crown; and those pretensions of the parliament, now branded with the title of innovations, are only a recovery of the just rights of the people.

These views, far from being odious, are surely large, and generous, and noble: To their prevalence and success the kingdom owes its liberty; perhaps its learning, its industry, commerce, and naval power: By them chiefly the ENGLISH name is distinguished among the society of nations, and aspires to a rivalship with that of the freest and most illustrious commonwealths of antiquity. But as all these mighty consequences could not reasonably be foreseen at the time when the contest began, the royalists of that age wanted not specious arguments on their side, by which they could justify their defence of the then established prerogatives of the prince. We shall state the question, as it might have appeared to them at the assembling of that parliament, which, by its violent encroachments on the crown, began the civil wars.

The only rule of government, they might have said, known and acknowledged among men, is use and practice:[128] Reason is so uncertain a guide that it will always be exposed to doubt and controversy: Could it ever render itself prevalent over the people, men had always retained it as their sole rule of conduct: They had still continued in the primitive, unconnected, state of nature, without submitting to political government, whose sole basis is, not pure reason, but authority and precedent. Dissolve these ties, you break all the bonds of civil society, and leave every man at liberty to consult his private interest, by those expedients, which his appetite, disguised under the appearance of reason, shall dictate to him. The spirit of innovation is in itself pernicious, however favourable its particular object may sometimes appear: A truth so obvious, that the popular party themselves are sensible of it; and therefore cover their encroachments on the crown by the plausible pretence of their recovering the ancient liberties of the people.

128. [In *The History of England*, Hume writes, "In the particular exertions of power, the question ought never to be forgotten, *What is best?* But in the general distribution of power among the several members of a constitution, there can seldom be admitted any other question, than *What is established?* . . . If any other rule than established practice be followed, factions and dissentions must multiply without end . . ." (vol. IV, pp. 354–55).]

But the present prerogatives of the crown, allowing all the suppositions of that party, have been incontestably established ever since the accession of the House of TUDOR;[129] a period, which, as it now comprehends a hundred and sixty years, may be allowed sufficient to give stability to any constitution. Would it not have appeared ridiculous, in the reign of the Emperor HADRIAN, to have talked of the republican constitution as the rule of government; or to have supposed, that the former rights of the senate, and consuls, and tribunes were still subsisting?[130]

But the present claims of the ENGLISH monarchs are much more favourable than those of the ROMAN emperors during that age. The authority of AUGUSTUS was a plain usurpation, grounded only on military violence, and forms such an epoch in the ROMAN history, as is obvious to every reader. But if HENRY VII. really, as some pretend, enlarged the power of the crown, it was only by insensible acquisitions, which escaped the apprehension of the people, and have scarcely been remarked even by historians and politicians. The new government, if it deserve the epithet, is an imperceptible transition from the former; is entirely engrafted on it; derives its title fully from that root; and is to be considered only as one of those gradual revolutions, to which human affairs, in every nation, will be for ever subject.

The House of TUDOR, and after them that of STUART,[131] exercised no prerogatives, but what had been claimed and exercised by the PLANTAGENETS.[132] Not a single branch of their authority can be said to be an innovation. The only difference is, that, perhaps, former kings exerted these powers only by intervals, and were not able, by reason of the opposition of their barons, to render them so steady a rule of administration. But the sole inference from this fact is, that those ancient times were more turbulent and seditious; and that royal authority, the constitution, and the laws have happily of late gained the ascendant.

Under what pretence can the popular party now speak of recovering the ancient constitution? The former controul over the kings was not

129. [Ruling family of England from Henry VII in 1485 to Elizabeth's death in 1603.]

130. [Hume is considering various Parliamentary debates that took place in the early 1640s, some 160 years after the accession of Henry VII. Hadrian was Emperor of Rome from A.D. 117 to 138, his rule ending some 160 years after the beginning of the Empire with Augustus.]

131. [The ruling family of England from 1603 to 1649 and from 1660 to 1714.]

132. [A name of the House of English kings who ruled from 1154 to 1399.]

placed in the commons, but in the barons: The people had no authority, and even little or no liberty; till the crown, by suppressing these factious tyrants, enforced the execution of the laws, and obliged all the subjects equally to respect each others rights, privileges, and properties. If we must return to the ancient barbarous and feudal constitution; let those gentlemen, who now behave themselves with so much insolence to their sovereign, set the first example. Let them make court to be admitted as retainers to a neighbouring baron; and by submitting to slavery under him, acquire some protection to themselves; together with the power of exercising rapine and oppression over their inferior slaves and villains. This was the condition of the commons among their remote ancestors.

But how far back must we go, in having recourse to ancient constitutions and governments? There was a constitution still more ancient than that to which these innovators affect so much to appeal. During that period there was no *magna charta:*[133] The barons themselves possessed few regular, stated privileges: And the house of commons probably had not an existence.

It is ridiculous to hear the commons, while they are assuming, by usurpation, the whole power of government, talk of reviving ancient institutions. Is it not known, that, though representatives received wages from their constituents; to be a member of the lower house was always considered as a burden, and an exemption from it as a privilege? Will they persuade us, that power, which, of all human acquisitions, is the most coveted, and in comparison of which even reputation and pleasure and riches are slighted, could ever be regarded as a burden by any man?

The property, acquired of late by the commons, it is said, entitles them to more power than their ancestors enjoyed. But to what is this encrease of their property owing, but to an encrease of their liberty and their security? Let them therefore acknowledge, that their ancestors, while the crown was restrained by the seditious barons, really enjoyed less liberty than they themselves have attained, after the sovereign acquired the ascendant: And let them enjoy that liberty with moderation; and not forfeit it by new exorbitant claims, and by rendering it a pretence for endless innovations.

The true rule of government is the present established practice of

133. [The Great Charter of 1215 between King John and Norman Barons. See Hume's discussion of this in *The History of England*, vol. I, pp. 442–49.]

the age. That has most authority, because it is recent: It is also best known, for the same reason. Who has assured those tribunes, that the PLANTAGENETS did not exercise as high acts of authority as the TUDORS? Historians, they say, do not mention them. But historians are also silent with regard to the chief exertions of prerogative by the TUDORS. Where any power or prerogative is fully and undoubtedly established, the exercise of it passes for a thing of course, and readily escapes the notice of history and annals. Had we no other monuments of ELIZABETH'S reign, than what are preserved even by CAMDEN, the most copious, judicious, and exact of our historians,[134] we should be entirely ignorant of the most important maxims of her government.

Was not the present monarchical government, in its full extent, authorized by lawyers, recommended by divines, acknowledged by politicians, acquiesced in, nay passionately cherished, by the people in general; and all this during a period of at least a hundred and sixty years, and till of late, without the smallest murmur or controversy? This general consent surely, during so long a time, must be sufficient to render a constitution legal and valid. If the origin of all power be derived, as is pretended, from the people; here is their consent in the fullest and most ample terms that can be desired or imagined.

But the people must not pretend, because they can, by their consent, lay the foundations of government, that therefore they are to be permitted, at their pleasure, to overthrow and subvert them. There is no end of these seditious and arrogant claims. The power of the crown is now openly struck at: The nobility are also in visible peril: The gentry will soon follow: The popular leaders, who will then assume the name of gentry, will next be exposed to danger: And the people themselves, having become incapable of civil government, and lying under the restraint of no authority, must, for the sake of peace, admit, instead of their legal and mild monarchs, a succession of military and despotic tyrants.

These consequences are the more to be dreaded, as the present fury of the people, though glossed over by pretensions to civil liberty, is in reality incited by the fanaticism of religion; a principle the most blind, headstrong, and ungovernable, by which human nature can possibly be actuated. Popular rage is dreadful, from whatever motive derived: But must be attended with the most pernicious consequences,

134. [William Camden (1551–1623), *The Historie of the most renowned and victorious princesse Elizabeth* (pt. I, 1615; pt. II 1625; English translation from Latin, 1635).]

when it arises from a principle, which disclaims all controul by human law, reason, or authority.

These are the arguments, which each party may make use of to justify the conduct of their predecessors, during that great crisis. The event, if that can be admitted as a reason, has shown, that the arguments of the popular party were better founded; but perhaps, according to the established maxims of lawyers and politicians, the views of the royalists ought, before-hand, to have appeared more solid, more safe, and more legal. But this is certain, that the greater moderation we now employ in representing past events; the nearer shall we be to produce a full coalition of the parties, and an entire acquiescence in our present establishment. Moderation is of advantage to every establishment: Nothing but zeal can overturn a settled power: And an over-active zeal in friends is apt to beget a like spirit in antagonists. The transition from a moderate opposition against an establishment, to an entire acquiescence in it, is easy and insensible.

There are many invincible arguments, which should induce the malcontent party to acquiesce entirely in the present settlement of the constitution. They now find, that the spirit of civil liberty, though at first connected with religious fanaticism, could purge itself from that pollution, and appear under a more genuine and engaging aspect; a friend to toleration, and an encourager of all the enlarged and generous sentiments that do honour to human nature. They may observe, that the popular claims could stop at a proper period; and after retrenching the high claims of prerogative, could still maintain a due respect to monarchy, to nobility, and to all ancient institutions. Above all, they must be sensible, that the very principle, which made the strength of their party, and from which it derived its chief authority, has now deserted them, and gone over to their antagonists. The plan of liberty is settled; its happy effects are proved by experience; a long tract of time has given it stability; and whoever would attempt to overturn it, and to recall the past government or abdicated family, would, besides other more criminal imputations, be exposed, in their turn, to the reproach of faction and innovation. While they peruse the history of past events, they ought to reflect, both that those rights of the crown are long since annihilated, and that the tyranny, and violence, and oppression, to which they often gave rise, are ills, from which the established liberty of the constitution has now at last happily protected the people. These reflections will prove a better security to our freedom and privileges, than to deny, contrary to the clearest evidence of facts, that such regal powers ever had an existence. There is not a more effectual method of betraying a cause, than to lay the stress of the argument on a wrong place, and by disputing an untenable post, enure the adversaries to success and victory.

Essay IX: Of the Protestant Succession

I suppose, that a member of parliament, in the reign of King WILLIAM or Queen ANNE, while the establishment of the *Protestant Succession*[135] was yet uncertain, were deliberating concerning the party he would chuse in that important question, and weighing, with impartiality, the advantages and disadvantages on each side. I believe the following particulars would have entered into his consideration.

He would easily perceive the great advantage resulting from the restoration of the STUART family; by which we should preserve the succession clear and undisputed, free from a pretender, with such a specious title as that of blood, which, with the multitude, is always the claim, the strongest and most easily comprehended. It is in vain to say, as many have done, that the question with regard to *governors*, independent of *government*, is frivolous, and little worth disputing, much less fighting about. The generality of mankind never will enter into these sentiments; and it is much happier, I believe, for society, that they do not, but rather continue in their natural prepossessions. How could stability be preserved in any monarchical government, (which, though, perhaps, not the best, is, and always has been, the most common

135. [James II, who converted to Catholicism in 1669, was King of England from 1685 to 1688. He fled England as a result of the invasion of William of Orange, who then succeeded to the throne with Mary, his wife, ruling until 1702 (Mary died in 1694), and reestablishing Protestant rule in England. William III was succeeded by Queen Anne, also Protestant, who ruled until her death in 1714. In "Of the Protestant Succession," Hume is intimating the question whether a Catholic can legitimately rule in a country whose religious practice is dominated by Protestants. Strikingly, Hume does not mention Jacobitism in this essay. Taking their name from the Latin for James, the Jacobites were adherents of James II after his abdication in 1688, or his son James Francis Edward Stuart ("the Old Pretender" to the throne); thus, by 1689 a division was formed between the Williamites—defenders of William as King of England — and the Jacobites. Following the Hanoverian Succession to the throne in 1714 with George I, the Jacobites aimed and schemed at returning the Stuarts to the Royal seat. There was a Jacobite uprising in 1745 led by Charles Edward Stuart ("the Young Pretender" to the throne) ultimately leading Hume to suppress "Of the Protestant Succession" from publication in 1748 until 1752, fearing that it might engender further violence.]

of any) unless men had so passionate a regard for the true heir of their royal family; and even though he be weak in understanding, or infirm in years, gave him so sensible a preference above persons the most accomplished in shining talents, or celebrated for great atchievements? Would not every popular leader put in his claim at every vacancy, or even without any vacancy; and the kingdom become the theatre of perpetual wars and convulsions? The condition of the ROMAN empire, surely, was not, in this respect, much to be envied; nor is that of the *Eastern* nations, who pay little regard to the titles of their sovereign, but sacrifice them, every day, to the caprice or momentary humour of the populace or soldiery. It is but a foolish wisdom, which is so carefully displayed, in undervaluing princes, and placing them on a level with the meanest of mankind. To be sure, an anatomist finds no more in the greatest monarch than in the lowest peasant or day-labourer; and a moralist may, perhaps, frequently find less. But what do all these reflections tend to? We, all of us, still retain these prejudices in favour of birth and family; and neither in our serious occupations, nor most careless amusements, can we ever get entirely rid of them. A tragedy, that should represent the adventures of sailors, or porters, or even of private gentlemen, would presently disgust us; but one that introduces kings and princes, acquires in our eyes an air of importance and dignity. Or should a man be able, by his superior wisdom, to get entirely above such prepossessions, he would soon, by means of the same wisdom, again bring himself down to them, for the sake of society, whose welfare he would perceive to be intimately connected with them. Far from endeavouring to undeceive the people in this particular, he would cherish such sentiments of reverence to their princes; as requisite to preserve a due subordination in society. And though the lives of twenty thousand men be often sacrificed to maintain a king in possession of his throne, or preserve the right of succession undisturbed, he entertains no indignation at the loss, on pretence that every individual of these was, perhaps, in himself, as valuable as the prince he served. He considers the consequences of violating the hereditary right of kings: Consequences, which may be felt for many centuries; while the loss of several thousand men brings so little prejudice to a large kingdom, that it may not be perceived a few years after.

The advantages of the HANOVER[136] succession are of an opposite

136. [Queen Anne was succeeded by George Ludwig, ruler of Hanover, who was crowned George I, establishing Hanoverian rule in England from 1714 to 1837.]

nature, and arise from this very circumstance, that it violates hereditary right; and places on the throne a prince, to whom birth gave no title to that dignity. It is evident, from the history of this island, that the privileges of the people have, during near two centuries, been continually upon the encrease, by the division of the church-lands, by the alienations of the barons' estates, by the progress of trade, and above all, by the happiness of our situation, which, for a long time, gave us sufficient security, without any standing army or military establishment. On the contrary, public liberty has, almost in every other nation of EUROPE, been, during the same period, extremely upon the decline; while the people were disgusted at the hardships of the old feudal militia, and rather chose to entrust their prince with mercenary armies, which he easily turned against themselves. It was nothing extraordinary, therefore, that some of our BRITISH sovereigns mistook the nature of the constitution, at least, the genius of the people; and as they embraced all the favourable precedents left them by their ancestors, they overlooked all those which were contrary, and which supposed a limitation in our government. They were encouraged in this mistake, by the example of all the neighbouring princes, who bearing the same title or appellation, and being adorned with the same ensigns of authority, naturally led them to claim the same powers and prerogatives. It appears from the speeches, and proclamations of JAMES I. and the whole train of that prince's actions, as well as his son's, that he regarded the ENGLISH government as a simple monarchy, and never imagined that any considerable part of his subjects entertained a contrary idea. This opinion made those monarchs discover their pretensions, without preparing any force to support them; and even without reserve or disguise, which are always employed by those, who enter upon any new project, or endeavour to innovate in any government. The flattery of courtiers farther confirmed their prejudices; and above all, that of the clergy, who from several passages of *scripture,* and these wrested too, had erected a regular and avowed system of arbitrary power. The only method of destroying, at once, all these high claims and pretensions, was to depart from the true hereditary line, and choose a prince, who, being plainly a creature of the public, and receiving the crown on conditions, expressed and avowed, found his authority established on the same bottom with the privileges of the people. By electing him in the royal line, we cut off all hopes of ambitious subjects, who might, in future emergencies, disturb the government by their cabals and pretensions: By rendering the crown hereditary in his family, we avoided all the inconveniencies of elective monarchy: And by excluding the lineal heir, we secured all our constitutional limitations, and rendered our government uniform and of a piece. The people cherish monarchy, because protected by it: The monarch favours liberty, because created by it. And thus every advantage is obtained by the new establishment, as far as human skill and wisdom can extend itself.

These are the separate advantages of fixing the succession, either in the house of STUART, or in that of HANOVER. There are also disadvantages in each establishment, which an impartial patriot would ponder and examine, in order to form a just judgment upon the whole.

The disadvantages of the protestant succession consist in the foreign dominions, which are possessed by the princes of the HANOVER line, and which, it might be supposed, would engage us in the intrigues and wars of the continent, and lose us, in some measure, the inestimable advantage we possess, of being surrounded and guarded by the sea, which we command. The disadvantages of recalling the abdicated family consist chiefly in their religion, which is more prejudicial to society than that established amongst us, is contrary to it, and affords no toleration, or peace, or security to any other communion.

It appears to me, that these advantages and disadvantages are allowed on both sides; at least, by every one who is at all susceptible of argument or reasoning. No subject, however loyal, pretends to deny, that the disputed title and foreign dominions of the present royal family are a loss. Nor is there any partizan of the STUARTS, but will confess, that the claim of hereditary, indefeasible right, and the Roman Catholic religion, are also disadvantages in that family. It belongs, therefore, to a philosopher alone, who is of neither party, to put all the circumstances in the scale, and assign to each of them its proper poise and influence. Such a one will readily, at first, acknowledge that all political questions are infinitely complicated, and that there scarcely ever occurs, in any deliberation, a choice, which is either purely good, or purely ill. Consequences, mixed and varied, may be foreseen to flow from every measure: And many consequences, unforeseen, do always, in fact, result from every one. Hesitation, and reserve, and suspence, are, therefore, the only sentiments he brings to this essay or trial. Or if he indulges any passion, it is that of derision against the ignorant multitude, who are always clamorous and dogmatical, even in the nicest questions, of which, from want of temper, perhaps still more than of understanding, they are altogether unfit judges.

But to say something more determinate on this head, the following reflections will, I hope, show the temper, if not the understanding of a philosopher.[137]

Were we to judge merely by first appearances, and by past experience, we must allow that the advantages of a parliamentary title in the house of HANOVER are greater than those of an undisputed hereditary title in the house of STUART; and that our fathers acted wisely in preferring the former to the latter. So long as the house of STUART ruled in GREAT BRITAIN, which, with some interruption, was above eighty years, the government was kept in a continual fever, by the contention between the privileges of the people and the prerogatives of the crown. If arms were dropped, the noise of disputes continued: Or if these were silenced, jealousy still corroded the heart, and threw the nation into an unnatural ferment and disorder. And while we were thus occupied in domestic disputes, a foreign power, dangerous to public liberty, erected itself in EUROPE, without any opposition from us, and even sometimes with our assistance.

But during these last sixty years, when a parliamentary establishment has taken place; whatever factions may have prevailed either among the people or in public assemblies, the whole force of our constitution has always fallen to one side, and an uninterrupted harmony has been preserved between our princes and our parliaments. Public liberty, with internal peace and order, has flourished almost without interruption: Trade and manufactures, and agriculture, have encreased: The arts, and sciences, and philosophy, have been cultivated. Even religious parties have been necessitated to lay aside their mutual rancour: And the glory of the nation has spread itself all over EUROPE; derived equally from our progress in the arts of peace, and from valour and success in war. So long and so glorious a period no nation almost can boast of: Nor is there another instance in the whole history of mankind, that so many millions of people have, during such a space of time, been held together, in a manner so free, so rational, and so suitable to the dignity of human nature.

But though this recent experience seems clearly to decide in favour of the present establishment, there are some circumstances to be thrown into the other scale; and it is dangerous to regulate our judgment by one event or example.

137. [For similar remarks on how a philosopher should reflect on political questions, see the opening sentence of "Of Civil Liberty" and the final four paragraphs "Of the Original Contract" (both in this edition).]

We have had two rebellions during the flourishing period above mentioned, besides plots and conspiracies without number. And if none of these have produced any very fatal event, we may ascribe our escape chiefly to the narrow genius of those princes who disputed our establishment; and we may esteem ourselves so far fortunate. But the claims of the banished family, I fear, are not yet antiquated; and who can foretel, that their future attempts will produce no greater disorder?

The disputes between privilege and prerogative may easily be composed by laws, and votes, and conferences, and concessions; where there is tolerable temper or prudence on both sides, or on either side. Among contending titles, the question can only be determined by the sword, and by devastation, and by civil war.

A prince, who fills the throne with a disputed title, dares not arm his subjects; the only method of securing a people fully, both against domestic oppression and foreign conquest.

Notwithstanding our riches and renown, what a critical escape did we make, by the late peace, from dangers, which were owing not so much to bad conduct and ill success in war, as to the pernicious practice of mortgaging our finances, and the still more pernicious maxim of never paying off our incumbrances? Such fatal measures would not probably have been embraced, had it not been to secure a precarious establishment.

But to convince us, that an hereditary title is to be embraced rather than a parliamentary one, which is not supported by any other views or motives; a man needs only transport himself back to the aera of the restoration, and suppose, that he had had a seat in that parliament which recalled the royal family, and put a period to the greatest disorders that ever arose from the opposite pretensions of prince and people. What would have been thought of one, that had proposed, at that time, to set aside CHARLES II. and settle the crown on the Duke of YORK, or GLOUCESTER,[138] merely in order to exclude all high claims, like those of their father and grandfather? Would not such a one have been regarded as an extravagant projector, who loved dangerous remedies,

138. [The Duke of York was James, King of England from 1685 to 1688, who was brother of Charles II and father of the soon to be Queen Mary. The Exclusion Crisis of 1679–81 was in large part due to the Catholicism of James (see n. 135). Henry, Duke of Gloucester, was the youngest brother of Charles II.]

and could tamper and play with a government and national constitution, like a quack with a sickly patient?

In reality, the reason assigned by the nation for excluding the race of STUART, and so many other branches of the royal family, is not on account of their hereditary title (a reason, which would, to vulgar apprehensions, have appeared altogether absurd), but on account of their religion. Which leads us to compare the disadvantages above mentioned in each establishment.

I confess, that, considering the matter in general, it were much to be wished, that our prince had no foreign dominions, and could confine all his attention to the government of this island. For not to mention some real inconveniencies that may result from territories on the continent, they afford such a handle for calumny and defamation, as is greedily seized by the people, always disposed to think ill of their superiors. It must, however, be acknowledged, that HANOVER, is, perhaps, the spot of ground in EUROPE the least inconvenient for a King of ENGLAND. It lies in the heart of GERMANY, at a distance from the great powers, which are our natural rivals: It is protected by the laws of the empire, as well as by the arms of its own sovereign: And it serves only to connect us more closely with the house of AUSTRIA, our natural ally.

The religious persuasion of the house of STUART is an inconvenience of a much deeper dye, and would threaten us with much more dismal consequences. The Roman Catholic religion, with its train of priests and friers, is more expensive than ours: Even though unaccompanied with its natural attendants of inquisitors, and stakes, and gibbets, it is less tolerating: And not content with dividing the sacerdotal from the regal office (which must be prejudicial to any state), it bestows the former on a foreigner, who has always a separate interest from that of the public, and may often have an opposite one.

But were this religion ever so advantageous to society, it is contrary to that which is established among us, and which is likely to keep possession, for a long time, of the minds of the people. And though it is much to be hoped, that the progress of reason will, by degrees, abate the acrimony of opposite religions all over EUROPE; yet the spirit of moderation has, as yet, made too slow advances to be entirely trusted.

Thus, upon the whole, the advantages of the settlement in the family of STUART, which frees us from a disputed title, seem to bear some proportion with those of the settlement in the family of HANOVER, which frees us from the claims of prerogative: But at the same time, its disadvantages, by placing on the throne a Roman Catholic, are greater than those of the other establishment, in settling the crown on a foreign prince. What party an impartial patriot, in the reign of K. WILLIAM or Q. ANNE, would have chosen amidst these opposite views, may, perhaps, to some appear hard to determine.[g]

But the settlement in the house of HANOVER has actually taken place. The princes of that family, without intrigue, without cabal, without solicitation on their part, have been called to mount our throne, by the united voice of the whole legislative body. They have, since their accession, displayed, in all their actions, the utmost mildness, equity, and regard to the laws and constitution. Our own ministers, our own parliaments, ourselves have governed us; and if aught ill has befallen us, we can only blame fortune or ourselves. What a reproach must we become among nations, if, disgusted with a settlement so deliberately made, and whose conditions have been so religiously observed, we should throw every thing again into confusion; and by our levity and rebellious disposition, prove ourselves totally unfit for any state but that of absolute slavery and subjection?

The greatest inconvenience, attending a disputed title, is, that it brings us in danger of civil wars and rebellions. What wise man, to avoid this inconvenience, would run directly into a civil war and rebellion? Not to mention, that so long possession, secured by so many laws, must, ere this time, in the apprehension of a great part of the nation, have begotten a title in the house of Hanover, independent of their present possession: So that now we should not, even by a revolution, obtain the end of avoiding a disputed title.

No revolution made by national forces, will ever be able, without some other great necessity, to abolish our debts and incumbrances, in which the interest of so many persons is concerned. And a revolution made by foreign forces, is a conquest: A calamity, with which the precarious balance of power threatens us, and which our civil dissentions are likely, above all other circumstances, to bring upon us.

Part III
The Critique of Speculative Politics

From *Essays, Moral, Political, and Literary*

Essay X: *Of Parties in General*

Of all men, that distinguish themselves by memorable atchievements, the first place of honour seems due to LEGISLATORS and founders of states, who transmit a system of laws and institutions to secure the peace, happiness, and liberty of future generations. The influence of useful inventions in the arts and sciences may, perhaps, extend farther than that of wise laws, whose effects are limited both in time and place; but the benefit arising from the former, is not so sensible as that which results from the latter. Speculative sciences do, indeed, improve the mind; but this advantage reaches only to a few persons, who have leisure to apply themselves to them. And as to practical arts, which encrease the commodities and enjoyments of life, it is well known, that men's happiness consists not so much in an abundance of these, as in the peace and security with which they possess them; and those blessings can only be derived from good government. Not to mention, that general virtue and good morals in a state, which are so requisite to happiness, can never arise from the most refined precepts of philosophy, or even the severest injunctions of religion; but must proceed entirely from the virtuous education of youth, the effect of wise laws and institutions. I must, therefore, presume to differ from Lord BACON[139] in this particular, and must regard antiquity as somewhat unjust in its distribution of honours, when it made gods of all the inventors of useful arts, such as CERES, BACCHUS, AESCULAPIUS; and dignify legislators, such as ROMULUS and THESEUS,[140] only with the appellation of demigods and heroes.

As much as legislators and founders of states ought to be honoured and respected among men, as much ought the founders of sects and factions to be detested and hated; because the influence of faction is

139. [Sir Francis Bacon (1561–1626), *The Advancement of Learning*, 2*nd* edition, ed. by W.A. Wright (Oxford: At the Clarendon Press, 1873), p. 52 (bk. I, sec. VII)]

140. [Ceres, Bacchus, and Aesculapius were Roman deities of corn, wine, and healing, respectively. Romulus (*c.* 735 B.C.) was the legendary founder and first king of Rome, while Theseus (*c.* 1200 B.C.) was the legendary hero and founder-king of Athens.]

directly contrary to that of laws. Factions subvert government, render laws impotent, and beget the fiercest animosities among men of the same nation, who ought to give mutual assistance and protection to each other. And what should render the founders of parties more odious is, the difficulty of extirpating these weeds, when once they have taken root in any state. They naturally propagate themselves for many centuries, and seldom end but by the total dissolution of that government, in which they are sown. They are, besides, plants which grow most plentifully in the richest soil; and though absolute governments be not wholly free from them, it must be confessed, that they rise more easily, and propagate themselves faster in free governments, where they always infect the legislature itself, which alone could be able, by the steady application of rewards and punishments, to eradicate them.

Factions may be divided into PERSONAL and REAL; that is, into factions, founded on personal friendship or animosity among such as compose the contending parties, and into those founded on some real difference of sentiment or interest. The reason of this distinction is obvious; though I must acknowledge, that parties are seldom found pure and unmixed, either of the one kind or the other. It is not often seen, that a government divides into factions, where there is no difference in the views of the constituent members, either real or apparent, trivial or material: And in those factions, which are founded on the most real and most material difference, there is always observed a great deal of personal animosity or affection. But notwithstanding this mixture, a party may be denominated either personal or real, according to that principle which is predominant, and is found to have the greatest influence.

Personal factions arise most easily in small republics. Every domestic quarrel, there, becomes an affair of state. Love, vanity, emulation, any passion, as well as ambition and resentment, begets public division. The NERI and BIANCHI of FLORENCE, the FREGOSI and ADORNI of GENOA, the COLONESI and ORSINI of modern ROME, were parties of this kind.[141]

Men have such a propensity to divide into personal factions, that the smallest appearance of real difference will produce them. What can be imagined more trivial than the difference between one colour

141. [Hume's three examples are drawn from early-thirteenth to late-fourteenth-century Italian history.]

of livery and another in horse races? Yet this difference begat two most inveterate factions in the GREEK empire,[142] the PRASINI and VENETI, who never suspended their animosities, till they ruined that unhappy government.[143]

We find in the ROMAN history a remarkable dissension between two tribes, the POLLIA and PAPIRIA, which continued for the space of near three hundred years, and discovered itself in their suffrages at every election of magistrates.[144] This faction was the more remarkable, as it could continue for so long a tract of time; even though it did not spread itself, nor draw any of the other tribes into a share of the quarrel. If mankind had not a strong propensity to such divisions, the indifference of the rest of the community must have suppressed this

142. [The Eastern Empire of Rome, that is, Byzantium.]

143. [In the circus at Rome and the hippodrome at Constantinople, charioteers were distinguished by the colors they wore, red, white, green, and blue. These chariot races were followed with frenzied passion, leading to political factions being formed on the basis of the colors of the most favored charioteers. Edward Gibbon (1737–94) reports, "Under the reign of Anastasius, this popular frenzy was inflamed by religious zeal; and the greens, who had treacherously concealed stones and daggers under baskets of fruit, massacred, at a solemn festival, three thousand of their blue adversaries" (*The History of the Decline and Fall of the Roman Empire*, ed. by J. B. Bury in 7 vols. (London: Methuen & Co. Ltd., 1896–1900), vol. IV, p. 220 {ch. XL}).]

144. As this fact has not been much observed by antiquaries or politicians, I shall deliver it in the words of the ROMAN historian. *Populus* TUSCULANUS *cum conjugibus ac liberis* ROMAM *venit: Ea multitudo, veste mutata, & specie reorum tribus circuit, genibus se omnium advolvens. Plus itaque misericordia ad paenoe veniam impetrandam, quam causa ad crimen purgandum valuit. Tribus omnes praeter* POLLIAM, *antiquarunt legem.* POLLIAE *sententia fuit, puberes verberatos necari, liberos conjugesque sub corona lege belli venire: Memoriamque ejus irae* TUSCULANIS *in paenoe tam atrocis auctores mansisse ad patris aetatem constat; nec quemquam fere ex* POLLIA *tribu candidatum* PAPIRAM *ferre solitam,* T. LIVII, lib. 8. 37. The CASTELANI and NICOLLOTI are two mobbish factions in VENICE, who frequently box together, and then lay aside their quarrels presently. [Titus Livius (59 B.C.–A.D. 17), *The History of Rome*, trans. by D. Spillan *et al.*, 4 vols. (London: G. Bell and Sons, Ltd., 1911), vol. I, p. 555 (8.37): "The Tusculans, with their wives and children, came to Rome. The whole party in mourning habits, like persons under accusation, went round the tribes, throwing themselves at the feet of the citizens. The compassion thus excited operated more effectually towards procuring them pardon, than all their arguments did towards clearing them of guilt. Every one of the tribes, except the Pollian, negatived the proposition. The sentence of the Pollian tribe, was that the grown-up males should be beaten and put to death, and their wives and children sold by auction, according to the rules of war. It appears that the resentment which rose against the advisers of so rigorous a measure, was retained in memory by the Tusculans down to the age of our fathers; and that hardly any candidate of the Pollian tribe could, ever since, gain the votes of the Papirian."]

foolish animosity, that had not any aliment of new benefits and injuries, of general sympathy and antipathy, which never fail to take place, when the whole state is rent into two equal factions.

Nothing is more usual than to see parties, which have begun upon a real difference, continue even after that difference is lost. When men are once inlisted on opposite sides, they contract an affection to the persons with whom they are united, and an animosity against their antagonists: And these passions they often transmit to their posterity. The real difference between GUELF and GHIBBELLINE was long lost in ITALY, before these factions were extinguished. The GUELFS adhered to the pope, the GHIBBELLINES to the emperor; yet the family of SFORZA, who were in alliance with the emperor, though they were GUELFS, being expelled MILAN by the king[145] of FRANCE, assisted by JACOMO TRIVULZIO and the GHIBBELLINES, the pope concurred with the latter, and they formed leagues with the pope against the emperor.

The civil wars which arose some few years ago in MOROCCO, between the *blacks* and *whites*, merely on account of their complexion, are founded on a pleasant difference. We laugh at them; but I believe, were things rightly examined, we afford much more occasion of ridicule to the MOORS. For, what are all the wars of religion,[146] which have prevailed in this polite and knowing part of the world? They are certainly more absurd than the MOORISH civil wars. The difference of complexion is a sensible and a real difference: But the controversy about an article of faith, which is utterly absurd and unintelligible, is not a difference in sentiment, but in a few phrases and expressions, which one party accepts of, without understanding them; and the other refuses in the same manner.

Real factions may be divided into those from *interest*, from *principle*, and from *affection*. Of all factions, the first are the most reasonable, and the most excusable. Where two orders of men, such as the nobles and people, have a distinct authority in a government, not very accurately balanced and modelled, they naturally follow a distinct interest; nor can we reasonably expect a different conduct, considering that degree of selfishness implanted in human nature. It requires great skill

145. LEWIS XII. [Louis XII ruled France from 1498 to 1515.]

146. [Hume has in mind the French religious wars of the last half of the sixteenth century, the English civil war in the seventeenth century and, perhaps, certain revolts led by the Anabaptists in Germany in the first half of the sixteenth century. See n. 184.]

in a legislator to prevent such parties; and many philosophers are of opinion, that this secret, like the *grand elixir,* or *perpetual motion,* may amuse men in theory, but can never possibly be reduced to practice. In despotic governments, indeed, factions often do not appear; but they are not the less real; or rather, they are more real and more pernicious, upon that very account. The distinct orders of men, nobles and people, soldiers and merchants, have all a distinct interest; but the more powerful oppresses the weaker with impunity, and without resistance; which begets a seeming tranquillity in such governments.

There has been an attempt in ENGLAND to divide the *landed* and *trading* part of the nation; but without success. The interests of these two bodies are not really distinct, and never will be so, till our public debts encrease to such a degree, as to become altogether oppressive and intolerable.

Parties from *principle,* especially abstract speculative principle, are known only to modern times, and are, perhaps, the most extraordinary and unaccountable *phenomenon,* that has yet appeared in human affairs. Where different principles beget a contrariety of conduct, which is the case with all different political principles, the matter may be more easily explained. A man, who esteems the true right of government to lie in one man, or one family, cannot easily agree with his fellow-citizen, who thinks that another man or family is possessed of this right. Each naturally wishes that right may take place, according to his own notions of it. But where the difference of principle is attended with no contrariety of action, but every one may follow his own way, without interfering with his neighbour, as happens in all religious controversies; what madness, what fury can beget such unhappy and such fatal divisions?

Two men travelling on the highway, the one east, the other west, can easily pass each other, if the way be broad enough: But two men, reasoning upon opposite principles of religion, cannot so easily pass, without shocking; though one should think, that the way were also, in that case, sufficiently broad, and that each might proceed, without interruption, in his own course. But such is the nature of the human mind, that it always lays hold on every mind that approaches it; and as it is wonderfully fortified by an unanimity of sentiments, so is it shocked and disturbed by any contrariety.[147] Hence the eagerness,

147. [This important principle of human nature does not appear in Hume's *Treatise.*]

which most people discover in a dispute; and hence their impatience of opposition, even in the most speculative and indifferent opinions.

This principle, however frivolous it may appear, seems to have been the origin of all religious wars and divisions. But as this principle is universal in human nature, its effects would not have been confined to one age, and to one sect of religion, did it not there concur with other more accidental causes, which raise it to such a height, as to produce the greatest misery and devastation. Most religions of the ancient world arose in the unknown ages of government, when men were as yet barbarous and uninstructed, and the prince, as well as peasant, was disposed to receive, with implicit faith, every pious tale or fiction, which was offered him. The magistrate embraced the religion of the people, and entering cordially into the care of sacred matters, naturally acquired an authority in them, and united the ecclesiastical with the civil power. But the *Christian* religion arising, while principles directly opposite to it were firmly established in the polite part of the world, who despised the nation that first broached this novelty; no wonder, that, in such circumstances, it was but little countenanced by the civil magistrate, and that the priesthood was allowed to engross all the authority in the new sect. So bad a use did they make of this power, even in those early times, that the primitive persecutions may, perhaps, *in part,*[148] be ascribed to the violence instilled by them into their follow-

148. I say, *in part;* For it is a vulgar error to imagine, that the ancients were as great friends to toleration as the ENGLISH or DUTCH are at present. The laws against external superstition, amongst the ROMANS, were as ancient as the time of the twelve tables; [Codified Roman Law, 451–450 B.C.; see n. 201.] and the JEWS as well as CHRISTIANS were sometimes punished by them; though, in general, these laws were not rigorously executed. Immediately after the conquest of Gaul, they forbad all but the natives to be initiated into the religion of the DRUIDS; and this was a kind of persecution. In about a century after this conquest, the emperor, CLAUDIUS, quite abolished that superstition by penal laws; which would have been a very grievous persecution, if the imitation of the ROMAN manners had not, before-hand, weaned the GAULS from their ancient prejudices. SUETONIUS *in vita* CLAUDII. [Suetonius (*c.* A.D. 70–141), "Life of Claudius," in *Lives of the Caesars*. Claudius was Emperor from A.D. 41 to 54.] PLINY ascribes the abolition of the Druidical superstitions to TIBERIUS, probably because that emperor had taken some steps towards restraining them (lib. xxx. cap. i. [Pliny, the Elder (A.D. 23–79), *Natural History*, 30.4. Tiberius was Emperor from A.D. 14 to 37). The Druids practiced human sacrifice.]). This is an instance of the usual caution and moderation of the ROMANS in such cases; and very different from their violent and sanguinary method of treating the *Christians.* Hence we may entertain a suspicion, that those furious persecutions of *Christianity* were in some measure owing

ers. And the same principles of priestly government continuing, after Christianity became the established religion, they have engendered a spirit of persecution, which has ever since been the poison of human society, and the source of the most inveterate factions in every government. Such divisions, therefore, on the part of the people, may justly be esteemed factions of *principle;* but, on the part of the priests, who are the prime movers, they are really factions of *interest.*

There is another cause (beside the authority of the priests, and the separation of the ecclesiastical and civil powers) which has contributed to render CHRISTENDOM the scene of religious wars and divisions. Religions, that arise in ages totally ignorant and barbarous, consist mostly of traditional tales and fictions, which may be different in every sect, without being contrary to each other; and even when they are contrary, every one adheres to the tradition of his own sect, without much reasoning or disputation. But as philosophy was widely spread over the world, at the time when Christianity arose, the teachers of the new sect were obliged to form a system of speculative opinions; to divide, with some accuracy, their articles of faith; and to explain, comment, confute, and defend with all the subtilty of argument and science. Hence naturally arose keenness in dispute, when the Christian religion came to be split into new divisions and heresies:[149] And this keenness assisted the priests in their policy, of begetting a mutual hatred and antipathy among their deluded followers. Sects of philosophy, in the ancient world, were more zealous than parties of religion; but in modern times, parties of religion are more furious and enraged than the most cruel factions that ever arose from interest and ambition.

I have mentioned parties from *affection* as a kind of *real* parties, beside those from *interest* and *principle.* By parties from affection, I understand those which are founded on the different attachments of men towards particular families and persons, whom they desire to rule over them. These factions are often very violent; though, I must own, it may seem unaccountable, that men should attach themselves so

---

to the imprudent zeal and bigotry of the first propagators of that sect; and Ecclesiastical history affords us many reasons to confirm this suspicion.[h]

149. [For a remarkably similar account to Hume's on the relationship between philosophy and the rise of Christianity, see Michael Oakeshott's essay "The Tower of Babel," in *Rationalism in Politics and Other Essays*, ed. by T. Fuller, new and expanded edition, (Indianapolis: Liberty Fund, 1991).]

strongly to persons, with whom they are no wise acquainted, whom perhaps they never saw, and from whom they never received, nor can ever hope for any favour. Yet this we often find to be the case, and even with men, who, on other occasions, discover no great generosity of spirit, nor are found to be easily transported by friendship beyond their own interest. We are apt to think the relation between us and our sovereign very close and intimate. The splendour of majesty and power bestows an importance on the fortunes even of a single person. And when a man's good-nature does not give him this imaginary interest, his ill-nature will, from spite and opposition to persons whose sentiments are different from his own.[150]

Essay XI: *Of the Original Contract*

As no party, in the present age, can well support itself, without a philosophical or speculative system of principles, annexed to its political or practical one; we accordingly find, that each of the factions, into which this nation is divided, has reared up a fabric of the former kind, in order to protect and cover that scheme of actions, which it pursues. The people being commonly very rude builders, especially in this speculative way, and more especially still, when actuated by party-zeal; it is natural to imagine, that their workmanship must be a little unshapely, and discover evident marks of that violence and hurry, in which it was raised. The one party, by tracing up government to the DEITY, endeavour to render it so sacred and inviolate, that it must be little less than sacrilege, however tyrannical it may become, to touch or invade it, in the smallest article. The other party, by founding government altogether on the consent of the PEOPLE, suppose that there is a kind of *original contract*, by which the subjects have tacitly reserved the power of resisting their sovereign, whenever they find themselves aggrieved by that authority, with which they have, for certain purposes, voluntarily entrusted him. These are the speculative principles of the two parties; and these too are the practical consequences deduced from them.

I shall venture to affirm, *That both these* systems *of speculative principles are just; though not in the sense, intended by the parties:* And, *That both*

150. [This essay, along with "Of the Independency of Parliament" and "Idea of a Perfect Commonwealth" (both in this edition), had a significant influence on the thought of James Madison, an influence that reveals itself especially in *The Federalist* no. 10.]

the schemes *of practical consequences are prudent; though not in the extremes, to which each party, in opposition to the other, has commonly endeavoured to carry them.*

That the DEITY is the ultimate author of all government, will never be denied by any, who admit a general providence, and allow, that all events in the universe are conducted by an uniform plan, and directed to wise purposes. As it is impossible for the human race to subsist, at least in any comfortable or secure state, without the protection of government; this institution must certainly have been intended by that beneficent Being, who means the good of all his creatures: And as it has universally, in fact, taken place, in all countries, and all ages; we may conclude, with still greater certainty, that it was intended by that omniscient Being, who can never be deceived by any event or operation. But since he gave rise to it, not by any particular or miraculous interposition, but by his concealed and universal efficacy; a sovereign cannot, properly speaking, be called his vice-gerent, in any other sense than every power or force, being derived from him, may be said to act by his commission. Whatever actually happens is comprehended in the general plan or intention of providence; nor has the greatest and most lawful prince any more reason, upon that account, to plead a peculiar sacredness or inviolable authority, than an inferior magistrate, or even an usurper, or even a robber and a pyrate. The same divine superintendant, who, for wise purposes, invested a TITUS or a TRAJAN with authority, did also, for purposes, no doubt, equally wise, though unknown, bestow power on a BORGIA or an ANGRIA.[151] The same causes, which gave rise to the sovereign power in every state, established likewise every petty jurisdiction in it, and every limited authority. A constable, therefore, no less than a king, acts by a divine commission, and possesses an indefeasible right.

When we consider how nearly equal all men are in their bodily force, and even in their mental powers and faculties, till cultivated by education; we must necessarily allow, that nothing but their own consent could, at first, associate them together, and subject them to any authority. The people, if we trace government to its first origin in the

151. [Titus was Roman Emperor from A.D. 79 to 81; Trajan was Roman Emperor from A.D. 98 to 117. Cesare Borgia, with the aid of his father, Pope Alexander VI, and Louis XII of France, subdued and ruled over the territory of Romagna, in northeast Italy, from 1501 to 1503. Machiavelli (1469–1527) describes Borgia's rise to power in chs. VII and XI of *The Prince*. Angria was an eighteenth-century pirate, operating south of Bombay, India.]

woods and desarts, are the source of all power and jurisdiction, and voluntarily, for the sake of peace and order, abandoned their native liberty, and received laws from their equal and companion. The conditions, upon which they were willing to submit, were either expressed, or were so clear and obvious, that it might well be esteemed superfluous to express them. If this, then, be meant by the *original contract,* it cannot be denied, that all government is, at first, founded on a contract, and that the most ancient rude combinations of mankind were formed chiefly by that principle. In vain, are we asked in what records this charter of our liberties is registered. It was not written on parchment, nor yet on leaves or barks of trees. It preceded the use of writing and all the other civilized arts of life. But we trace it plainly in the nature of man, and in the equality, or something approaching equality, which we find in all the individuals of that species. The force, which now prevails, and which is founded on fleets and armies, is plainly political, and derived from authority, the effect of established government. A man's natural force consists only in the vigour of his limbs, and the firmness of his courage; which could never subject multitudes to the command of one. Nothing but their own consent, and their sense of the advantages resulting from peace and order, could have had that influence.

Yet even this consent was long very imperfect, and could not be the basis of a regular administration. The chieftain, who had probably acquired his influence during the continuance of war, ruled more by persuasion than command; and till he could employ force to reduce the refractory and disobedient, the society could scarcely be said to have attained a state of civil government. No compact or agreement, it is evident, was expressly formed for general submission; an idea far beyond the comprehension of savages: Each exertion of authority in the chieftain must have been particular, and called forth by the present exigencies of the case: The sensible utility, resulting from his interposition, made these exertions become daily more frequent; and their frequency gradually produced an habitual, and, if you please to call it so, a voluntary, and therefore precarious, acquiescence in the people.

But philosophers, who have embraced a party (if that be not a contradiction in terms)[152] are not contented with these concessions. They assert, not only that government in its earliest infancy arose from

152. [Hume also comments on the philosopher's proper stance toward politics in the opening paragraph of "Of Civil Liberty" and "Of the Protestant Succession" (p. 152) (both in this edition).]

consent or rather the voluntary acquiescence of the people; but also, that, even at present, when it has attained full maturity, it rests on no other foundation.[153] They affirm, that all men are still born equal, and owe allegiance to no prince or government, unless bound by the obligation and sanction of a *promise.* And as no man, without some equivalent, would forego the advantages of his native liberty, and subject himself to the will of another; this promise is always understood to be conditional, and imposes on him no obligation, unless he meet with justice and protection from his sovereign. These advantages the sovereign promises him in return; and if he fail in the execution, he has broken, on his part, the articles of engagement, and has thereby freed his subject from all obligations to allegiance. Such, according to these philosophers, is the foundation of authority in every government; and such the right of resistance, possessed by every subject.

But would these reasoners look abroad into the world, they would meet with nothing that, in the least, corresponds to their ideas, or can warrant so refined and philosophical a system. On the contrary, we find, every where, princes, who claim their subjects as their property, and assert their independent right of sovereignty, from conquest or succession. We find also, every where, subjects, who acknowledge this right in their prince, and suppose themselves born under obligations of obedience to a certain sovereign, as much as under the ties of reverence and duty to certain parents. These connexions are always conceived to be equally independent of our consent, in PERSIA and CHINA; in FRANCE and SPAIN; and even in HOLLAND and ENGLAND, wherever the doctrines above-mentioned have not been carefully inculcated. Obedience or subjection becomes so familiar, that most men never make any enquiry about its origin or cause, more than about the principle of gravity, resistance, or the most universal laws of nature. Or if curiosity ever move them; as soon as they learn, that they themselves and their ancestors have, for several ages, or from time immemorial, been subject to such a form of government or such a family; they immediately acquiesce, and acknowledge their obligation to allegiance. Were you to preach, in most parts of the world, that political connexions are founded altogether on voluntary consent or a mutual promise, the magistrate would soon imprison you, as seditious,

153. [Hume has various Whig thinkers in mind, most especially John Locke (1632–1704). See Locke's *Two Treatises of Government*, ed. by P. Laslett, student edition (Cambridge: Cambridge University Press, 1988), pp. 269–76 and 330–33.]

for loosening the ties of obedience; if your friends did not before shut you up as delirious, for advancing such absurdities. It is strange, that an act of the mind, which every individual is supposed to have formed, and after he came to the use of reason too, otherwise it could have no authority; that this act, I say, should be so much unknown to all of them, that, over the face of the whole earth, there scarcely remain any traces or memory of it.

But the contract, on which government is founded, is said to be the *original contract;* and consequently may be supposed too old to fall under the knowledge of the present generation. If the agreement, by which savage men first associated and conjoined their force, be here meant, this is acknowledged to be real; but being so ancient, and being obliterated by a thousand changes of government and princes, it cannot now be supposed to retain any authority. If we would say any thing to the purpose, we must assert, that every particular government, which is lawful, and which imposes any duty of allegiance on the subject, was, at first, founded on consent and a voluntary compact. But besides that this supposes the consent of the fathers to bind the children, even to the most remote generations,[154] (which republican writers will never allow) besides this, I say, it is not justified by history or experience, in any age or country of the world.

Almost all the governments, which exist at present, or of which there remains any record in story, have been founded originally, either on usurpation or conquest, or both, without any pretence of a fair consent, or voluntary subjection of the people. When an artful and bold man is placed at the head of an army or faction, it is often easy for him, by employing, sometimes violence, sometimes false pretences, to establish his dominion over a people a hundred times more numerous than his partizans. He allows no such open communication, that his enemies can know, with certainty, their number or force. He gives them no leisure to assemble together in a body to oppose him. Even all those, who are the instruments of his usurpation, may wish his fall; but their ignorance of each other's intention keeps them in awe, and is the sole cause of his security. By such arts as these, many governments have

154. [The criticism that is implicit here was also made by Sir Robert Filmer (1588–1653)—the proponent of the Divine Right of Kings—in his *The Anarchy of a Limited or Mixed Monarchy*. See Filmer, *Patriarcha and Other Writings*, ed. by J. P. Sommerville (Cambridge: Cambridge University Press, 1991).]

been established; and this is all the *original contract,* which they have to boast of.

The face of the earth is continually changing, by the encrease of small kingdoms into great empires, by the dissolution of great empires into smaller kingdoms, by the planting of colonies, by the migration of tribes. Is there any thing discoverable in all these events, but force and violence? Where is the mutual agreement or voluntary association so much talked of?

Even the smoothest way, by which a nation may receive a foreign master, by marriage or a will, is not extremely honourable for the people; but supposes them to be disposed of, like a dowry or a legacy, according to the pleasure or interest of their rulers.

But where no force interposes, and election takes place; what is this election so highly vaunted? It is either the combination of a few great men, who decide for the whole, and will allow of no opposition: Or it is the fury of a multitude, that follow a seditious ringleader, who is not known, perhaps, to a dozen among them, and who owes his advancement merely to his own impudence, or to the momentary caprice of his fellows.

Are these disorderly elections, which are rare too, of such mighty authority, as to be the only lawful foundation of all government and allegiance?

In reality, there is not a more terrible event, than a total dissolution of government, which gives liberty to the multitude, and makes the determination or choice of a new establishment depend upon a number, which nearly approaches to that of the body of the people: For it never comes entirely to the whole body of them. Every wise man, then, wishes to see, at the head of a powerful and obedient army, a general, who may speedily seize the prize, and give to the people a master, which they are so unfit to chuse for themselves. So little correspondent is fact and reality to those philosophical notions.

Let not the establishment at the *Revolution*[155] deceive us, or make us so much in love with a philosophical origin to government, as to imagine all others monstrous and irregular. Even that event was far from corresponding to these refined ideas. It was only the succession, and that only in the regal part of the government, which was then changed: And it was only the majority of seven hundred, who deter-

155. [See n. 25.]

mined that change for near ten millions. I doubt not, indeed, but the bulk of those ten millions acquiesced willingly in the determination: But was the matter left, in the least, to their choice? Was it not justly supposed to be, from that moment, decided, and every man punished, who refused to submit to the new sovereign? How otherwise could the matter have ever been brought to any issue or conclusion?

The republic of ATHENS was, I believe, the most extensive democracy, that we read of in history: Yet if we make the requisite allowances for the women, the slaves, and the strangers, we shall find, that that establishment was not, at first, made, nor any law ever voted, by a tenth part of those who were bound to pay obedience to it: Not to mention the islands and foreign dominions, which the ATHENIANS claimed as theirs by right of conquest. And as it is well known, that popular assemblies in that city were always full of licence and disorder, notwithstanding the institutions and laws by which they were checked: How much more disorderly must they prove, where they form not the established constitution, but meet tumultuously on the dissolution of the ancient government, in order to give rise to a new one? How chimerical must it be to talk of a choice in such circumstances?

The ACHAEANS enjoyed the freest and most perfect democracy of all antiquity; yet they employed force to oblige some cities to enter into their league, as we learn from POLYBIUS.[156]

HARRY the IVth and HARRY the VIIth of ENGLAND,[157] had really no title to the throne but a parliamentary election; yet they never would acknowledge it, lest they should thereby weaken their authority. Strange, if the only real foundation of all authority be consent and promise!

It is in vain to say, that all governments are or should be, at first, founded on popular consent, as much as the necessity of human affairs will admit. This favours entirely my pretension. I maintain, that human affairs will never admit of this consent; seldom of the appearance of it. But that conquest or usurpation, that is, in plain terms, force, by dissolving the ancient governments, is the origin of almost all the new ones, which were ever established in the world. And that in the few cases, where consent may seem to have taken place, it was commonly

156. Lib. ii. cap. 38. [Polybius (*c.* 200–118 B.C.), *Histories*, 2.38.]

157. [Henry IV was King of England from 1399 to 1413, and Henry VII was King from 1485 to 1509.]

so irregular, so confined, or so much intermixed either with fraud or violence, that it cannot have any great authority.

My intention here is not to exclude the consent of the people from being one just foundation of government where it has place. It is surely the best and most sacred of any. I only pretend, that it has very seldom had place in any degree, and never almost in its full extent. And that therefore some other foundation of government must also be admitted.

Were all men possessed of so inflexible a regard to justice, that, of themselves, they would totally abstain from the properties of others; they had for ever remained in a state of absolute liberty, without subjection to any magistrate or political society: But this is a state of perfection, of which human nature is justly deemed incapable. Again; were all men possessed of so perfect an understanding, as always to know their own interests, no form of government had ever been submitted to, but what was established on consent, and was fully canvassed by every member of the society: But this state of perfection is likewise much superior to human nature. Reason, history, and experience shew us, that all political societies have had an origin much less accurate and regular; and were one to choose a period of time, when the people's consent was the least regarded in public transactions, it would be precisely on the establishment of a new government. In a settled constitution, their inclinations are often consulted; but during the fury of revolutions, conquests, and public convulsions, military force or political craft usually decides the controversy.

When a new government is established, by whatever means, the people are commonly dissatisfied with it, and pay obedience more from fear and necessity, than from any idea of allegiance or of moral obligation. The prince is watchful and jealous, and must carefully guard against every beginning or appearance of insurrection. Time, by degrees, removes all these difficulties, and accustoms the nation to regard, as their lawful or native princes, that family, which, at first, they considered as usurpers or foreign conquerors. In order to found this opinion, they have no recourse to any notion of voluntary consent or promise, which, they know, never was, in this case, either expected or demanded. The original establishment was formed by violence, and submitted to from necessity. The subsequent administration is also supported by power, and acquiesced in by the people, not as a matter of choice, but of obligation. They imagine not, that their consent gives their prince a title: But they willingly consent, because they think, that, from long possession, he has acquired a title, independent of their choice or inclination.

Should it be said, that, by living under the dominion of a prince, which one might leave, every individual has given a *tacit* consent to his authority, and promised him obedience; it may be answered, that such an implied consent can only have place, where a man imagines, that the matter depends on his choice. But where he thinks (as all mankind do who are born under established governments) that by his birth he owes allegiance to a certain prince or certain form of government; it would be absurd to infer a consent or choice, which he expressly, in this case, renounces and disclaims.

Can we seriously say, that a poor peasant or artizan has a free choice to leave his country, when he knows no foreign language or manners, and lives from day to day, by the small wages which he acquires? We may as well assert, that a man, by remaining in a vessel, freely consents to the dominion of the master; though he was carried on board while asleep, and must leap into the ocean, and perish, the moment he leaves her.

What if the prince forbid his subjects to quit his dominions; as in TIBERIUS'S time,[158] it was regarded as a crime in a ROMAN knight that he had attempted to fly to the PARTHIANS, in order to escape the tyranny of that emperor?[159] Or as the ancient MUSCOVITES prohibited all travelling under pain of death? And did a prince observe, that many of his subjects were seized with the frenzy of migrating to foreign countries, he would doubtless, with great reason and justice, restrain them, in order to prevent the depopulation of his own kingdom. Would he forfeit the allegiance of all his subjects, by so wise and reasonable a law? Yet the freedom of their choice is surely, in that case, ravished from them.

A company of men, who should leave their native country, in order to people some uninhabited region, might dream of recovering their native freedom; but they would soon find, that their prince still laid claim to them, and called them his subjects, even in their new settlement. And in this he would but act conformably to the common ideas of mankind.

The truest *tacit* consent of this kind, that is ever observed, is when

158. [Tiberius was Emperor of Rome from A.D. 14 to 37.]

159. TACIT. Ann. vi. cap. 14. [Tacitus (*c.* A.D. 56–120), *Annals*, 4.14.]

a foreigner settles in any country, and is beforehand acquainted with the prince, and government, and laws, to which he must submit: Yet is his allegiance, though more voluntary, much less expected or depended on, than that of a natural born subject. On the contrary, his native prince still asserts a claim to him. And if he punish not the renegade, when he seizes him in war with his new prince's commission; this clemency is not founded on the municipal law, which in all countries condemns the prisoner; but on the consent of princes, who have agreed to this indulgence, in order to prevent reprisals.

Did one generation of men go off the stage at once, and another succeed, as is the case with silk-worms and butterflies, the new race, if they had sense enough to choose their government, which surely is never the case with men, might voluntarily, and by general consent, establish their own form of civil polity, without any regard to the laws or precedents, which prevailed among their ancestors. But as human society is in perpetual flux, one man every hour going out of the world, another coming into it, it is necessary, in order to preserve stability in government, that the new brood should conform themselves to the established constitution, and nearly follow the path which their fathers, treading in the footsteps of theirs, had marked out to them. Some innovations must necessarily have place in every human institution, and it is happy where the enlightened genius of the age give these a direction to the side of reason, liberty, and justice: but violent innovations no individual is entitled to make: they are even dangerous to be attempted by the legislature: more ill than good is ever to be expected from them: and if history affords examples to the contrary, they are not to be drawn into precedent, and are only to be regarded as proofs, that the science of politics affords few rules, which will not admit of some exception, and which may not sometimes be controuled by fortune and accident. The violent innovations in the reign of HENRY VIII.[160] proceeded from an imperious monarch, seconded by the appearance of legislative authority: Those in the reign of CHARLES I.[161] were derived from faction and fanaticism; and both of them have proved happy in the issue: But even the former were long the source of many

160. [King of England from 1509 to 1547. In the early 1530s, Henry removed England from papal jurisdiction, establishing the king of England as the supreme head of the Church of England, now understood to be the Anglican Church.]

161. [See n. 84.]

disorders, and still more dangers; and if the measures of allegiance were to be taken from the latter, a total anarchy must have place in human society, and a final period at once be put to every government.

Suppose, that an usurper, after having banished his lawful prince and royal family, should establish his dominion for ten or a dozen years in any country, and should preserve so exact a discipline in his troops, and so regular a disposition in his garrisons, that no insurrection had ever been raised, or even murmur heard, against his administration: Can it be asserted, that the people, who in their hearts abhor his treason, have tacitly consented to his authority, and promised him allegiance, merely because, from necessity, they live under his dominion? Suppose again their native prince restored, by means of an army, which he levies in foreign countries: They receive him with joy and exultation, and shew plainly with what reluctance they had submitted to any other yoke. I may now ask, upon what foundation the prince's title stands? Not on popular consent surely: For though the people willingly acquiesce in his authority, they never imagine, that their consent made him sovereign. They consent; because they apprehend him to be already, by birth, their lawful sovereign. And as to that tacit consent, which may now be inferred from their living under his dominion, this is no more than what they formerly gave to the tyrant and usurper.

When we assert, that all lawful government arises from the consent of the people, we certainly do them a great deal more honour than they deserve, or even expect and desire from us. After the ROMAN dominions became too unwieldly for the republic to govern them, the people, over the whole known world, were extremely grateful to AUGUSTUS[162] for that authority, which, by violence, he had established over them; and they shewed an equal disposition to submit to the successor, whom he left them, by his last will and testament. It was afterwards their misfortune, that there never was, in one family, any long regular succession; but that their line of princes was continually broken, either by private assassinations or public rebellions. The *praetorian* bands, on the failure of every family, set up one emperor; the legions in the East a second; those in GERMANY, perhaps, a third: And the sword alone could decide the controversy. The condition of the people, in that mighty monarchy, was to be lamented, not because the choice of the emperor was never left to them; for that was impracticable: But because they never fell under any succession of masters,

162. [Augustus was the first Emperor of the Roman Empire. See n. 20.]

who might regularly follow each other. As to the violence and wars and bloodshed, occasioned by every new settlement; these were not blameable, because they were inevitable.

The house of LANCASTER ruled in this island about sixty years;[163] yet the partizans of the white rose seemed daily to multiply in ENGLAND. The present establishment has taken place during a still longer period. Have all views of right in another family been utterly extinguished; even though scarce any man now alive had arrived at years of discretion, when it was expelled, or could have consented to its dominion, or have promised it allegiance? A sufficient indication surely of the general sentiment of mankind on this head. For we blame not the partizans of the abdicated family, merely on account of the long time, during which they have preserved their imaginary loyalty. We blame them for adhering to a family, which, we affirm, has been justly expelled, and which, from the moment the new settlement took place, had forfeited all title to authority.

But would we have a more regular, at least a more philosophical, refutation of this principle of an original contract or popular consent; perhaps, the following observations may suffice.

All *moral* duties may be divided into two kinds.[164] The *first* are those, to which men are impelled by a natural instinct or immediate propensity, which operates on them, independent of all ideas of obligation, and of all views, either to public or private utility. Of this nature are, love of children, gratitude to benefactors, pity to the unfortunate. When we reflect on the advantage, which results to society from such humane instincts, we pay them the just tribute of moral approbation and esteem: But the person, actuated by them, feels their power and influence, antecedent to any such reflection.

The *second* kind of moral duties are such as are not supported by any original instinct of nature, but are performed entirely from a sense of obligation, when we consider the necessities of human society, and the impossibility of supporting it, if these duties were neglected. It is thus *justice* or a regard to the property of others, *fidelity* or the observance of promises, become obligatory, and acquire an authority over mankind. For as it is evident, that every man loves himself better than any other person, he is naturally impelled to extend his acquisitions

163. [From 1399 to 1461 and from 1470 to 1471.]

164. [These two kinds of duties correspond to the distinction that Hume draws in the *Treatise* between natural and artificial virtues. See n. 1.]

as much as possible; and nothing can restrain him in this propensity, but reflection and experience, by which he learns the pernicious effects of that licence, and the total dissolution of society which must ensue from it. His original inclination, therefore, or instinct, is here checked and restrained by a subsequent judgment or observation.

The case is precisely the same with the political or civil duty of *allegiance,* as with the natural duties of justice and fidelity.[165] Our primary instincts lead us, either to indulge ourselves in unlimited freedom, or to seek dominion over others: And it is reflection only, which engages us to sacrifice such strong passions to the interests of peace and public order. A small degree of experience and observation suffices to teach us, that society cannot possibly be maintained without the authority of magistrates, and that this authority must soon fall into contempt, where exact obedience is not payed to it. The observation of these general and obvious interests is the source of all allegiance, and of that moral obligation, which we attribute to it.

What necessity, therefore, is there to found the duty of *allegiance* or obedience to magistrates on that of *fidelity* or a regard to promises, and to suppose, that it is the consent of each individual, which subjects him to government; when it appears, that both allegiance and fidelity stand precisely on the same foundation, and are both submitted to by mankind, on account of the apparent interests and necessities of human society? We are bound to obey our sovereign, it is said; because we have given a tacit promise to that purpose. But why are we bound to observe our promise? It must here be asserted, that the commerce and intercourse of mankind, which are of such mighty advantage, can have no security where men pay no regard to their engagements. In like manner, may it be said, that men could not live at all in society, at least in a civilized society, without laws and magistrates and judges, to prevent the encroachments of the strong upon the weak, of the violent upon the just and equitable. The obligation to allegiance being of like force and authority with the obligation to fidelity, we gain nothing by

165. [In the *Treatise,* Hume classifies justice, allegiance, and fidelity as *artificial* virtues. However, both here and in his *An Enquiry Concerning the Principles of Morals,* Hume writes of these virtues or duties as *natural.* Nevertheless, Hume has not changed his position. Critics of the *Treatise* often conflated the artificial with the arbitrary, claiming that, for Hume, justice is simply an arbitrary feature of human affairs. To circumvent this criticism that he took to be entirely unfounded, Hume altered the words that he used to express the distinction between those virtues and duties for which there is an original instinct and those for which there is not.]

resolving the one into the other. The general interests or necessities of society are sufficient to establish both.

If the reason be asked of that obedience, which we are bound to pay to government, I readily answer, *because society could not otherwise subsist:* And this answer is clear and intelligible to all mankind. Your answer is, *because we should keep our word.* But besides, that no body, till trained in a philosophical system, can either comprehend or relish this answer: Besides this, I say, you find yourself embarrassed, when it is asked, *why we are bound to keep our word?* Nor can you give any answer, but what would, immediately, without any circuit, have accounted for our obligation to allegiance.

But *to whom is allegiance due? And who is our lawful sovereign?*[166] This question is often the most difficult of any, and liable to infinite discussions. When people are so happy, that they can answer, *Our present sovereign, who inherits, in a direct line, from ancestors, that have governed us for many ages;* this answer admits of no reply; even though historians, in tracing up to the remotest antiquity, the origin of that royal family, may find, as commonly happens, that its first authority was derived from usurpation and violence. It is confessed, that private justice, or the abstinence from the properties of others, is a most cardinal virtue: Yet reason tells us, that there is no property in durable objects, such as lands or houses, when carefully examined in passing from hand to hand, but must, in some period, have been founded on fraud and injustice. The necessities of human society, neither in private nor public life, will allow of such an accurate enquiry: And there is no virtue or moral duty, but what may, with facility, be refined away, if we indulge a false philosophy, in sifting and scrutinizing it, by every captious rule of logic, in every light or position, in which it may be placed.

The questions with regard to private property have filled infinite volumes of law and philosophy, if in both we add the commentators to the original text; and in the end, we may safely pronounce, that many of the rules, there established, are uncertain, ambiguous, and arbitrary. The like opinion may be formed with regard to the succession and rights of princes and forms of government. Several cases, no doubt, occur, especially in the infancy of any constitution, which admit of no determination from the laws of justice and equity: And our historian

166. [Hume discusses these questions in greater detail in the *Treatise*, pp. 62–73 (in this edition).]

RAPIN pretends, that the controversy between EDWARD the Third and PHILIP DE VALOIS was of this nature, and could be decided only by an appeal to heaven, that is, by war and violence.[167]

Who shall tell me, whether GERMANICUS or DRUSUS ought to have succeeded to TIBERIUS,[168] had he died, while they were both alive, without naming any of them for his successor? Ought the right of adoption to be received as equivalent to that of blood, in a nation, where it had the same effect in private families, and had already, in two instances, taken place in the public? Ought GERMANICUS to be esteemed the elder son because he was born before DRUSUS; or the younger, because he was adopted after the birth of his brother? Ought the right of the elder to be regarded in a nation, where he had no advantage in the succession of private families? Ought the ROMAN empire at that time to be deemed hereditary, because of two examples; or ought it, even so early, to be regarded as belonging to the stronger or to the present possessor, as being founded on so recent an usurpation?

COMMODUS mounted the throne after a pretty long succession of excellent emperors, who had acquired their title, not by birth, or public election, but by the fictitious rite of adoption. That bloody debauchee being murdered by a conspiracy suddenly formed between his wench and her gallant, who happened at that time to be *Praetorian Praefect;* these immediately deliberated about choosing a master to human kind, to speak in the style of those ages; and they cast their eyes on PERTINAX. Before the tyrant's death was known, the *Praefect* went secretly to that senator, who, on the appearance of the soldiers, imagined that his execution had been ordered by COMMODUS. He was immediately saluted emperor by the officer and his attendants; chearfully proclaimed by the populace; unwillingly submitted to by the guards; formally recognized by the senate; and passively received by the provinces and armies of the empire.

The discontent of the *Praetorian* bands broke out in a sudden sedition, which occasioned the murder of that excellent prince: And the world being now without a master and without government, the guards

167. [Paul de Rapin-Thoyras (1661–1725) wrote a ten-volume history of England that was the standard work on this subject prior to Hume's. The controversy Rapin is discussing concerns who will succeed Charles IV of France upon his death in 1328.]

168. [Tiberius was Emperor of Rome from A.D. 14 to 37. Germanicus, born in 24 B.C., was adopted by his uncle Tiberius in A.D. 4. Drusus, the biological son of Tiberius, was born in 13 B.C.]

thought proper to set the empire formally to sale. JULIAN, the purchaser, was proclaimed by the soldiers, recognized by the senate, and submitted to by the people; and must also have been submitted to by the provinces, had not the envy of the legions begotten opposition and resistance. PESCENNIUS NIGER in SYRIA elected himself emperor, gained the tumultuary consent of his army, and was attended with the secret good-will of the senate and people of ROME. ALBINUS in BRITAIN found an equal right to set up his claim; but SEVERUS, who governed PANNONIA, prevailed in the end above both of them. That able politician and warrior, finding his own birth and dignity too much inferior to the imperial crown, professed, at first, an intention only of revenging the death of PERTINAX. He marched as general into ITALY; defeated JULIAN; and without our being able to fix any precise commencement even of the soldiers' consent, he was from necessity acknowledged emperor by the senate and people; and fully established in his violent authority by subduing NIGER and ALBINUS.[169]

Inter haec Gordianus CAESAR (says CAPITOLINUS, speaking of another period) *sublatus a militibus.* Imperator *est appellatus, quia non erat alius in proesenti,*[170] It is to be remarked, that GORDIAN was a boy of fourteen years of age.

Frequent instances of a like nature occur in the history of the emperors; in that of ALEXANDER'S[171] successors; and of many other countries: Nor can any thing be more unhappy than a despotic government of this kind; where the succession is disjointed and irregular, and must be determined, on every vacancy, by force or election. In a free

169. HERODIAN, lib. ii. [Herodian (third century A.D.), *History of the Empire from the Time of Marcus Aurelius*, 2. Commodus, the elder son of Marcus Aurelius (the Emperor and philosopher), was Emperor of Rome from A.D. 180 to 192. Following Commodus' assassination, Pertinax became Emperor and he attempted to honor what he took to be the principles of government of Marcus Aurelius. Pertinax was himself assassinated in March of A.D. 193. Julian, Pescennius Niger, Albinus, and Severus were all vying to be Emperor, with Severus winning out and holding the position until A.D. 211.]

170. [Julius Capitolinus (n.d.), *Maximus and Balbinus*, sec. 14, in *Scriptores Historiae Augustae*: "In the meantime Gordian Caesar was lifted up by the soldiers {in A.D. 238} and hailed emperor (that is, Augustus), there being no one else at hand" (trans. by D. Magie).]

171. [Alexander the Great of Macedon (356–323 B.C.) established a vast Greek empire that extended into Asia, Persia, Egypt, and India.]

government, the matter is often unavoidable, and is also much less dangerous. The interests of liberty may there frequently lead the people, in their own defence, to alter the succession of the crown. And the constitution, being compounded of parts, may still maintain a sufficient stability, by resting on the aristocratical or democratical members, though the monarchical be altered, from time to time, in order to accommodate it to the former.

In an absolute government, when there is no legal prince, who has a title to the throne, it may safely be determined to belong to the first occupant. Instances of this kind are but too frequent, especially in the eastern monarchies. When any race of princes expires, the will or destination of the last sovereign will be regarded as a title. Thus the edict of LEWIS the XIVth,[172] who called the bastard princes to the succession in case of the failure of all the legitimate princes, would, in such an event, have some authority.[173] Thus the will of CHARLES the Second[174] disposed of the whole SPANISH monarchy. The cession of the ancient proprietor, especially when joined to conquest, is likewise deemed a good title. The general obligation, which binds us to government, is the interest and necessities of society; and this obligation is very strong. The determination of it to this or that particular prince or form of government is frequently more uncertain and dubious.

172. [Louis XIV's (1638–1715) government ruled from 1643 to 1715, with Louis assuming direct power in 1661.]

173. It is remarkable, that, in the remonstrance of the duke of BOURBON and the legitimate princes, against this destination of LOUIS the XIVth, the doctrine of the *original contract* is insisted on, even in that absolute government. The FRENCH nation, say they, chusing HUGH CAPET [Elected king of the Franks in 987.] and his posterity to rule over them and their posterity, where the former line fails, there is a tacit right reserved to choose a new royal family; and this right is invaded by calling the bastard princes to the throne, without the consent of the nation. But the Comte de BOULAINVILLIERS, who wrote in defence of the bastard princes, ridicules this notion of an original contract, especially when applied to HUGH CAPET; who mounted the throne, says he, by the same arts, which have ever been employed by all conquerors and usurpers. He got his title, indeed, recognized by the states after he had put himself in possession: But is this a choice or contract? The Comte de BOULAINVILLIERS, we may observe, was a noted republican; but being a man of learning, and very conversant in history, he knew that the people were never almost consulted in these revolutions and new establishments, and that time alone bestowed right and authority on what was commonly at first founded on force and violence. See *Etat de la France,* Vol. III. [Henri de Boulainvilliers (1658–1722), *Etat de la France*, 3 vols., 1727.]

174. [King of Spain from 1665 to 1700.]

Present possession has considerable authority in these cases, and greater than in private property; because of the disorders which attend all revolutions and changes of government.

We shall only observe, before we conclude, that, though an appeal to general opinion may justly, in the speculative sciences of metaphysics, natural philosophy, or astronomy, be deemed unfair and inconclusive, yet in all questions with regard to morals, as well as criticism, there is really no other standard, by which any controversy can ever be decided. And nothing is a clearer proof, that a theory of this kind is erroneous, than to find, that it leads to paradoxes, repugnant to the common sentiments of mankind, and to the practice and opinion of all nations and all ages. The doctrine, which founds all lawful government on an *original contract*, or consent of the people, is plainly of this kind; nor has the most noted of its partizans, in prosecution of it, scrupled to affirm, *that absolute monarchy is inconsistent with civil society, and so can be no form of civil government at all;*[175] and that *the supreme power in a state cannot take from any man, by taxes and impositions, any part of his property, without his own consent or that of his representatives.*[176] What authority any moral reasoning can have, which leads into opinions so wide of the general practice of mankind, in every place but this single kingdom, it is easy to determine.

The only passage I meet with in antiquity, where the obligation of obedience to government is ascribed to a promise, is in PLATO'S *Crito:* where SOCRATES refuses to escape from prison, because he had tacitly promised to obey the laws.[177] Thus he builds a *tory* consequence of passive obedience, on a *whig* foundation of the original contract.

New discoveries are not to be expected in these matters. If scarce any man, till very lately, ever imagined that government was founded on compact, it is certain, that it cannot, in general, have any such foundation.

The crime of rebellion among the ancients was commonly expressed by the terms *νεωτερίζειν, novas res moliri.*[178]

175. See LOCKE on Government, chap. vii. sec. 90. [John Locke (1632–1704), *Two Treatises of Government*, ed. by P. Laslett, student edition (Cambridge: Cambridge University Press, 1988), p. 326.]

176. Id. chap. xi. sec. 138, 139, 140. [Locke, *Two Treatises of Government*, pp. 360–62.]

177. [In Plato's (428–348 B.C.) dialogue *Crito*, Crito comes to Socrates (469–399 B.C.) offering him the chance to escape from his prison cell after he has been condemned to death.]

178. [The terms refer to innovation, especially political innovation.]

Essay XII: *Of Passive Obedience*

In the former essay, we endeavoured to refute the *speculative* systems of politics advanced in this nation; as well the religious system of the one party, as the philosophical of the other. We come now to examine the *practical* consequences, deduced by each party, with regard to the measures of submission due to sovereigns.

As the obligation to justice is founded entirely on the interests of society, which require mutual abstinence from property, in order to preserve peace among mankind; it is evident, that, when the execution of justice would be attended with very pernicious consequences, that virtue must be suspended, and give place to public utility, in such extraordinary and such pressing emergencies. The maxim, *fiat Justitia et ruat Coelum,* let justice be performed, though the universe be destroyed, is apparently false, and by sacrificing the end to the means, shews a preposterous idea of the subordination of duties. What governor of a town makes any scruple of burning the suburbs, when they facilitate the approaches of the enemy? Or what general abstains from plundering a neutral country, when the necessities of war require it, and he cannot otherwise subsist his army? The case is the same with the duty of allegiance; and common sense teaches us, that, as government binds us to obedience only on account of its tendency to public utility, that duty must always, in extraordinary cases, when public ruin would evidently attend obedience, yield to the primary and original obligation. *Salus populi suprema Lex,* the safety of the people is the supreme law. This maxim is agreeable to the sentiments of mankind in all ages: Nor is any one, when he reads of the insurrections against NERO[179] or PHILIP the Second,[180] so infatuated with party-systems, as not to wish success to the enterprize, and praise the undertakers. Even our high monarchical party, in spite of their sublime theory, are forced, in such cases, to judge, and feel, and approve, in conformity to the rest of mankind.

Resistance, therefore, being admitted in extraordinary emergencies, the question can only be among good reasoners, with regard to the degree of necessity, which can justify resistance, and render it lawful or commendable. And here I must confess, that I shall always incline

179. [Roman Emperor from A.D. 54 to 68.]

180. [King of Spain from 1556 to 1598.]

to their side, who draw the bond of allegiance very close, and consider an infringement of it, as the last refuge in desperate cases, when the public is in the highest danger, from violence and tyranny. For besides the mischiefs of a civil war, which commonly attends insurrection; it is certain, that, where a disposition to rebellion appears among any people, it is one chief cause of tyranny in the rulers, and forces them into many violent measures which they never would have embraced, had every one been inclined to submission and obedience. Thus the *tyrannicide* or assassination, approved of by ancient maxims, instead of keeping tyrants and usurpers in awe, made them ten times more fierce and unrelenting; and is now justly, upon that account, abolished by the laws of nations, and universally condemned as a base and treacherous method of bringing to justice these disturbers of society.

Besides we must consider, that, as obedience is our duty in the common course of things, it ought chiefly to be inculcated; nor can any thing be more preposterous than an anxious care and solicitude in stating all the cases, in which resistance may be allowed. In like manner, though a philosopher reasonably acknowledges, in the course of an argument, that the rules of justice may be dispensed with in cases of urgent necessity; what should we think of a preacher or casuist, who should make it his chief study to find out such cases, and enforce them with all the vehemence of argument and eloquence? Would he not be better employed in inculcating the general doctrine, than in displaying the particular exceptions, which we are, perhaps, but too much inclined, of ourselves, to embrace and to extend?

There are, however, two reasons, which may be pleaded in defence of that party among us, who have, with so much industry, propagated the maxims of resistance; maxims, which, it must be confessed, are, in general, so pernicious, and so destructive of civil society. The *first* is, that their antagonists carrying the doctrine of obedience to such an extravagant height, as not only never to mention the exceptions in extraordinary cases (which might, perhaps, be excusable) but even positively to exclude them; it became necessary to insist on these exceptions, and defend the rights of injured truth and liberty. The *second*, and, perhaps, better reason, is founded on the nature of the BRITISH constitution and form of government.

It is almost peculiar to our constitution to establish a first magistrate with such high pre-eminence and dignity, that, though limited by the laws, he is, in a manner, so far as regards his own person, above the laws, and can neither be questioned nor punished for any injury or wrong, which may be committed by him. His ministers alone, or those who act by his commission, are obnoxious to justice; and while the prince is thus allured, by the prospect of personal safety, to give the laws their free course, an equal security is, in effect, obtained by the punishment of lesser offenders, and at the same time a civil war is avoided, which would be the infallible consequence, were an attack, at every turn, made directly upon the sovereign. But though the constitution pays this salutary compliment to the prince, it can never reasonably be understood, by that maxim, to have determined its own destruction, or to have established a tame submission, where he protects his ministers, perseveres in injustice, and usurps the whole power of the commonwealth. This case, indeed, is never expressly put by the laws; because it is impossible for them, in their ordinary course, to provide a remedy for it, or establish any magistrate, with superior authority, to chastise the exorbitancies of the prince. But as a right without a remedy would be an absurdity; the remedy in this case, is the extraordinary one of resistance, when affairs come to that extremity, that the constitution can be defended by it alone. Resistance therefore must, of course, become more frequent in the BRITISH government, than in others, which are simpler, and consist of fewer parts and movements. Where the king is an absolute sovereign, he has little temptation to commit such enormous tyranny as may justly provoke rebellion: But where he is limited, his imprudent ambition, without any great vices, may run him into that perilous situation. This is frequently supposed to have been the case with CHARLES the First;[181] and if we may now speak truth, after animosities are ceased, this was also the case with JAMES the Second.[182] These were harmless, if not, in their private character, good men; but mistaking the nature of our constitution, and engrossing the whole legislative power, it became necessary to oppose them with some vehemence; and even to deprive the latter formally of that authority, which he had used with such imprudence and indiscretion.

Essay XIII: *Of Superstition and Enthusiasm*

That the corruption of the best things produces the worst, is grown into a maxim, and is commonly proved, among other instances, by the pernicious effects of *superstition* and *enthusiasm,* the corruptions of true religion.

181. [See n. 84.]
182. [See n. 135.]

These two species of false religion, though both pernicious, are yet of a very different, and even of a contrary nature. The mind of man is subject to certain unaccountable terrors and apprehensions, proceeding either from the unhappy situation of private or public affairs, from ill health, from a gloomy and melancholy disposition, or from the concurrence of all these circumstances. In such a state of mind, infinite unknown evils are dreaded from unknown agents; and where real objects of terror are wanting, the soul, active to its own prejudice, and fostering its predominant inclination, finds imaginary ones, to whose power and malevolence it sets no limits. As these enemies are entirely invisible and unknown, the methods taken to appease them are equally unaccountable, and consist in ceremonies, observances, mortifications, sacrifices, presents, or in any practice, however absurd or frivolous, which either folly or knavery recommends to a blind and terrified credulity. Weakness, fear, melancholy, together with ignorance, are, therefore, the true sources of SUPERSTITION.

But the mind of man is also subject to an unaccountable elevation and presumption, arising from prosperous success, from luxuriant health, from strong spirits, or from a bold and confident disposition. In such a state of mind, the imagination swells with great, but confused conceptions, to which no sublunary beauties or enjoyments can correspond. Every thing mortal and perishable vanishes as unworthy of attention. And a full range is given to the fancy in the invisible regions or world of spirits, where the soul is at liberty to indulge itself in every imagination, which may best suit its present taste and disposition. Hence arise raptures, transports, and surprising flights of fancy; and confidence and presumption still encreasing, these raptures, being altogether unaccountable, and seeming quite beyond the reach of our ordinary faculties, are attributed to the immediate inspiration of that Divine Being, who is the object of devotion. In a little time, the inspired person comes to regard himself as a distinguished favourite of the Divinity; and when this frenzy once takes place, which is the summit of enthusiasm, every whimsy is consecrated: Human reason, and even morality are rejected as fallacious guides: And the fanatic madman delivers himself over, blindly, and without reserve, to the supposed illapses of the spirit, and to inspiration from above. Hope, pride, presumption, a warm imagination, together with ignorance, are, therefore, the true sources of ENTHUSIASM.

These two species of false religion might afford occasion to many speculations; but I shall confine myself, at present, to a few reflections concerning their different influence on government and society.

My first reflection is, *That superstition is favourable to priestly power, and enthusiasm not less or rather more contrary to it, than sound reason and philosophy.* As superstition is founded on fear, sorrow, and a depression of spirits, it represents the man to himself in such despicable colours, that he appears unworthy, in his own eyes, of approaching the divine presence, and naturally has recourse to any other person, whose sanctity of life, or, perhaps, impudence and cunning, have made him be supposed more favoured by the Divinity. To him the superstitious entrust their devotions: To his care they recommend their prayers, petitions, and sacrifices: And by his means, they hope to render their addresses acceptable to their incensed Deity. Hence the origin of PRIESTS, who may justly be regarded as an invention of a timorous and abject superstition, which, ever diffident of itself, dares not offer up its own devotions, but ignorantly thinks to recommend itself to the Divinity, by the mediation of his supposed friends and servants. As superstition is a considerable ingredient in almost all religions, even the most fanatical; there being nothing but philosophy able entirely to conquer these unaccountable terrors; hence it proceeds, that in almost every sect of religion there are priests to be found: But the stronger mixture there is of superstition, the higher is the authority of the priesthood.

On the other hand, it may be observed, that all enthusiasts have been free from the yoke of ecclesiastics, and have expressed great independence in their devotion; with a contempt of forms, ceremonies, and traditions. The *quakers* are the most egregious, though, at the same time, the most innocent enthusiasts that have yet been known; and are, perhaps, the only sect, that have never admitted priests amongst them. The *independents,*[183] of all the ENGLISH sectaries, approach nearest to the *quakers* in fanaticism, and in their freedom from priestly bondage. The *presbyterians*[184] follow after, at an equal distance in both

183. [Hume vividly discusses the place of Independents in the English Civil War of 1642–52 in *The History of England*, volume V, pp. 441–45. There he says, "The fanaticism of the independents, exalted to a higher pitch {than the presbyterians}, abolished ecclesiastical government, disdained creeds and systems, neglected every ceremony, and confounded all ranks and orders. The soldier, the merchant, the mechanic, indulging the fervors of zeal, and guided by the illapses of the spirit, resigned himself to an inward and superior direction, and was consecrated, in a manner, by an immediate intercourse and communication with heaven" (p. 442). Despite this zeal, Hume reports, the independents were also constant defenders of some form of religious toleration.]

184. [Presbyterians were opposed to Episcopacy (church rule by Bishops who owed their appointment to the Crown) and favored a return to a more primitive form of church

particulars. In short this observation is founded in experience; and will also appear to be founded in reason, if we consider, that, as enthusiasm arises from a presumptuous pride and confidence, it thinks itself sufficiently qualified to *approach* the Divinity, without any human mediator. Its rapturous devotions are so fervent, that it even imagines itself *actually* to *approach* him by the way of contemplation and inward converse; which makes it neglect all those outward ceremonies and observances, to which the assistance of the priests appears so requisite in the eyes of their superstitious votaries. The fanatic consecrates himself, and bestows on his own person a sacred character, much superior to what forms and ceremonious institutions can confer on any other.

My *second* reflection with regard to these species of false religion is, *that religions, which partake of enthusiasm are, on their first rise, more furious and violent than those which partake of superstition; but in a little time become more gentle and moderate.* The violence of this species of religion, when excited by novelty, and animated by opposition, appears from numberless instances; of the *anabaptists* in GERMANY, the *camisars* in FRANCE, the *levellers* and other fanatics in ENGLAND, and the *covenanters* in SCOTLAND.[185] Enthusiasm being founded on strong spirits, and a presumptuous boldness of character, it naturally begets the most extreme resolutions; especially after it rises to that height as to inspire the deluded fanatic with the opinion of divine illuminations, and with a contempt for the common rules of reason, morality, and prudence.

It is thus enthusiasm produces the most cruel disorders in human society; but its fury is like that of thunder and tempest, which exhaust themselves in a little time, and leave the air more calm and serene

---

organization. They played a significant role in the English Civil War. See Hume's *The History of England*, vols. V and VI, generally.]

185. [The Anabaptists, so-called because they were opposed to baptism at birth, favoring instead baptism only for repenting adults, led several peasant uprisings in Germany and Switzerland from 1525 to 1534. The Camisards were French Calvinists who rebelled against the persecution that resulted from Louis XIV's revocation of the Edict of Nantes (1685). The Levellers came into existence during the English Civil War in opposition to any form of aristocracy and hierarchical relationship; many of the Levellers were Anabaptists. The Covenanters were adherents of a Covenant agreed to in Edinburgh, partially in opposition to Charles I (see n. 84), and partially in opposition to popery. Hume remarks that the covenant was "fitted to inflame the minds of men against their fellow creatures." Defenders of the covenant thought that only "rebels to God, and traitors to their country" could oppose the covenant (*The History of England*, vol. V, p. 258; see pp. 249–82, generally).]

than before. When the first fire of enthusiasm is spent, men naturally, in all fanatical sects, sink into the greatest remissness and coolness in sacred matters; there being no body of men among them, endowed with sufficient authority, whose interest is concerned to support the religious spirit: No rites, no ceremonies, no holy observances, which may enter into the common train of life, and preserve the sacred principles from oblivion. Superstition, on the contrary, steals in gradually and insensibly; renders men tame and submissive; is acceptable to the magistrate, and seems inoffensive to the people: Till at last the priest, having firmly established his authority, becomes the tyrant and disturber of human society, by his endless contentions, persecutions, and religious wars. How smoothly did the ROMISH church advance in her acquisition of power? But into what dismal convulsions did she throw all EUROPE, in order to maintain it? On the other hand, our sectaries who were formerly such dangerous bigots, are now become very free reasoners; and the *quakers* seem to approach nearly the only regular body of *deists* in the universe, the *literati*, or the disciples of CONFUCIUS in CHINA.[186]

My *third* observation on this head is, *that superstition is an enemy to civil liberty, and enthusiasm a friend to it.* As superstition groans under the dominion of priests, and enthusiasm is destructive of all ecclesiastical power, this sufficiently accounts for the present observation. Not to mention, that enthusiasm, being the infirmity of bold and ambitious tempers, is naturally accompanied with a spirit of liberty; as superstition, on the contrary, renders men tame and abject, and fits them for slavery. We learn from ENGLISH history, that, during the civil wars, the *independents* and *deists*, though the most opposite in their religious principles; yet were united in their political ones, and were alike passionate for a commonwealth. And since the origin of *whig* and *tory*,[187] the leaders of the *whigs* have either been *deists* or profest *latitudinarians* in their principles; that is, friends to toleration, and indifferent to any particular sect of *christians:* While the sectaries, who have all a strong tincture of enthusiasm, have always, without exception, concurred with that party, in defence of civil liberty. The resemblance in their superstitions long united the high-church *tories*, and the *Roman catholics*, in support of prerogative

186. The CHINESE Literati have no priests or ecclesiastical establishment. [Confucius (551–479 B.C.) was an important Chinese thinker, whose views on virtue are close in certain respects to those of Aristotle (384–22 B.C.).]

187. [See n. 86.]

and kingly power; though experience of the tolerating spirit of the *whigs* seems of late to have reconciled the *catholics* to that party.

The *molinists* and *jansenists* in FRANCE have a thousand unintelligible disputes, which are not worthy the reflection of a man of sense: But what principally distinguishes these two sects, and alone merits attention, is the different spirit of their religion. The *molinists* conducted by the *jesuits*, are great friends to superstition, rigid observers of external forms and ceremonies, and devoted to the authority of the priests, and to tradition. The *jansenists* are enthusiasts, and zealous promoters of the passionate devotion, and of the inward life; little influenced by authority; and, in a word, but half catholics. The consequences are exactly conformable to the foregoing reasoning. The *jesuits* are the tyrants of the people, and the slaves of the court: And the *jansenists* preserve alive the small sparks of the love of liberty, which are to be found in the FRENCH nation.[188]

Essay XIV: *Of Moral Prejudices*

There is a Set of Men lately sprung up amongst us, who endeavour to distinguish themselves by ridiculing every Thing, that has hitherto appear'd sacred and venerable in the Eyes of Mankind. Reason, Sobriety, Honour, Friendship, Marriage, are the perpetual Subjects of their insipid Raillery: And even public Spirit, and a Regard to our Country, are treated as chimerical and romantic. Were the Schemes of these Anti-reformers to take Place, all the Bonds of Society must be broke, to make Way for the Indulgence of a licentious Mirth and Gaiety: The Companion of our drunken Frollics must be prefer'd to a Friend or Brother: Dissolute Prodigality must be supply'd at the Expence of every Thing valuable, either in public or private: And Men shall have so little Regard to any Thing beyond themselves, that, at last, a free Constitution of Government must become a Scheme perfectly impracticable among Mankind, and must degenerate into one universal System of Fraud and Corruption.

There is another Humour, which may be observ'd in some Pretenders to Wisdom, and which, if not so pernicious as the idle petulant Humour above-mention'd, must, however, have a very bad Effect on those, who indulge it. I mean that grave philosophic Endeavour after

188. [For more on this seventeenth-century theological dispute, see R.A. Knox, *Enthusiasm: A Chapter in the History of Religion* (Oxford: At the Clarendon Press, 1950).]

Perfection, which, under Pretext of reforming Prejudices and Errors, strikes at all the most endearing Sentiments of the Heart, and all the most useful Byasses and Instincts, which can govern a human Creature. The *Stoics*[189] were remarkable for this Folly among the Antients; and I wish some of more venerable Characters in latter Times had not copy'd them too faithfully in this Particular. The virtuous and tender Sentiments, or Prejudices, if you will, have suffer'd mightily by these Reflections; while a certain sullen Pride or Contempt of Mankind has prevail'd in their Stead, and has been esteem'd the greatest Wisdom; tho', in Reality, it be the most egregious Folly of all others. *Statilius* being sollicited by *Brutus* to make one of that noble Band, who struck the GOD-like Stroke for the Liberty of *Rome,* refus'd to accompany them, saying, *That all Men were Fools or Mad, and did not deserve that a wise Man should trouble his Head about them.*[190]

My learned Reader will here easily recollect the Reason, which an antient Philosopher gave, why he wou'd not be reconcil'd to his Brother, who sollicited his Friendship. He was too much a Philosopher to think, that the Connexion of having sprung from the same Parent, ought to have any Influence on a reasonable Mind, and exprest his Sentiment after such a Manner as I think not proper to repeat. When your Friend is in Affliction, says *Epictetus,* you may counterfeit a Sympathy with him, if it give him Relief; but take Care not to allow any Compassion to sink into your Heart, or disturb that Tranquillity, which is the Perfection of Wisdom. *Diogenes* being ask'd by his Friends in his Sickness, What should be done with him after his Death? *Why,* says he, *throw me out into the Fields.* "What! reply'd they, to the Birds or Beasts." *No: Place a Cudgel by me, to defend myself withal.* "To what Purpose, say they, you will not have any Sense, nor any Power of making Use of it." *Then if the Beasts shou'd devour me,* cries he, *shall I be any more*

189. [Stoicism was a Hellenistic school of philosophy that began with Zeno around 300 B.C. and continued into the first century of the Roman Empire. Stoicism also exercised some influence in Europe in the sixteenth through seventeenth centuries. Hume draws from four of the ancient schools of philosophy in his essays: "The Epicurean," "The Stoic," "The Platonist," and "The Sceptic" (See *Essays, Moral, Political, and Literary*).]

190. [Hume is citing a line from Plutarch's life of Brutus. Brutus is unsure whether to let Statilius know of his conspiracy against Caesar. Under the cover of a philosophical dispute, Brutus learns what Statilius's sentiments would be based on the remark that Hume cites, and he decides to leave Statilius in the dark. See *Plutarch's Lives*, trans. by J. Langhorne and W. Langhorne, 6 vols. (London: Sharpe and Son, 1819), vol. VI, p. 70.]

sensible of it? I know none of the Sayings of that Philosopher, which shews more evidently both the Liveliness and Ferocity of his Temper.

How different from these are the Maxims by which *Eugenius* conducts himself! In his Youth he apply'd himself, with the most unwearied Labour, to the Study of Philosophy; and nothing was ever able to draw him from it, except when an Opportunity offer'd of serving his Friends, or doing a Pleasure to some Man of Merit. When he was about thirty Years of Age, he was determin'd to quit the free Life of a Batchelor (in which otherwise he wou'd have been inclin'd to remain) by considering, that he was the last Branch of an antient Family, which must have been extinguish'd had he died without Children. He made Choice of the virtuous and beautiful *Emira* for his Consort, who, after being the Solace of his Life for many Years, and having made him the Father of several Children, paid at last the general Debt to Nature. Nothing cou'd have supported him under so severe an Affliction, but the Consolation he receiv'd from his young Family, who were now become dearer to him on account of their deceast Mother. One Daughter in particular is his Darling, and the secret Joy of his Soul; because her Features, her Air, her Voice recal every Moment the tender Memory of his Spouse, and fill his Eyes with Tears. He conceals this Partiality as much as possible; and none but his intimate Friends are acquainted with it. To them he reveals all his Tenderness; nor is he so affectedly Philosophical, as even to call it by the Name of *Weakness*. They know, that he still keeps the Birth-day of *Emira* with Tears, and a more fond and tender Recollection of past Pleasures; in like Manner as it was celebrated in her Lifetime with Joy and Festivity. They know, that he preserves her Picture with the utmost Care, and has one Picture in Minature, which he always wears next to his Bosom: That he has left Orders in his last Will, that, in whatever Part of the World he shall happen to die, his Body shall be transported, and laid in the same Grave with her's: And that a Monument shall be erected over them, and their mutual Love and Happiness celebrated in an Epitaph, which he himself has compos'd for that Purpose.

A few Years ago I receiv'd a Letter from a Friend, who was abroad on his Travels, and shall here communicate it to the Public. It contains such an Instance of a Philosophic Spirit, as I think pretty extraordinary, and may serve as an Example, not to depart too far from the receiv'd Maxims of Conduct and Behaviour, by a refin'd Search after Happiness or Perfection. The Story I have been since assur'd of as Matter of Fact.

Paris, Aug. 2, 1737.

SIR,—I know you are more curious of Accounts of Men than of Buildings, and are more desirous of being inform'd of private History than of public Transactions; for which Reason, I thought the following Story, which is the common Topic of Conversation in this City, wou'd be no unacceptable Entertainment to you.

A young Lady of Birth and Fortune, being left intirely at her own Disposal, persisted long in a Resolution of leading a single Life, notwithstanding several advantageous Offers that had been made to her. She had been determin'd to embrace this Resolution, by observing the many unhappy Marriages among her Acquaintance, and by hearing the Complaints, which her Female Friends made of the Tyranny, Inconstancy, Jealousy or Indifference of their Husbands. Being a Woman of strong Spirit and an uncommon Way of thinking, she found no Difficulty either in forming or maintaining this Resolution, and cou'd not suspect herself of such Weakness, as ever to be induc'd, by any Temptation, to depart from it. She had, however, entertain'd a strong Desire of having a Son, whose Education she was resolv'd to make the principal Concern of her Life, and by that Means supply the Place of those other Passions, which she was resolv'd for ever to renounce. She push'd her Philosophy to such an uncommon Length, as to find no Contradiction betwixt such a Desire and her former Resolution; and accordingly look'd about, with great Deliberation, to find, among all her Male-Acquaintance, one whose Character and Person were agreeable to her, without being able to satisfy herself on that Head. At Length, being in the Play-house one Evening, she sees in the *Parterre,* a young Man of a most engaging Countenance and modest Deportment; and feels such a Prepossession in his Favour, that she had Hopes this must be the Person she had long sought for in vain. She immediately dispatches a Servant to him; desiring his Company, at her Lodgings, next Morning. The young Man was over-joy'd at the Message, and cou'd not command his Satisfaction, upon receiving such an Advance from a Lady of so great Beauty, Reputation and Quality. He was, therefore, much disappointed, when he found a Woman, who wou'd allow him no Freedoms; and amidst all her obliging Behaviour, confin'd and over-aw'd him to the Bounds of rational Discourse and Conversation. She seem'd, however, willing to commence a Friendship with him; and told him, that his Company wou'd always be acceptable to her, whenever he had a leisure Hour to bestow. He needed not much Entreaty to renew his Visits, being so struck with her Wit and Beauty, that he must have been unhappy, had he been debarr'd her Company. Every Conversation serv'd only the more to inflame his Passion, and gave him more Occasion to admire her Person and Understanding, as well as to rejoice in his own Good-fortune. He was not, however, without Anxiety, when he consider'd the Disproportion of their Birth and Fortune; nor was his Uneasiness allay'd even when he reflected on the extraordinary Manner in which their Acquaintance had commenc'd. Our Philosophical Heroine, in the mean Time, discover'd, that her Lover's personal Qualities did not belye his Phisiognomy; so that, judging there was no Occasion for any farther Trial, she takes a proper Opportunity of communicating to him her whole Intention. Their Intercourse continu'd for sometime, till at last her Wishes were crown'd, and she was now Mother of a Boy, who was to be the Object of her future Care and Concern. Gladly wou'd she have continu'd her Friendship with the Father; but finding him too passionate a Lover to remain within the Bounds of Friendship, she was oblig'd to put a Violence upon herself. She sends him a Letter, in which she had inclos'd a Bond of Annuity for a Thousand Crowns; desiring him, at the same Time, never to see her more, and to forget, if possible, all past Favours and Familiarities. He was Thunder-struck at receiving this Message; and, having tried, in vain, all the Arts that might win upon the Resolution of a Woman, resolv'd at last to attack her by her *Foible.* He commences a Law-suit against her before the Parliament of *Paris;* and claims his Son, whom he pretends a Right to educate as he pleas'd, according to the usual Maxims of the Law in such Cases. She pleads, on the other Hand, their express Agreement before their Commerce, and pretends, that he had renounc'd all Claim to any Offspring that might arise from their Embraces. It is not yet known, how the Parliament will determine in this extraordinary Case, which puzzles all the Lawyers, as much as it does the Philosophers. As soon as they come to any Issue, I shall inform you of it, and shall embrace any Opportunity of subscribing myself, as I do at present.

SIR,

Your most humble Servant.

Part IV
The Evolution of Civilization and Society

From *Essays, Moral, Political, and Literary*

Essay XV: *Of the Origin of Government*

Man, born in a family, is compelled to maintain society, from necessity, from natural inclination, and from habit. The same creature, in his farther progress, is engaged to establish political society, in order to administer justice; without which there can be no peace among them, nor safety, nor mutual intercourse. We are, therefore, to look upon all the vast apparatus of our government, as having ultimately no other object or purpose but the distribution of justice, or, in other words, the support of the twelve judges. Kings and parliaments, fleets and armies, officers of the court and revenue, ambassadors, ministers, and privy-counsellors, are all subordinate in their end to this part of administration. Even the clergy, as their duty leads them to inculcate morality, may justly be thought, so far as regards this world, to have no other useful object of their institution.

All men are sensible of the necessity of justice to maintain peace and order; and all men are sensible of the necessity of peace and order for the maintenance of society. Yet, notwithstanding this strong and obvious necessity, such is the frailty or perverseness of our nature! it is impossible to keep men, faithfully and unerringly, in the paths of justice. Some extraordinary circumstances may happen, in which a man finds his interests to be more promoted by fraud or rapine, than hurt by the breach which his injustice makes in the social union. But much more frequently, he is seduced from his great and important, but distant interests, by the allurement of present, though often very frivolous temptations. This great weakness is incurable in human nature.

Men must, therefore, endeavour to palliate what they cannot cure. They must institute some persons, under the appellation of magistrates, whose peculiar office it is, to point out the decrees of equity, to punish transgressors, to correct fraud and violence, and to oblige men, however reluctant, to consult their own real and permanent interests. In a word, OBEDIENCE is a new duty which must be invented to support that of JUSTICE; and the tyes of equity must be corroborated by those of allegiance.

But still, viewing matters in an abstract light, it may be thought, that nothing is gained by this alliance, and that the factitious duty of obedience, from its very nature, lays as feeble a hold of the human mind, as the primitive and natural duty of justice. Peculiar interests and present temptations may overcome the one as well as the other. They are equally exposed to the same inconvenience. And the man, who is inclined to be a bad neighbour, must be led by the same motives, well or ill understood, to be a bad citizen and subject. Not to mention, that the magistrate himself may often be negligent, or partial, or unjust in his administration.

Experience, however, proves, that there is a great difference between the cases. Order in society, we find, is much better maintained by means of government; and our duty to the magistrate is more strictly guarded by the principles of human nature, than our duty to our fellow-citizens. The love of dominion is so strong in the breast of man, that many, not only submit to, but court all the dangers, and fatigues, and cares of government; and men, once raised to that station, though often led astray by private passions, find, in ordinary cases, a visible interest in the impartial administration of justice. The persons, who first attain this distinction by the consent, tacit or express, of the people, must be endowed with superior personal qualities of valour, force, integrity, or prudence, which command respect and confidence: and after government is established, a regard to birth, rank, and station has a mighty influence over men, and enforces the decrees of the magistrate. The prince or leader exclaims against every disorder, which disturbs his society. He summons all his partizans and all men of probity to aid him in correcting and redressing it: and he is readily followed by all indifferent persons in the execution of his office. He soon acquires the power of rewarding these services; and in the progress of society, he establishes subordinate ministers and often a military force, who find an immediate and a visible interest, in supporting his authority. Habit soon consolidates what other principles of human nature had imperfectly founded; and men, once accustomed to obedience, never think of departing from that path, in which they and their ancestors have constantly trod, and to which they are confined by so many urgent and visible motives.

But though this progress of human affairs may appear certain and inevitable, and though the support which allegiance brings to justice, be founded on obvious principles of human nature, it cannot be expected that men should beforehand be able to discover them, or foresee their operation. Government commences more casually and more imperfectly. It is probable, that the first ascendant of one man over multitudes begun during a state of war; where the superiority of courage and of genius discovers itself most visibly, where unanimity and concert are most requisite, and where the pernicious effects of disorder are most sensibly felt. The long continuance of that state, an incident common among savage tribes, enured the people to submission; and if the chieftain possessed as much equity as prudence and valour, he became, even during peace, the arbiter of all differences, and could gradually, by a mixture of force and consent, establish his authority. The benefit sensibly felt from his influence, made it be cherished by the people, at least by the peaceable and well disposed among them; and if his son enjoyed the same good qualities, government advanced the sooner to maturity and perfection; but was still in a feeble state, till the farther progress of improvement procured the magistrate a revenue, and enabled him to bestow rewards on the several instruments of his administration, and to inflict punishments on the refractory and disobedient. Before that period, each exertion of his influence must have been particular, and founded on the peculiar circumstances of the case. After it, submission was no longer a matter of choice in the bulk of the community, but was rigorously exacted by the authority of the supreme magistrate.

In all governments, there is a perpetual intestine struggle, open or secret, between AUTHORITY and LIBERTY;[191] and neither of them can ever absolutely prevail in the contest. A great sacrifice of liberty must necessarily be made in every government; yet even the authority, which confines liberty, can never, and perhaps ought never, in any constitution, to become quite entire and uncontroulable. The sultan is master of the life and fortune of any individual; but will not be permitted to impose new taxes on his subjects: a French monarch can impose taxes at pleasure; but would find it dangerous to attempt the lives and fortunes of individuals. Religion also, in most countries, is commonly found to be a very intractable principle; and other principles or prejudices frequently resist all the authority of the civil magistrate; whose power, being founded on opinion, can never subvert other opin-

191. [This struggle is a constant theme of Hume's *The History of England*.]

ions, equally rooted with that of his title to dominion. The government, which, in common appellation, receives the appellation of free, is that which admits of a partition of power among several members, whose united authority is no less, or is commonly greater than that of any monarch; but who, in the usual course of administration, must act by general and equal laws, that are previously known to all the members and to all their subjects. In this sense, it must be owned, that liberty is the perfection of civil society; but still authority must be acknowledged essential to its very existence: and in those contests, which so often take place between the one and the other, the latter may, on that account, challenge the preference. Unless perhaps one may say (and it may be said with some reason) that a circumstance, which is essential to the existence of civil society, must always support itself, and needs be guarded with less jealousy, than one that contributes only to its perfection, which the indolence of men is so apt to neglect, or their ignorance to overlook.[192]

Essay XVI: *Of the Rise and Progress of the Arts and Sciences*

Nothing requires greater nicety, in our enquiries concerning human affairs, than to distinguish exactly what is owing to *chance,* and what proceeds from *causes;* nor is there any subject, in which an author is more liable to deceive himself by false subtilties and refinements. To say, that any event is derived from chance, cuts short all farther enquiry concerning it, and leaves the writer in the same state of ignorance with the rest of mankind. But when the event is supposed to proceed from certain and stable causes, he may then display his ingenuity, in assigning these causes; and as a man of any subtilty can never be at a loss in this particular, he has thereby an opportunity of swelling his volumes, and discovering his profound knowledge, in observing what escapes the vulgar and ignorant.[193]

The distinguishing between chance and causes must depend upon every particular man's sagacity, in considering every particular incident. But, if I were to assign any general rule to help us in applying this

192. [Hume discusses some of the themes in this essay in greater detail in the *Treatise,* bk. III, pt. II, sec. 7 (in this edition).]

193. [Hume looks at similar matters in the first two paragraphs of "Of Commerce" (in this edition).]

distinction, it would be the following, *What depends upon a few persons is, in a great measure, to be ascribed to chance, or secret and unknown causes: What arises from a great number, may often be accounted for by determinate and known causes.*

Two natural reasons may be assigned for this rule. *First,* If you suppose a dye to have any biass, however small, to a particular side, this biass, though, perhaps, it may not appear in a few throws, will certainly prevail in a great number, and will cast the balance entirely to that side. In like manner, when any *causes* beget a particular inclination or passion, at a certain time, and among a certain people; though many individuals may escape the contagion, and be ruled by passions peculiar to themselves; yet the multitude will certainly be seized by the common affection, and be governed by it in all their actions.

Secondly, Those principles or causes, which are fitted to operate on a multitude, are always of a grosser and more stubborn nature, less subject to accidents, and less influenced by whim and private fancy, than those which operate on a few only. The latter are commonly so delicate and refined, that the smallest incident in the health, education, or fortune of a particular person, is sufficient to divert their course, and retard their operation; nor is it possible to reduce them to any general maxims or observations. Their influence at one time will never assure us concerning their influence at another; even though all the general circumstances should be the same in both cases.

To judge by this rule, the domestic and the gradual revolutions of a state must be a more proper subject of reasoning and observation, than the foreign and the violent, which are commonly produced by single persons, and are more influenced by whim, folly, or caprice, than by general passions and interests. The depression of the lords, and rise of the commons in ENGLAND, after the statutes of alienation and the encrease of trade and industry, are more easily accounted for by general principles, than the depression of the SPANISH, and rise of the FRENCH monarchy, after the death of CHARLES QUINT.[194] Had HARRY IV., Cardinal RICHLIEU, and LOUIS XIV. been SPANIARDS; and PHILIP II. III. and IV. and CHARLES II.[195] been

194. [Charles V, Holy Roman Emperor from 1519 to 1556 and, as Charles I, king of Spain.]

195. [Henry IV was king of France from 1589 to 1610. Richelieu was the chief minister of and power behind Louis XIII of France from 1624 to 1642. The government of Louis XIV ruled France from 1643 to 1715. The three Philips and Charles II ruled Spain from 1665 until 1700.]

FRENCHMEN, the history of these two nations had been entirely reversed.

For the same reason, it is more easy to account for the rise and progress of commerce in any kingdom, than for that of learning; and a state, which should apply itself to the encouragement of the one, would be more assured of success, than one which should cultivate the other. Avarice, or the desire of gain, is an universal passion, which operates at all times, in all places, and upon all persons: But curiosity, or the love of knowledge, has a very limited influence, and requires youth, leisure, education, genius, and example, to make it govern any person. You will never want booksellers, while there are buyers of books: But there may frequently be readers where there are no authors. Multitudes of people, necessity and liberty, have begotten commerce in HOLLAND: But study and application have scarcely produced any eminent writers.

We may, therefore, conclude, that there is no subject, in which we must proceed with more caution, than in tracing the history of the arts and sciences; lest we assign causes which never existed, and reduce what is merely contingent to stable and universal principles. Those who cultivate the sciences in any state, are always few in number: The passion, which governs them, limited: Their taste and judgment delicate and easily perverted: And their application disturbed with the smallest accident. Chance, therefore, or secret and unknown causes, must have a great influence on the rise and progress of all the refined arts.

But there is a reason, which induces me not to ascribe the matter altogether to chance. Though the persons, who cultivate the sciences with such astonishing success, as to attract the admiration of posterity, be always few, in all nations and all ages; it is impossible but a share of the same spirit and genius must be antecedently diffused throughout the people among whom they arise, in order to produce, form, and cultivate, from their earliest infancy, the taste and judgment of those eminent writers. The mass cannot be altogether insipid, from which such refined spirits are extracted. *There is a God within us,* says OVID, *who breathes that divine fire, by which we are animated.*[196] Poets, in all ages, have advanced this claim to inspiration. There is not, however,

196. Est Deus in nobis; agitante calescimus illo:
Impetus hic, sacrae semina mentis habet.
OVID, *Fast. lib.* vi. 5.
[Ovid (43 B.C.–A.D.17), *Fasti*, 6.5–6.]

any thing supernatural in the case. Their fire is not kindled from heaven. It only runs along the earth; is caught from one breast to another; and burns brightest, where the materials are best prepared, and most happily disposed. The question, therefore, concerning the rise and progress of the arts and sciences, is not altogether a question concerning the taste, genius, and spirit of a few, but concerning those of a whole people; and may, therefore, be accounted for, in some measure, by general causes and principles. I grant, that a man, who should enquire, why such a particular poet, as HOMER,[197] for instance, existed, at such a place, in such a time, would throw himself headlong into chimaera, and could never treat of such a subject, without a multitude of false subtilties and refinements. He might as well pretend to give a reason, why such particular generals, as FABIUS and SCIPIO,[198] lived in ROME at such a time, and why FABIUS came into the world before SCIPIO. For such incidents as these, no other reason can be given than that of HORACE:

> *Scit genius, natale comes, qui temperat astrum*
> *Naturae Deus humanae, mortalis in unum—*
> *—Quodque caput, vultu mutabilis, albus & ater.*[199]

But I am persuaded, that in many cases good reasons might be given, why such a nation is more polite and learned, at a particular time, than any of its neighbours. At least, this is so curious a subject, that it were a pity to abandon it entirely, before we have found whether it be susceptible of reasoning, and can be reduced to any general principles.

My first observation on this head is, *That it is impossible for the arts and sciences to arise, at first, among any people unless that people enjoy the blessing of a free government.*

In the first ages of the world, when men are as yet barbarous and ignorant, they seek no farther security against mutual violence and

197. [The *Odyssey* and *Iliad* are attributed to Homer, about whom we know next to nothing.]

198. [Hume probably means Fabius Cunctator (died 203 B.C.) and Scipio Africanus Major (236–184/3 B.C.), both generals during the Second Punic War (218–201 B.C.)]

199. [Horace (65–8 B.C.), *Epistles*, 2.2.187–89: "The Genius alone knows—that companion who rules our star of birth, the god of human nature, though mortal for each single life, and changing in countenance, white or black" (trans. by H. R. Fairclough).]

injustice, than the choice of some rulers, few or many, in whom they place an implicit confidence, without providing any security, by laws or political institutions, against the violence and injustice of these rulers. If the authority be centered in a single person, and if the people, either by conquest, or by the ordinary course of propagation, encrease to a great multitude, the monarch, finding it impossible, in his own person, to execute every office of sovereignty, in every place, must delegate his authority to inferior magistrates, who preserve peace and order in their respective districts. As experience and education have not yet refined the judgments of men to any considerable degree, the prince, who is himself unrestrained, never dreams of restraining his ministers, but delegates his full authority to every one, whom he sets over any portion of the people. All general laws are attended with inconveniencies, when applied to particular cases; and it requires great penetration and experience, both to perceive that these inconveniencies are fewer than what result from full discretionary powers in every magistrate; and also to discern what general laws are, upon the whole, attended with fewest inconveniencies. This is a matter of so great difficulty, that men may have made some advances, even in the sublime arts of poetry and eloquence, where a rapidity of genius and imagination assists their progress, before they have arrived at any great refinement in their municipal laws, where frequent trials and diligent observation can alone direct their improvements. It is not, therefore, to be supposed, that a barbarous monarch, unrestrained and uninstructed, will ever become a legislator, or think of restraining his *Bashaws*, in every province, or even his *Cadis* in every village. We are told, that the late *Czar*,[200] though actuated with a noble genius, and smit with the love and admiration of EUROPEAN arts; yet professed an esteem for the TURKISH policy in this particular, and approved of such summary decisions of causes, as are practised in that barbarous monarchy, where the judges are not restrained by any methods, forms, or laws. He did not perceive, how contrary such a practice would have been to all his other endeavours for refining his people. Arbitrary power, in all cases, is somewhat oppressive and debasing; but it is altogether ruinous and intolerable, when contracted into a small compass; and becomes still worse, when the person, who possesses it, knows that the time of his authority is

200. [Peter the Great of Russia, ruler of Russia from 1689 to 1725.]

limited and uncertain. *Habet subjectos tanquam suos; viles, ut alienos.*[201] He governs the subjects with full authority, as if they were his own; and with negligence or tyranny, as belonging to another. A people, governed after such a manner, are slaves in the full and proper sense of the word; and it is impossible they can ever aspire to any refinements of taste or reason. They dare not so much as pretend to enjoy the necessaries of life in plenty or security.

To expect, therefore, that the arts and sciences should take their first rise in a monarchy, is to expect a contradiction. Before these refinements have taken place, the monarch is ignorant and uninstructed; and not having knowledge sufficient to make him sensible of the necessity of balancing his government upon general laws, he delegates his full power to all inferior magistrates. This barbarous policy debases the people, and for ever prevents all improvements. Were it possible, that, before science were known in the world, a monarch could possess so much wisdom as to become a legislator, and govern his people by law, not by the arbitrary will of their fellow-subjects, it might be possible for that species of government to be the first nursery of arts and sciences. But that supposition seems scarcely to be consistent or rational.

It may happen, that a republic, in its infant state, may be supported by as few laws as a barbarous monarchy, and may entrust as unlimited an authority to its magistrates or judges. But, besides that the frequent elections by the people, are a considerable check upon authority; it is impossible, but, in time, the necessity of restraining the magistrates, in order to preserve liberty, must at last appear, and give rise to general laws and statutes. The ROMAN Consuls, for some time, decided all causes, without being confined by any positive statutes, till the people, bearing this yoke with impatience, created the *decemvirs,* who promulgated the *twelve tables;* a body of laws, which, though, perhaps, they were not equal in bulk to one ENGLISH act of parliament, were almost the only written rules, which regulated property and punishment, for some ages, in that famous republic.[202] They were, however, suffi-

201. TACIT. hist. lib. i. 37. [Tacitus (*c.* A.D. 56–120), *The Histories*, 1.37: "Now he keeps us under his heel as if we were his slaves and regards us as cheap because we belong to another" (trans. by C. H. Moore).]

202. [The Twelve Tables were the earliest code of Roman law, and the foundation of its development. These tables that collected and attempted to codify customary law were drawn up by a special commission of *decemvirs* in 451–450 B.C.]

cient, together with the forms of a free government, to secure the lives and properties of the citizens, to exempt one man from the dominion of another; and to protect every one against the violence or tyranny of his fellow-citizens. In such a situation the sciences may raise their heads and flourish: But never can have being amidst such a scene of oppression and slavery, as always results from barbarous monarchies, where the people alone are restrained by the authority of the magistrates, and the magistrates are not restrained by any law or statute. An unlimited despotism of this nature, while it exists, effectually puts a stop to all improvements, and keeps men from attaining that knowledge, which is requisite to instruct them in the advantages, arising from a better police, and more moderate authority.

Here then are the advantages of free states. Though a republic should be barbarous, it necessarily, by an infallible operation, gives rise to LAW, even before mankind have made any considerable advances in the other sciences. From law arises security: From security curiosity: And from curiosity knowledge. The latter steps of this progress may be more accidental; but the former are altogether necessary. A republic without laws can never have any duration. On the contrary, in a monarchical government, law arises not necessarily from the forms of government. Monarchy, when absolute, contains even something repugnant to law. Great wisdom and reflexion can alone reconcile them. But such a degree of wisdom can never be expected, before the greater refinements and improvements of human reason. These refinements require curiosity, security, and law. The *first* growth, therefore, of the arts and sciences can never be expected in despotic governments.

There are other causes, which discourage the rise of the refined arts in despotic governments; though I take the want of laws, and the delegation of full powers to every petty magistrate, to be the principal. Eloquence certainly springs up more naturally in popular governments: Emulation too in every accomplishment must there be more animated and enlivened: And genius and capacity have a fuller scope and career. All these causes render free governments the only proper *nursery* for the arts and sciences.

The next observation, which I shall make on this head, is, *That nothing is more favourable to the rise of politeness and learning, than a number of neighbouring and independent states, connected together by commerce and policy.* The emulation, which naturally arises among those neighbouring states, is an obvious source of improvement: But what I would chiefly insist on is the stop, which such limited territories give both to *power* and to *authority*.

Extended governments, where a single person has great influence, soon become absolute; but small ones change naturally into commonwealths. A large government is accustomed by degrees to tyranny; because each act of violence is at first performed upon a part, which, being distant from the majority, is not taken notice of, nor excites any violent ferment. Besides, a large government, though the whole be discontented, may, by a little art, be kept in obedience; while each part, ignorant of the resolutions of the rest, is afraid to begin any commotion or insurrection. Not to mention, that there is a superstitious reverence for princes, which mankind naturally contract when they do not often see the sovereign, and when many of them become not acquainted with him so as to perceive his weaknesses. And as large states can afford a great expence, in order to support the pomp of majesty; this is a kind of fascination on men, and naturally contributes to the enslaving of them.

In a small government, any act of oppression is immediately known throughout the whole: The murmurs and discontents, proceeding from it, are easily communicated: And the indignation arises the higher, because the subjects are not apt to apprehend in such states, that the distance is very wide between themselves and their sovereign. "No man," said the prince of CONDE,[203] "is a hero to his *Valet de Chambre.*" It is certain that admiration and acquaintance are altogether incompatible towards any mortal creature. Sleep and love convinced even ALEXANDER[204] himself that he was not a God: But I suppose that such as daily attended him could easily, from the numberless weaknesses to which he was subject, have given him many still more convincing proofs of his humanity.

But the divisions into small states are favourable to learning, by stopping the progress of *authority* as well as that of *power*. Reputation is often as great a fascination upon men as sovereignty, and is equally destructive to the freedom of thought and examination. But where a number of neighbouring states have a great intercourse of arts and commerce, their mutual jealousy keeps them from receiving too lightly the law from each other, in matters of taste and of reasoning, and

203. [Louis II de Bourbon (1621–86).]

204. [Alexander the Great (356–323 B.C.) of Macedonia, established in thirteen years an immense Greco-Macedonian Empire.]

makes them examine every work of art with the greatest care and accuracy. The contagion of popular opinion spreads not so easily from one place to another. It readily receives a check in some state or other, where it concurs not with the prevailing prejudices. And nothing but nature and reason, or, at least, what bears them a strong resemblance, can force its way through all obstacles, and unite the most rival nations into an esteem and admiration of it.

GREECE was a cluster of little principalities, which soon became republics; and being united both by their near neighbourhood, and by the ties of the same language and interest, they entered into the closest intercourse of commerce and learning. There concurred a happy climate, a soil not unfertile, and a most harmonious and comprehensive language; so that every circumstance among that people seemed to favour the rise of the arts and sciences. Each city produced its several artists and philosophers, who refused to yield the preference to those of the neighbouring republics: Their contention and debates sharpened the wits of men: A variety of objects was presented to the judgment, while each challenged the preference to the rest: and the sciences, not being dwarfed by the restraint of authority, were enabled to make such considerable shoots, as are, even at this time, the objects of our admiration. After the ROMAN *christian,* or *catholic* church had spread itself over the civilized world, and had engrossed all the learning of the times; being really one large state within itself, and united under one head; this variety of sects immediately disappeared, and the PERIPATETIC[205] philosophy was alone admitted into all the schools, to the utter depravation of every kind of learning. But mankind, having at length thrown off this yoke, affairs are now returned nearly to the same situation as before, and EUROPE is at present a copy at large, of what GREECE was formerly a pattern in miniature. We have seen the advantage of this situation in several instances. What checked the progress of the CARTESIAN philosophy,[206] to which the FRENCH nation shewed such a strong propensity towards the end of the last century, but the opposition made to it by the other nations of EUROPE, who soon discovered the weak sides of that philosophy? The severest scrutiny, which NEWTON'S[207] theory has undergone, proceeded not

205. [See n. 14.]

206. [René Descartes (1596–1650) and those who were influenced by him.]

207. [Sir Isaac Newton (1642–1727). Several Hume scholars believe that Newton had a significant influence on him, and that Hume attempted to carry out a Newtonian

from his own countrymen, but from foreigners; and if it can overcome the obstacles, which it meets with at present in all parts of EUROPE, it will probably go down triumphant to the latest posterity. The ENGLISH are become sensible of the scandalous licentiousness of their stage, from the example of the FRENCH decency and morals. The FRENCH are convinced, that their theatre has become somewhat effeminate, by too much love and gallantry; and begin to approve of the more masculine taste of some neighbouring nations.

In CHINA, there seems to be a pretty considerable stock of politeness and science, which, in the course of so many centuries, might naturally be expected to ripen into something more perfect and finished, than what has yet arisen from them. But CHINA is one vast empire, speaking one language, governed by one law, and sympathizing in the same manners. The authority of any teacher, such as CONFUCIUS,[208] was propagated easily from one corner of the empire to the other. None had courage to resist the torrent of popular opinion. And posterity was not bold enough to dispute what had been universally received by their ancestors. This seems to be one natural reason, why the sciences have made so slow a progress in that mighty empire.[209]

If we consider the face of the globe, EUROPE, of all the four parts of the world, is the most broken by seas, rivers, and mountains; and

program in moral subjects in *A Treatise of Human Nature.* The subtitle of that work is "Being an Attempt to introduce the experimental Method of Reasoning into Moral Subjects."]

208. [See n. 186.]

209. If it be asked how we can reconcile to the foregoing principles the happiness, riches, and good police of the CHINESE, who have always been governed by a monarch, and can scarcely form an idea of a free government; I would answer, that though the CHINESE government be a pure monarchy, it is not, properly speaking, absolute. This proceeds from a peculiarity in the situation of that country: They have no neighbours, except the TARTARS, from whom they were, in some measure, secured, at least seemed to be secured, by their famous wall, and by the great superiority of their numbers. By this means, military discipline has always been much neglected amongst them; and their standing forces are mere militia, of the worst kind; and unfit to suppress any general insurrection in countries so extremely populous. The sword, therefore, may properly be said to be always in the hands of the people, which is a sufficient restraint upon the monarch, and obliges him to lay his *mandarins* or governors of provinces under the restraint of general laws, in order to prevent those rebellions, which we learn from history to have been so frequent and dangerous in that government. Perhaps, a pure monarchy of this kind, were it fitted for defence against foreign enemies, would be the best of all governments, as having both the tranquillity attending kingly power, and the moderation and liberty of popular assemblies.

GREECE of all countries of EUROPE. Hence these regions were naturally divided into several distinct governments. And hence the sciences arose in GREECE; and EUROPE has been hitherto the most constant habitation of them.

I have sometimes been inclined to think, that interruptions in the periods of learning, were they not attended with such a destruction of ancient books, and the records of history, would be rather favourable to the arts and sciences, by breaking the progress of authority, and dethroning the tyrannical usurpers over human reason. In this particular, they have the same influence, as interruptions in political governments and societies. Consider the blind submission of the ancient philosophers to the several masters in each school, and you will be convinced, that little good could be expected from a hundred centuries of such a servile philosophy. Even the ECLECTICS, who arose about the age of AUGUSTUS,[210] notwithstanding their professing to chuse freely what pleased them from every different sect, were yet, in the main, as slavish and dependent as any of their brethren; since they sought for truth not in nature, but in the several schools; where they supposed she must necessarily be found, though not united in a body, yet dispersed in parts. Upon the revival of learning, those sects of STOICS and EPICUREANS, PLATONISTS[211] and PYTHAGORICIANS,[212] could never regain any credit or authority; and, at the same time, by the example of their fall, kept men from submitting, with such blind deference, to those new sects, which have attempted to gain an ascendant over them.

The *third* observation, which I shall form on this head, of the rise and progress of the arts and sciences, is, *That though the only proper* Nursery *of these noble plants be a free state; yet may they be transplanted into any government; and that a republic is most favourable to the growth of the sciences, a civilized monarchy*[213] *to that of the polite arts.*

To balance a large state or society, whether monarchical or republi-

210. [Augustus was the first Emperor of Rome. See n. 20.]

211. [See n. 188.]

212. [Beginning with Pythagoras at the end of the sixth century B.C. and lasting until the start of the fourth century B.C., the Pythagoreans were as much a religious brotherhood as a school of philosophy.]

213. [Hume implicitly distinguishes the civilized monarchies of the West, for example, France, from the barbarous monarchies of the East, for example, Turkey. On Hume's distinction between a monarchy and a republic, see n. 41.]

can, on general laws, is a work of so great difficulty, that no human genius, however comprehensive, is able, by the mere dint of reason and reflection, to effect it. The judgments of many must unite in this work: Experience must guide their labour: Time must bring it to perfection: And the feeling of inconveniencies must correct the mistakes, which they inevitably fall into, in their first trials and experiments. Hence appears the impossibility, that this undertaking should be begun and carried on in any monarchy; since such a form of government, ere civilized, knows no other secret or policy, than that of entrusting unlimited powers to every governor or magistrate, and subdividing the people into so many classes and orders of slavery. From such a situation, no improvement can ever be expected in the sciences, in the liberal arts, in laws, and scarcely in the manual arts and manufactures. The same barbarism and ignorance, with which the government commences, is propagated to all posterity, and can never come to a period by the efforts or ingenuity of such unhappy slaves.

But though law, the source of all security and happiness, arises late in any government, and is the slow product of order and of liberty, it is not preserved with the same difficulty, with which it is produced; but when it has once taken root, is a hardy plant, which will scarcely ever perish through the ill culture of men, or the rigour of the seasons. The arts of luxury, and much more the liberal arts, which depend on a refined taste or sentiment, are easily lost; because they are always relished by a few only, whose leisure, fortune, and genius fit them for such amusements. But what is profitable to every mortal, and in common life, when once discovered, can scarcely fall into oblivion, but by the total subversion of society, and by such furious inundations of barbarous invaders, as obliterate all memory of former arts and civility. Imitation also is apt to transport these coarser and more useful arts from one climate to another, and make them precede the refined arts in their progress; though perhaps they sprang after them in their first rise and propagation. From these causes proceed civilized monarchies; where the arts of government, first invented in free states, are preserved to the mutual advantage and security of sovereign and subject.

However perfect, therefore, the monarchical form may appear to some politicians, it owes all its perfection to the republican; nor is it possible, that a pure despotism, established among a barbarous people, can ever, by its native force and energy, refine and polish itself. It must borrow its laws, and methods, and institutions, and consequently its stability and order, from free governments. These advantages are the sole growth of republics. The extensive despotism of a barbarous monarchy, by entering into the detail of the government, as well as into the principal points of administration, for ever prevents all such improvements.

In a civilized monarchy, the prince alone is unrestrained in the exercise of his authority, and possesses alone a power, which is not bounded by any thing but custom, example, and the sense of his own interest. Every minister or magistrate, however eminent, must submit to the general laws, which govern the whole society, and must exert the authority delegated to him after the manner, which is prescribed. The people depend on none but their sovereign, for the security of their property. He is so far removed from them, and is so much exempt from private jealousies or interests, that this dependence is scarcely felt. And thus a species of government arises, to which, in a high political rant, we may give the name of *Tyranny,* but which, by a just and prudent administration, may afford tolerable security to the people, and may answer most of the ends of political society.

But though in a civilized monarchy, as well as in a republic, the people have security for the enjoyment of their property; yet in both these forms of government, those who possess the supreme authority have the disposal of many honours and advantages, which excite the ambition and avarice of mankind. The only difference is, that, in a republic, the candidates for office must look downwards, to gain the suffrages of the people; in a monarchy, they must turn their attention upwards, to court the good graces and favour of the great. To be successful in the former way, it is necessary for a man to make himself *useful,* by his industry, capacity, or knowledge: To be prosperous in the latter way, it is requisite for him to render himself *agreeable,*[214] by his wit, complaisance, or civility. A strong genius succeeds best in republics: A refined taste in monarchies. And consequently the sciences are the more natural growth of the one, and the polite arts of the other.

Not to mention, that monarchies, receiving their chief stability from a superstitious reverence to priests and princes, have commonly abridged the liberty of reasoning, with regard to religion, and politics,

214. [Hume's understanding of virtue relies on a recognition of mental qualities that are *either* useful to ourselves or others *or* agreeable to ourselves or others. See *An Enquiry Concerning the Principles of Morals*, pp. 51–72.]

and consequently metaphysics and morals. All these form the most considerable branches of science. Mathematics and natural philosophy, which only remain, are not half so valuable.

Among the arts of conversation, no one pleases more than mutual deference or civility, which leads us to resign our own inclinations to those of our companion, and to curb and conceal that presumption and arrogance, so natural to the human mind. A good-natured man, who is well educated, practises this civility to every mortal, without premeditation or interest. But in order to render that valuable quality general among any people, it seems necessary to assist the natural disposition by some general motive. Where power rises upwards from the people to the great, as in all republics, such refinements of civility are apt to be little practised; since the whole state is, by that means, brought near to a level, and every member of it is rendered, in a great measure, independent of another. The people have the advantage, by the authority of their suffrages: The great, by the superiority of their station. But in a civilized monarchy, there is a long train of dependence from the prince to the peasant, which is not great enough to render property precarious, or depress the minds of the people; but is sufficient to beget in every one an inclination to please his superiors, and to form himself upon those models, which are most acceptable to people of condition and education. Politeness of manners, therefore, arises most naturally in monarchies and courts; and where that flourishes, none of the liberal arts will be altogether neglected or despised.

The republics in EUROPE are at present noted for want of politeness. *The good-manners of a* SWISS *civilized in* HOLLAND,[215] is an expression for rusticity among the FRENCH. The ENGLISH, in some degree, fall under the same censure, notwithstanding their learning and genius. And if the VENETIANS be an exception to the rule, they owe it, perhaps, to their communication with the other ITALIANS, most of whose governments beget a dependence more than sufficient for civilizing their manners.

It is difficult to pronounce any judgment concerning the refinements of the ancient republics in this particular: But I am apt to suspect, that

215. C'est la politesse d'un Suisse
En HOLLANDE civilisé.
ROUSSEAU.

[Jean-Baptiste Rousseau (1671–1741), *Poesies Diverses*, in *Oeuvres* (Paris, 1820), vol. II, p. 366).]

the arts of conversation were not brought so near to perfection among them as the arts of writing and composition. The scurrility of the ancient orators, in many instances, is quite shocking, and exceeds all belief. Vanity too is often not a little offensive in authors of those ages;[216] as well as the common licentiousness and immodesty of their stile, *Quicunque impudicus, adulter, ganeo, manu, ventre,* pene, *bona patria laceraverat,* says SALLUST[217] in one of the gravest and most moral passages of his history. *Nam fuit ante Helenam Cunnus teterrima belli Causa,* is an expression of HORACE,[218] in tracing the origin of moral good and evil. OVID[219] and LUCRETIUS[220] are almost as licentious in their stile as Lord ROCHESTER;[221] though the former were fine gentlemen and delicate writers, and the latter, from the corruptions of that court, in which he lived, seems to have thrown off all regard to shame and decency. JUVENAL[222] inculcates modesty with great zeal; but sets a very bad example of it, if we consider the impudence of his expressions.

I shall also be bold to affirm, that among the ancients, there was

216. It is needless to cite CICERO or PLINY on this head: They are too much noted: But one is a little surprised to find ARRIAN, a very grave, judicious writer, interrupt the thread of his narration all of a sudden, to tell his readers that he himself is as eminent among the GREEKS for eloquence as ALEXANDER was for arms. Lib. i. 12. [Arrian (second century A.D.), *Anabasis of Alexander & Indica*, 1.12.]

217. [Sallust (probably 86–35 B.C.), *The War with Catiline*, 14.2: "Whatever wanton, glutton, or gamester had wasted his patrimony in play, feasting, or debauchery" and murderers, perjurers, and those with an evil conscience, {"all these were nearest and dearest to Catiline"} (trans. by J. C. Rolfe).]

218. [Horace, *Satires*, 1.3.107: "Before Helen's day a wench was the most dreadful cause of war" (trans. by H. R. Fairclough).]

219. [Hume is probably referring Ovid's (43 B.C.–A.D. 17) *Amores*, three books of love poems.]

220. This poet (See lib. iv. 1175.) recommends a very extraordinary cure for love, and what one expects not to meet with in so elegant and philosophical a poem. It seems to have been the original of some of Dr. SWIFT'S images. The elegant CATULLUS and PHAEDRUS fall under the same censure. [Lucretius (*c.* early half of first century B.C.), recommends emphasizing the faults of the women (*De Rerum Natura*, 4.1145–1190). Jonathan Swift (1667–1745) is most famous for *Gulliver's Travels*. Catullus (84–54 B.C.) was a Roman poet, and Phaedrus (*c.* 15 B.C.–A.D. 50) was a writer of verse fables.]

221. [John Wilmot (1647–80), the second earl of Rochester.]

222. [Juvenal (between A.D. 50 and 65–after 127) is remembered for his five books of *Satires*.]

not much delicacy of breeding, or that polite deference and respect, which civility obliges us either to express or counterfeit towards the persons with whom we converse. CICERO was certainly one of the finest gentlemen of his age; yet I must confess I have frequently been shocked with the poor figure under which he represents his friend Atticus, in those dialogues, where he himself is introduced as a speaker. That learned and virtuous ROMAN, whose dignity, though he was only a private gentleman, was inferior to that of no one in ROME, is there shewn in rather a more pitiful light than PHILALETHES'S friend in our modern dialogues. He is a humble admirer of the orator, pays him frequent compliments, and receives his instructions, with all the deference which a scholar owes to his master.[223] Even CATO is treated in somewhat of a cavalier manner in the dialogues *de finibus.*

One of the most particular details of a real dialogue, which we meet with in antiquity, is related by POLYBIUS;[224] when PHILIP, king of MACEDON, a prince of wit and parts, met with TITUS FLAMININUS, one of the politest of the ROMANS, as we learn from PLUTARCH,[225] accompanied with ambassadors from almost all the GREEK cities. The AETOLIAN ambassador very abruptly tells the king, that he talked like a fool or a madman (ληρεῖν). *That's evident,* says his majesty, *even to a blind man;* which was a raillery on the blindness of his excellency. Yet all this did not pass the usual bounds: For the conference was not disturbed; and FLAMININUS was very well diverted with these strokes of humour. At the end, when PHILIP craved a little time to consult with his friends, of whom he had none present, the ROMAN general, being desirous also to shew his wit, as the historian says, tells him, *that perhaps the reason, why he had none of his friends with him, was because he had murdered them all;* which was actually the case. This unprovoked piece of rusticity is not condemned

223. ATT. Non mihi videtur ad beate vivendum satis esse virtutem. MAR. At hercule BRUTO meo videtur; cujus ego judicium, pace tua dixerim, longe antepono tuo. Tusc. Quaest. lib. v. 5. [Cicero (106–43 B.C.), *Tusculan Disputations*, 5.5.12: "*Atticus.* It does not appear to me that virtue can be sufficient for leading a happy life. *Marcus.* But, I can assure you, my friend Brutus thinks it sufficient and with your permission I put his judgment far above yours" (trans. by J. E. King). Cicero's *Letters to Atticus* are of great significance in understanding the Roman world from 68–44 B.C.]

224. Lib. xvii. 4. [Polybius (*c.* 200–118 B.C.), *The Histories*, 17.4–7.]

225. *In vita* FLAMIN., c. 2. [*Plutarch's Lives*, "The Life of Flamininus (died 174 B.C.)," trans. by J. Langhorne and W. Langhorne, 6 vols. (London: Sharpe and Son, 1819), vol. III, pp. 31–32.]

by the historian; caused no farther resentment in PHILIP, than to excite a SARDONIAN smile, or what we call a grin; and hindered him not from renewing the conference next day. PLUTARCH[226] too mentions this raillery amongst the witty and agreeable sayings of FLAMININUS.

Cardinal WOLSEY[227] apologized for his famous piece of insolence, in saying, EGO ET REX MEUS, *I and my king,* by observing, that this expression was conformable to the *Latin* idiom, and that a ROMAN always named himself before the person to whom, or of whom he spake. Yet this seems to have been an instance of want of civility among that people. The ancients made it a rule, that the person of the greatest dignity should be mentioned first in the discourse; insomuch, that we find the spring of a quarrel and jealousy between the ROMANS and AETOLIANS, to have been a poet's naming the AETOLIANS before the ROMANS, in celebrating a victory gained by their united arms over the MACEDONIANS.[228] Thus LIVIA disgusted TIBERIUS by placing her own name before his in an inscription.[229]

No advantages in this world are pure and unmixed. In like manner, as modern politeness, which is naturally so ornamental, runs often into affectation and foppery, disguise and insincerity; so the ancient simplicity, which is naturally so amiable and affecting, often degenerates into rusticity and abuse, scurrility and obscenity.

If the superiority in politeness should be allowed to modern times, the modern notions of *gallantry,* the natural produce of courts and monarchies, will probably be assigned as the causes of this refinement. No one denies this invention to be modern:[230] But some of the more zealous partizans of the ancients, have asserted it to be foppish and ridiculous, and a reproach, rather than a credit, to the present age.[231] It may here be proper to examine this question.

226. PLUT. *in vita* FLAMIN. c. 17. [*Plutarch's Lives*, p. 55.]

227. [Thomas Wolsey (1475?–1530) was one of the most powerful leaders England ever had, but he lost his power in 1529 as a result of failing to secure the divorce of Henry VIII from Catherine of Aragon.]

228. PLUT. *in vita* FLAMIN. c. 9. [*Plutarch's Lives*, p. 42.]

229. TACIT. *Ann. lib.* iii. cap. 64. [Tacitus (*c.* A.D. 56–120), *Annals*, 3.64.]

230. In the *Self-Tormentor* of TERENCE, CLINIAS, whenever he comes to town, instead of waiting on his mistress, sends for her to come to him. [Terence (*c.* 190–159 B.C.) was a Roman comic playwright who influenced Cicero and Montaigne (1533–92).]

231. LORD SHAFTESBURY, see his *Moralists.* [Anthony Ashley Cooper, Third Earl of Shaftesbury (1671–1713), *Characteristics*, ed. by J. M. Robertson, 2 vols. (London:

Nature has implanted in all living creatures an affection between the sexes, which, even in the fiercest and most rapacious animals, is not merely confined to the satisfaction of the bodily appetite, but begets a friendship and mutual sympathy, which runs through the whole tenor of their lives. Nay, even in those species, where nature limits the indulgence of this appetite to one season and to one object, and forms a kind of marriage or association between a single male and female, there is yet a visible complacency and benevolence, which extends farther, and mutually softens the affections of the sexes towards each other. How much more must this have place in man, where the confinement of the appetite is not natural; but either is derived accidentally from some strong charm of love, or arises from reflections on duty and convenience? Nothing, therefore, can proceed less from affectation than the passion of gallantry. It is *natural* in the highest degree. Art and education, in the most elegant courts, make no more alteration on it, than on all the other laudable passions. They only turn the mind more towards it; they refine it; they polish it; and give it a proper grace and expression.

But gallantry is as *generous* as it is *natural*. To correct such gross vices, as lead us to commit real injury on others, is the part of morals, and the object of the most ordinary education. Where *that* is not attended to, in some degree, no human society can subsist. But in order to render conversation, and the intercourse of minds more easy and agreeable, good-manners have been invented, and have carried the matter somewhat farther. Wherever nature has given the mind a propensity to any vice, or to any passion disagreeable to others, refined breeding has taught men to throw the biass on the opposite side, and to preserve, in all their behaviour, the appearance of sentiments different from those to which they naturally incline. Thus, as we are commonly proud and selfish, and apt to assume the preference above others, a polite man learns to behave with deference towards his companions, and to yield the superiority to them in all the common incidents of society. In like manner, wherever a person's situation may naturally beget any disagreeable suspicion in him, it is the part of good-manners to prevent it, by a studied display of sentiments, directly contrary to those of which he is apt to be jealous. Thus, old men know their infirmities, and naturally dread contempt from the youth: Hence, well-

---

Grant Richards, 1900), vol. II, pp. 10–11 (Treatise V, "The Moralists, A Philosophical Rhapsody").]

educated youth redouble the instances of respect and deference to their elders. Strangers and foreigners are without protection: Hence, in all polite countries, they receive the highest civilities, and are entitled to the first place in every company. A man is lord in his own family, and his guests are, in a manner, subject to his authority: Hence, he is always the lowest person in the company; attentive to the wants of every one; and giving himself all the trouble, in order to please, which may not betray too visible an affectation, or impose too much constraint on his guests.[232] Gallantry is nothing but an instance of the same generous attention. As nature has given *man* the superiority above *woman,* by endowing him with greater strength both of mind and body; it is his part to alleviate that superiority, as much as possible, by the generosity of his behaviour, and by a studied deference and complaisance for all her inclinations and opinions. Barbarous nations display this superiority, by reducing their females to the most abject slavery; by confining them, by beating them, by selling them, by killing them. But the male sex, among a polite people, discover their authority in a more generous, though not a less evident manner; by civility, by respect, by complaisance, and, in a word, by gallantry. In good company, you need not ask, Who is the master of the feast? The man, who sits in the lowest place, and who is always industrious in helping every one, is certainly the person. We must either condemn all such instances of generosity, as foppish and affected, or admit of gallantry among the rest. The ancient MUSCOVITES wedded their wives with a whip, instead of a ring. The same people, in their own houses, took always the precedency above foreigners, even[233] foreign ambassadors. These two instances of their generosity and politeness are much of a piece.

Gallantry is not less compatible with *wisdom* and *prudence,* than with

232. The frequent mention in ancient authors of that ill-bred custom of the master of the family's eating better bread or drinking better wine at table, than he afforded his guests, is but an indifferent mark of the civility of those ages. See JUVENAL, sat. 5. PLINII lib. xiv. cap. 13. [Pliny the Elder (A.D. 23–79), *Natural History,* 14.14.91.] Also PLINII *Epist.* [Pliny the Younger (A.D. 61–112?), *Letters.*] *Lucian de mercede conductis, Saturnalia &c.* [Lucian, *On Salaried Posts in Great Houses, Saturnalia, &c.*] There is scarcely any part of EUROPE at present so uncivilized as to admit of such a custom.

233. See *Relation of three Embassies,* by the Earl of CARLISLE. [The First Earl of Carlisle (1629–85) was England's ambassador to Russia, Sweden, and Denmark in the 1660s. *A Relation of Three Embassies from His Sacred Majestie Charles II to the Great Duke of Muscovite, the King of Sweden, and the King of Denmark* was actually written by Guy Miege, who accompanied Carlisle to his posts.]

nature and *generosity;* and when under proper regulations, contributes more than any other invention, to the *entertainment* and *improvement* of the youth of both sexes. Among every species of animals, nature has founded on the love between the sexes their sweetest and best enjoyment. But the satisfaction of the bodily appetite is not alone sufficient to gratify the mind; and even among brute-creatures, we find, that their play and dalliance, and other expressions of fondness, form the greatest part of the entertainment. In rational beings, we must certainly admit the mind for a considerable share. Were we to rob the feast of all its garniture of reason, discourse, sympathy, friendship, and gaiety, what remains would scarcely be worth acceptance, in the judgment of the truly elegant and luxurious.

What better school for manners, than the company of virtuous women; where the mutual endeavour to please must insensibly polish the mind, where the example of the female softness and modesty must communicate itself to their admirers, and where the delicacy of that sex puts every one on his guard, lest he give offence by any breach of decency.

Among the ancients, the character of the fair-sex was considered as altogether domestic; nor were they regarded as part of the polite world or of good company. This, perhaps, is the true reason why the ancients have not left us one piece of pleasantry that is excellent, (unless one may except the Banquet of XENOPHON,[234] and the Dialogues of LUCIAN[235]) though many of their serious compositions are altogether inimitable. HORACE condemns the coarse railleries and cold jests of PLAUTUS:[236] But, though the most easy, agreeable, and judicious writer in the world, is his own talent for ridicule very striking or refined? This, therefore, is one considerable improvement, which the polite arts have received from gallantry, and from courts, where it first arose.

But, to return from this digression, I shall advance it as a *fourth* observation on this subject, of the rise and progress of the arts and sciences, *That when the arts and sciences come to perfection in any state,*

234. [Xenophon (*c.* 428/7–354 B.C.), *Symposium*.]

235. [Lucian's (*c.* A.D. 120–180) principal writings are in dialogue form. One of these is the *Dialogue of the Dead*, a work Hume was reading and musing about some three weeks before his death. See Adam Smith's moving letter about Hume's death and character in *The Correspondence of Adam Smith*, ed. by E. C. Mossner and I. S. Ross, 2*nd* ed. (Oxford: Clarendon Press, 1987), pp. 217–21.]

236. [Horace (65–8 B.C.) criticizes the third-century-B.C. playwright Plautus in his *Ars Poetica*.]

from that moment they naturally, or rather necessarily decline, and seldom or never revive in that nation, where they formerly flourished.

It must be confessed, that this maxim, though conformable to experience, may, at first sight, be esteemed contrary to reason. If the natural genius of mankind be the same in all ages, and in almost all countries, (as seems to be the truth) it must very much forward and cultivate this genius, to be possessed of patterns in every art, which may regulate the taste, and fix the objects of imitation. The models left us by the ancients gave birth to all the arts about 200 years ago, and have mightily advanced their progress in every country of EUROPE: Why had they not a like effect during the reign of TRAJAN[237] and his successors; when they were much more entire, and were still admired and studied by the whole world? So late as the emperor JUSTINIAN,[238] the POET, by way of distinction, was understood, among the GREEKS, to be HOMER;[239] among the ROMANS, VIRGIL.[240] Such admiration still remained for these divine geniuses; though no poet had appeared for many centuries, who could justly pretend to have imitated them.

A man's genius is always, in the beginning of life, as much unknown to himself as to others; and it is only after frequent trials, attended with success, that he dares think himself equal to those undertakings, in which those, who have succeeded, have fixed the admiration of mankind. If his own nation be already possessed of many models of eloquence, he naturally compares his own juvenile exercises with these; and being sensible of the great disproportion, is discouraged from any farther attempts, and never aims at a rivalship with those authors, whom he so much admires. A noble emulation is the source of every excellence. Admiration and modesty naturally extinguish this emulation. And no one is so liable to an excess of admiration and modesty, as a truly great genius.

Next to emulation, the greatest encourager of the noble arts is praise

237. [Roman Emperor from A.D. 98 to 117.]

238. [Justinian (*c.* A.D. 482–565), Emperor from 527 to 565, attempted to restore the former greatness of the Roman Empire by recovering lost provinces in the West and, especially, by codifying Roman law.]

239. [The *Odyssey* and *Iliad* are attributed to Homer, about whom we know next to nothing.]

240. [Virgil's (70–19 B.C.) principal work is the *Aeneid*. Before leaving on a trip to Greece, Virgil ordered his literary executor to burn the work if anything should happen to him before his return home. Virgil died; however, the Emperor Augustus ordered the work to be made public.]

and glory. A writer is animated with new force, when he hears the applauses of the world for his former productions; and, being roused by such a motive, he often reaches a pitch of perfection, which is equally surprizing to himself and to his readers. But when the posts of honour are all occupied, his first attempts are but coldly received by the public; being compared to productions, which are both in themselves more excellent, and have already the advantage of an established reputation. Were MOLIERE and CORNEILLE[241] to bring upon the stage at present their early productions, which were formerly so well received, it would discourage the young poets, to see the indifference and disdain of the public. The ignorance of the age alone could have given admission to the *Prince* of TYRE; but it is to that we owe *the Moor*:[242] Had *Every man in his humour* been rejected, we had never seen VOLPONE.[243]

Perhaps, it may not be for the advantage of any nation to have the arts imported from their neighbours in too great perfection. This extinguishes emulation, and sinks the ardour of the generous youth. So many models of ITALIAN painting brought into ENGLAND, instead of exciting our artists, is the cause of their small progress in that noble art. The same, perhaps, was the case of ROME, when it received the arts from GREECE. That multitude of polite productions in the FRENCH language, dispersed all over GERMANY and the NORTH, hinder these nations from cultivating their own language, and keep them still dependent on their neighbours for those elegant entertainments.

It is true, the ancients had left us models in every kind of writing, which are highly worthy of admiration. But besides that they were written in languages, known only to the learned; besides this, I say, the comparison is not so perfect or entire between modern wits, and those who lived in so remote an age. Had WALLER[244] been born in ROME, during the reign of TIBERIUS,[245] his first productions had been despised, when compared to the finished odes of HORACE. But

241. [Moliere and Corneille were two prominent seventeenth-century French dramatists, the former leaning to comedy and the latter to tragedy.]

242. [Hume is referring to plays by William Shakespeare (1564–1616).]

243. [Hume is referring to plays by Ben Jonson (1572–1637).]

244. [A moderate Royalist in his politics, Edmund Waller (1606–87) was credited by Restoration poets with making certain innovations in meter and diction in his poetry.]

245. [Emperor of Rome from A.D. 14 to 37.]

in this island the superiority of the ROMAN poet diminished nothing from the fame of the ENGLISH. We esteemed ourselves sufficiently happy, that our climate and language could produce but a faint copy of so excellent an original.

In short, the arts and sciences, like some plants, require a fresh soil; and however rich the land may be, and however you may recruit it by art or care, it will never, when once exhausted, produce any thing that is perfect or finished in the kind.[246]

Essay XVII: *Of Commerce*

The greater part of mankind may be divided into two classes; that of *shallow* thinkers, who fall short of the truth; and that of *abstruse* thinkers, who go beyond it. The latter class are by far the most rare: and I may add, by far the most useful and valuable. They suggest hints, at least, and start difficulties, which they want, perhaps, skill to pursue; but which may produce fine discoveries, when handled by men who have a more just way of thinking. At worst, what they say is uncommon; and if it should cost some pains to comprehend it, one has, however, the pleasure of hearing something that is new. An author is little to be valued, who tells us nothing but what we can learn from every coffee-house conversation.

All people of *shallow* thought are apt to decry even those *of solid* understanding, as *abstruse* thinkers, and metaphysicians, and refiners; and never will allow any thing to be just which is beyond their own weak conceptions. There are some cases, I own, where an extraordinary refinement affords a strong presumption of falsehood, and where no reasoning is to be trusted but what is natural and easy. When a man deliberates concerning his conduct in any *particular* affair, and forms schemes in politics, trade, economy, or any business in life, he never ought to draw his arguments too fine, or connect too long a chain of consequences together. Something is sure to happen, that will disconcert his reasoning, and produce an event different from what he expected. But when we reason upon *general* subjects, one may justly affirm, that our speculations can scarcely ever be too fine, provided they be just; and that the difference between a common man and a man of genius is chiefly seen in the shallowness or depth of the princi-

246. [It is worth comparing Jean-Jacques Rousseau's (1712–78) *Discourse on the Sciences and the Arts* to "Of the Rise and Progress of the Arts and Sciences." See n. 35.]

ples upon which they proceed. General reasonings seem intricate, merely because they are general; nor is it easy for the bulk of mankind to distinguish, in a great number of particulars, that common circumstance in which they all agree, or to extract it, pure and unmixed, from the other superfluous circumstances. Every judgment or conclusion, with them, is particular. They cannot enlarge their view to those universal propositions, which comprehend under them an infinite number of individuals, and include a whole science in a single theorem. Their eye is confounded with such an extensive prospect; and the conclusions, derived from it, even though clearly expressed, seem intricate and obscure. But however intricate they may seem, it is certain, that general principles, if just and sound, must always prevail in the general course of things, though they may fail in particular cases; and it is the chief business of philosophers to regard the general course of things. I may add, that it is also the chief business of politicians; especially in the domestic government of the state, where the public good, which is, or ought to be their object, depends on the concurrence of a multitude of causes; not, as in foreign politics, on accidents and chances, and the caprices of a few persons. This therefore makes the difference between *particular* deliberations and *general* reasonings, and renders subtilty and refinement much more suitable to the latter than to the former.[247]

I thought this introduction necessary before the following discourses on *commerce, money, interest, balance of trade, &c.*[248] where, perhaps, there will occur some principles which are uncommon, and which may seem too refined and subtile for such vulgar subjects. If false, let them be rejected: But no one ought to entertain a prejudice against them, merely because they are out of the common road.

The greatness of a state, and the happiness of its subjects, how independent soever they may be supposed in some respects, are commonly allowed to be inseparable with regard to commerce; and as private men receive greater security, in the possession of their trade and riches, from the power of the public, so the public becomes powerful in

247. [For a similar series of remarks, see the opening paragraphs of "Of the Rise and Progress of the Arts and Sciences" (in this edition).]

248. ["Of Commerce" was the lead essay in a collection of twelve that Hume published in 1752 under the title of *Political Discourses*. Many of these essays deal with what is now called economics, and they had some influence on Adam Smith (1723–90), author of *An Inquiry into the Nature and Causes of the Wealth of Nations* (first ed., 1776). For a discussion of Hume's economic writings, see Eugene Rotwein's lengthy introduction to *David Hume: Writings on Economics* (London: Nelson, 1955).]

proportion to the opulence and extensive commerce of private men. This maxim is true in general; though I cannot forbear thinking, that it may possibly admit of exceptions, and that we often establish it with too little reserve and limitation. There may be some circumstances, where the commerce and riches and luxury of individuals, instead of adding strength to the public, will serve only to thin its armies, and diminish its authority among the neighbouring nations. Man is a very variable being, and susceptible of many different opinions, principles, and rules of conduct. What may be true, while he adheres to one way of thinking, will be found false, when he has embraced an opposite set of manners and opinions.

The bulk of every state may be divided into *husbandmen* and *manufacturers*. The former are employed in the culture of the land; the latter work up the materials furnished by the former, into all the commodities which are necessary or ornamental to human life. As soon as men quit their savage state, where they live chiefly by hunting and fishing, they must fall into these two classes; though the arts of agriculture employ *at first* the most numerous part of the society.[249] Time and experience improve so much these arts, that the land may easily maintain a much greater number of men, than those who are immediately employed in its culture, or who furnish the more necessary manufactures to such as are so employed.

If these superfluous hands apply themselves to the finer arts, which are commonly denominated the arts of *luxury*, they add to the happiness of the state; since they afford to many the opportunity of receiving enjoyments, with which they would otherwise have been unacquainted. But may not another scheme be proposed for the employment of these superfluous hands? May not the sovereign lay claim to them, and employ them in fleets and armies, to encrease the dominions of the state abroad, and spread its fame over distant nations? It is certain that the fewer desires and wants are found in the proprietors and labourers of land, the fewer hands do they employ; and consequently the superfluities of the land, instead of maintaining tradesmen and manufacturers, may support fleets

249. Mons. MELON, in his political essay on commerce, asserts, that even at present, if you divide FRANCE into 20 parts, 16 are labourers or peasants; two only artizans; one belonging to the law, church, and military; and one merchants, financiers, and bourgeois. This calculation is certainly very erroneous. In FRANCE, ENGLAND, and indeed most parts of EUROPE, half of the inhabitants live in cities; and even of those who live in the country, a great number are artizans, perhaps above a third. [Jean-François Melon (died 1738), *Essai politique sur le commerce* (1734; 2nd ed., 1736).]

and armies to a much greater extent, than where a great many arts are required to minister to the luxury of particular persons. Here therefore seems to be a kind of opposition between the greatness of the state and the happiness of the subject. A state is never greater than when all its superfluous hands are employed in the service of the public. The ease and convenience of private persons require, that these hands should be employed in their service. The one can never be satisfied, but at the expence of the other. As the ambition of the sovereign must entrench on the luxury of individuals; so the luxury of individuals must diminish the force, and check the ambition of the sovereign.

Nor is this reasoning merely chimerical; but is founded on history and experience. The republic of SPARTA was certainly more powerful than any state now in the world, consisting of an equal number of people; and this was owing entirely to the want of commerce and luxury. The HELOTES[250] were the labourers: The SPARTANS were the soldiers or gentlemen. It is evident, that the labour of the HELOTES could not have maintained so great a number of SPARTANS, had these latter lived in ease and delicacy, and given employment to a great variety of trades and manufactures. The like policy may be remarked in ROME. And indeed, throughout all ancient history, it is observable, that the smallest republics raised and maintained greater armies, than states consisting of triple the number of inhabitants, are able to support at present. It is computed, that, in all EUROPEAN nations, the proportion between soldiers and people does not exceed one to a hundred. But we read, that the city of ROME alone, with its small territory, raised and maintained, in early times, ten legions against the LATINS.[251] ATHENS, the whole of whose dominions was not larger than YORKSHIRE, sent to the expedition against SICILY near forty thousand men.[252] DIONYSIUS the elder, it is said, maintained a standing army of a hundred thousand foot and ten thousand horse, besides a large fleet of four hundred sail;[253] though his territories

250. [A servile group of people who were neither free nor slaves, occupying a position somewhere in between.]

251. [Titus Livy (59 B.C.–A.D. 17), *The History of Rome*, trans. by D. Spillan *et al.*, 4 vols. (London: G. Bell and Sons, Ltd., 1911), vol. I, p. 477 (bk. VII, ch. 25).]

252. THUCYDIDES, lib. vii. 75. [Thucydides (*c.* 460–400 B.C.), *History of the Peloponnesian War*, 7.75.]

253. DIOD. SIC. lib. ii. 5. This account, I own, is somewhat suspicious, not to say worse; chiefly because this army was not composed of citizens, but of mercenary forces. [Diodorus Siculus (first century B.C.), *Library of History*, 2.5.]

extended no farther than the city of SYRACUSE, about a third of the island of SICILY, and some sea-port towns and garrisons on the coast of ITALY and ILLYRICUM. It is true, the ancient armies, in time of war, subsisted much upon plunder: But did not the enemy plunder in their turn? which was a more ruinous way of levying a tax, than any other that could be devised. In short, no probable reason can be assigned for the great power of the more ancient states above the modern, but their want of commerce and luxury. Few artizans were maintained by the labour of the farmers, and therefore more soldiers might live upon it. LIVY says, that ROME, in his time, would find it difficult to raise as large an army as that which, in her early days, she sent out against the GAULS and LATINS.[254] Instead of those soldiers who fought for liberty and empire in CAMILLUS'S[255] time, there were, in AUGUSTUS'S days,[256] musicians, painters, cooks, players, and tailors; and if the land was equally cultivated at both periods, it could certainly maintain equal numbers in the one profession as in the other. They added nothing to the mere necessaries of life, in the latter period more than in the former.

It is natural on this occasion to ask, whether sovereigns may not return to the maxims of ancient policy, and consult their own interest in this respect, more than the happiness of their subjects? I answer, that it appears to me, almost impossible; and that because ancient policy was violent, and contrary to the more natural and usual course of things. It is well known with what peculiar laws SPARTA was governed, and what a prodigy that republic is justly esteemed by every one, who has considered human nature as it has displayed itself in other nations, and other ages. Were the testimony of history less positive and circumstantial, such a government would appear a mere philosophical whim or fiction, and impossible ever to be reduced to practice. And though the ROMAN and other ancient republics were supported on principles somewhat more natural, yet was there an extraordinary

254. TITI LIVII, lib. vii. cap. 25. "Adeo in quae laboramus," says he, "sola crevimus, divitias luxuriemque." [Titus Livius (59 B.C.–A.D. 17), *The History of Rome*, trans. by D. Spillan *et al.*, 4 vols. (London: G. Bell and Sons, Ltd., 1911), vol. I, p. 477 (7.25): "So true it is, we have improved in those particulars only about which we are solicitous, riches and luxury."]

255. [Camillus, termed the second founder of Rome, was a powerful military figure in the Roman Republic, especially in the first quarter of the fourth century B.C.]

256. [Augustus was the first Emperor of Rome. See n. 20.]

concurrence of circumstances to make them submit to such grievous burthens. They were free states; they were small ones; and the age being martial, all their neighbours were continually in arms. Freedom naturally begets public spirit, especially in small states; and this public spirit, this *amor patriae*, must encrease, when the public is almost in continual alarm, and men are obliged, every moment, to expose themselves to the greatest dangers for its defence. A continual succession of wars makes every citizen a soldier: He takes the field in his turn: And during his service he is chiefly maintained by himself. This service is indeed equivalent to a heavy tax; yet is it less felt by a people addicted to arms, who fight for honour and revenge more than pay, and are unacquainted with gain and industry as well as pleasure.[257] Not to mention the great equality of fortunes among the inhabitants of the ancient republics, where every field, belonging to a different proprietor, was able to maintain a family, and rendered the numbers of citizens very considerable, even without trade and manufactures.

But though the want of trade and manufactures, among a free and very martial people, may *sometimes* have no other effect than to render the public more powerful, it is certain, that, in the common course of human affairs, it will have a quite contrary tendency. Sovereigns must take mankind as they find them, and cannot pretend to introduce any violent change in their principles and ways of thinking. A long course of time, with a variety of accidents and circumstances, are requisite to produce those great revolutions, which so much diversify the face of human affairs. And the less natural any set of principles are, which support a particular society, the more difficulty will a legislator meet with in raising and cultivating them. It is his best policy to comply with

257. The more antient ROMANS lived in perpetual war with all their neighbours: And in old LATIN, the term *hostis*, expressed both a stranger and an enemy. This is remarked by CICERO; but by him is ascribed to the humanity of his ancestors, who softened, as much as possible, the denomination of an enemy, by calling him by the same appellation which signified a stranger. *De Off.* lib. i. 12. [Cicero (106–43 B.C.), *De Officiis*, 1.12.] 'Tis however much more probable, from the manners of the times, that the ferocity of those people was so great as to make them regard all strangers as enemies, and call them by the same name. It is not, besides, consistent with the most common maxims of policy or of nature, that any state should regard its public enemies with a friendly eye, or preserve any such sentiments for them as the ROMAN orator would ascribe to his ancestors. Not to mention, that the early ROMANS really exercised piracy, as we learn from their first treaties with CARTHAGE, preserved by POLYBIUS, lib. 3. [Polybius (*c.* 200–118 B.C.), *The Histories*, 3.22–27.] and consequently, like the SALLEE and ALGERINE rovers, were actually at war with most nations, and a stranger and an enemy were with them almost synonimous.

the common bent of mankind, and give it all the improvements of which it is susceptible. Now, according to the most natural course of things, industry and arts and trade encrease the power of the sovereign as well as the happiness of the subjects; and that policy is violent, which aggrandizes the public by the poverty of individuals. This will easily appear from a few considerations, which will present to us the consequences of sloth and barbarity.

Where manufactures and mechanic arts are not cultivated, the bulk of the people must apply themselves to agriculture; and if their skill and industry encrease, there must arise a great superfluity from their labour beyond what suffices to maintain them. They have no temptation, therefore, to encrease their skill and industry; since they cannot exchange that superfluity for any commodities, which may serve either to their pleasure or vanity. A habit of indolence naturally prevails. The greater part of the land lies uncultivated. What is cultivated, yields not its utmost for want of skill and assiduity in the farmers. If at any time the public exigencies require, that great numbers should be employed in the public service, the labour of the people furnishes now no superfluities, by which these numbers can be maintained. The labourers cannot encrease their skill and industry on a sudden. Lands uncultivated cannot be brought into tillage for some years. The armies, mean while, must either make sudden and violent conquests, or disband for want of subsistence. A regular attack or defence, therefore, is not to be expected from such a people, and their soldiers must be as ignorant and unskilful as their farmers and manufacturers.

Every thing in the world is purchased by labour; and our passions are the only causes of labour. When a nation abounds in manufactures and mechanic arts, the proprietors of land, as well as the farmers, study agriculture as a science, and redouble their industry and attention. The superfluity, which arises from their labour, is not lost; but is exchanged with manufactures for those commodities, which men's luxury now makes them covet. By this means, land furnishes a great deal more of the necessaries of life, than what suffices for those who cultivate it. In times of peace and tranquillity, this superfluity goes to the maintenance of manufacturers, and the improvers of liberal arts. But it is easy for the public to convert many of these manufacturers into soldiers, and maintain them by that superfluity, which arises from the labour of the farmers. Accordingly we find, that this is the case in all civilized governments. When the sovereign raises an army, what is the consequence? He imposes a tax. This tax obliges all the people to retrench what is least necessary to their subsistence. Those, who labour in such commodities, must either enlist in the troops, or turn themselves to agriculture, and thereby oblige some labourers to enlist for want of business. And to consider the matter abstractedly, manufactures encrease the power of the state only as they store up so much labour, and that of a kind to which the public may lay claim, without depriving any one of the necessaries of life. The more labour, therefore, is employed beyond mere necessaries, the more powerful is any state; since the persons engaged in that labour may easily be converted to the public service. In a state without manufactures, there may be the same number of hands; but there is not the same quantity of labour, nor of the same kind. All the labour is there bestowed upon necessaries, which can admit of little or no abatement.

Thus the greatness of the sovereign and the happiness of the state are, in a great measure, united with regard to trade and manufactures. It is a violent method, and in most cases impracticable, to oblige the labourer to toil, in order to raise from the land more than what subsists himself and family. Furnish him with manufactures and commodities, and he will do it of himself. Afterwards you will find it easy to seize some part of his superfluous labour, and employ it in the public service, without giving him his wonted return. Being accustomed to industry, he will think this less grievous, than if, at once, you obliged him to an augmentation of labour without any reward. The case is the same with regard to the other members of the state. The greater is the stock of labour of all kinds, the greater quantity may be taken from the heap, without making any sensible alteration in it.

A public granary of corn, a storehouse of cloth, a magazine of arms; all these must be allowed real riches and strength in any state. Trade and industry are really nothing but a stock of labour, which, in times of peace and tranquillity, is employed for the ease and satisfaction of individuals; but in the exigencies of state, may, in part, be turned to public advantage. Could we convert a city into a kind of fortified camp, and infuse into each breast so martial a genius, and such a passion for public good, as to make every one willing to undergo the greatest hardships for the sake of the public; these affections might now, as in ancient times, prove alone a sufficient spur to industry, and support the community. It would then be advantageous, as in camps, to banish all arts and luxury; and, by restrictions on equipage and tables, make the provisions and forage last longer than if the army were loaded with a number of superfluous retainers. But as these principles are too disinterested and too difficult to support, it is requisite to govern men by other passions, and animate them with a spirit of avarice and industry, art and luxury. The camp is, in this case, loaded with a superfluous retinue; but the provisions flow in proportionably larger. The harmony of the whole is still supported; and the natural bent of the mind being more complied with, individuals, as well as the public, find their account in the observance of those maxims.

The same method of reasoning will let us see the advantage of *foreign* commerce, in augmenting the power of the state, as well as the riches and happiness of the subject. It encreases the stock of labour in the nation; and the sovereign may convert what share of it he finds necessary to the service of the public. Foreign trade, by its imports, furnishes materials for new manufactures; and by its exports, it produces labour in particular commodities, which could not be consumed at home. In short, a kingdom, that has a large import and export, must abound more with industry, and that employed upon delicacies and luxuries, than a kingdom which rests contented with its native commodities. It is, therefore, more powerful, as well as richer and happier. The individuals reap the benefit of these commodities, so far as they gratify the senses and appetites. And the public is also a gainer, while a greater stock of labour is, by this means, stored up against any public exigency; that is, a greater number of laborious men are maintained, who may be diverted to the public service, without robbing any one of the necessaries, or even the chief conveniencies of life.

If we consult history, we shall find, that, in most nations, foreign trade has preceded any refinement in home manufactures, and given birth to domestic luxury. The temptation is stronger to make use of foreign commodities, which are ready for use, and which are entirely new to us, than to make improvements on any domestic commodity, which always advance by slow degrees, and never affect us by their novelty. The profit is also very great, in exporting what is superfluous at home, and what bears no price, to foreign nations, whose soil or climate is not favourable to that commodity. Thus men become acquainted with the *pleasures* of luxury and the *profits* of commerce; and their *delicacy* and *industry*, being once awakened, carry them on to farther improvements, in every branch of domestic as well as foreign trade.[258] And this perhaps is the chief advantage which arises from a commerce with strangers. It rouses men from their indolence; and presenting the gayer and more opulent part of the nation with objects of luxury, which they never before dreamed of, raises in them a desire

258. [See Hume's *An Enquiry Concerning the Principles of Morals*, pp. 89–90 (this edition).]

of a more splendid way of life than what their ancestors enjoyed. And at the same time, the few merchants, who possess the secret of this importation and exportation, make great profits; and becoming rivals in wealth to the ancient nobility, tempt other adventurers to become their rivals in commerce. Imitation soon diffuses all those arts; while domestic manufactures emulate the foreign in their improvements, and work up every home commodity to the utmost perfection of which it is susceptible. Their own steel and iron, in such laborious hands, become equal to the gold and rubies of the INDIES.

When the affairs of the society are once brought to this situation, a nation may lose most of its foreign trade, and yet continue a great and powerful people. If strangers will not take any particular commodity of ours, we must cease to labour in it. The same hands will turn themselves towards some refinement in other commodities, which may be wanted at home. And there must always be materials for them to work upon; till every person in the state, who possesses riches, enjoys as great plenty of home commodities, and those in as great perfection, as he desires; which can never possibly happen. CHINA is represented as one of the most flourishing empires in the world; though it has very little commerce beyond its own territories.

It will not, I hope, be considered as a superfluous digression, if I here observe, that, as the multitude of mechanical arts is advantageous, so is the great number of persons to whose share the productions of these arts fall. A too great disproportion among the citizens weakens any state. Every person, if possible, ought to enjoy the fruits of his labour, in a full possession of all the necessaries, and many of the conveniencies of life. No one can doubt, but such an equality is most suitable to human nature, and diminishes much less from the *happiness* of the rich than it adds to that of the poor. It also augments the *power of the state*, and makes any extraordinary taxes or impositions be paid with more chearfulness. Where the riches are engrossed by a few, these must contribute very largely to the supplying of the public necessities. But when the riches are dispersed among multitudes, the burthen feels light on every shoulder, and the taxes make not a very sensible difference on any one's way of living.

Add to this, that, where the riches are in few hands, these must enjoy all the power, and will readily conspire to lay the whole burthen on the poor, and oppress them still farther, to the discouragement of all industry.

In this circumstance consists the great advantage of ENGLAND above any nation at present in the world, or that appears in the records of any story. It is true, the ENGLISH feel some disadvantages in foreign trade by the high price of labour, which is in part the effect of the riches of their artisans, as well as of the plenty of money: But as foreign trade is not the most material circumstance, it is not to be put in competition with the happiness of so many millions. And if there were no more to endear to them that free government under which they live, this alone were sufficient. The poverty of the common people is a natural, if not an infallible effect of absolute monarchy; though I doubt, whether it be always true, on the other hand, that their riches are an infallible result of liberty. Liberty must be attended with particular accidents, and a certain turn of thinking, in order to produce that effect. Lord BACON, accounting for the great advantages obtained by the ENGLISH in their wars with FRANCE, ascribes them chiefly to the superior ease and plenty of the common people amongst the former;[259] yet the government of the two kingdoms was, at that time, pretty much alike. Where the labourers and artisans are accustomed to work for low wages, and to retain but a small part of the fruits of their labour, it is difficult for them, even in a free government, to better their condition, or conspire among themselves to heighten their wages. But even where they are accustomed to a more plentiful way of life, it is easy for the rich, in an arbitrary government, to conspire against *them,* and throw the whole burthen of the taxes on their shoulders.

It may seem an odd position, that the poverty of the common people in FRANCE, ITALY, and SPAIN, is, in some measure, owing to the superior riches of the soil and happiness of the climate; yet there want not reasons to justify this paradox. In such a fine mould or soil as that of those more southern regions, agriculture is an easy art; and one man, with a couple of sorry horses, will be able, in a season, to cultivate as much land as will pay a pretty considerable rent to the proprietor. All the art, which the farmer knows, is to leave his ground fallow for a year, as soon as it is exhausted; and the warmth of the sun alone and temperature of the climate enrich it, and restore its fertility. Such poor peasants, therefore, require only a simple maintenance for their labour. They have no stock or riches, which claim more; and at the same time, they are for ever dependant on their landlord, who gives no leases, nor fears that his land will be spoiled by the ill methods of cultivation. In ENGLAND, the land is rich, but coarse; must be cultivated at a great expence; and produces slender crops, when not carefully

259. [Sir Francis Bacon (1561–1626), *The Essayes or Counsels, Civill and Morall,* ed. by M. Kiernan (Cambridge: Harvard University Press, 1985), p. 93 (Essay 29).]

managed, and by a method which gives not the full profit but in a course of several years. A farmer, therefore, in ENGLAND must have a considerable stock, and a long lease; which beget proportional profits. The fine vineyards of CHAMPAGNE and BURGUNDY, that often yield to the landlord above five pounds *per* acre, are cultivated by peasants, who have scarcely bread: The reason is, that such peasants need no stock but their own limbs, with instruments of husbandry, which they can buy for twenty shillings. The farmers are commonly in some better circumstances in those countries. But the grasiers are most at their ease of all those who cultivate the land. The reason is still the same. Men must have profits proportionable to their expence and hazard. Where so considerable a number of the labouring poor as the peasants and farmers are in very low circumstances, all the rest must partake of their poverty, whether the government of that nation be monarchical or republican.

We may form a similar remark with regard to the general history of mankind. What is the reason, why no people, living between the tropics, could ever yet attain to any art or civility, or reach even any police in their government, and any military discipline; while few nations in the temperate climates have been altogether deprived of these advantages? It is probable that one cause of this phenomenon is the warmth and equality of weather in the torrid zone, which render clothes and houses less requisite for the inhabitants, and thereby remove, in part, that necessity, which is the great spur to industry and invention. *Curis acuens mortalia corda.*[260] Not to mention, that the fewer goods or possessions of this kind any people enjoy, the fewer quarrels are likely to arise amongst them, and the less necessity will there be for a settled police or regular authority to protect and defend them from foreign enemies, or from each other.

Essay XVIII: *Of Refinement in the Arts*[261]

Luxury is a word of an uncertain signification, and may be taken in a good as well as in a bad sense. In general, it means great refinement

260. [Virgil (70–19 B.C.), *Georgics*, 1.123: "sharpening men's wits by care" (trans. by H.R. Fairclough).]

261. [Hume changed the title of this essay in 1760 from "Of Luxury" to "Of Refinement in the Arts," thus underscoring the idea that luxury refines or polishes or civilizes both an individual and a country. For a discussion of the relationship in the

in the gratification of the senses; and any degree of it may be innocent or blameable, according to the age, or country, or condition of the person. The bounds between the virtue and the vice cannot here be exactly fixed, more than in other moral subjects. To imagine, that the gratifying of any sense, or the indulging of any delicacy in meat, drink, or apparel, is of itself a vice, can never enter into a head, that is not disordered by the frenzies of enthusiasm. I have, indeed, heard of a monk abroad, who, because the windows of his cell opened upon a noble prospect, made a *covenant with his eyes* never to turn that way, or receive so sensual a gratification. And such is the crime of drinking CHAMPAGNE or BURGUNDY, preferably to small beer or porter. These indulgences are only vices, when they are pursued at the expence of some virtue, as liberality or charity; in like manner as they are follies, when for them a man ruins his fortune, and reduces himself to want and beggary. Where they entrench upon no virtue, but leave ample subject whence to provide for friends, family, and every proper object of generosity or compassion, they are entirely innocent, and have in every age been acknowledged such by almost all moralists. To be entirely occupied with the luxury of the table, for instance, without any relish for the pleasures of ambition, study, or conversation, is a mark of stupidity, and is incompatible with any vigour of temper or genius. To confine one's expence entirely to such a gratification, without regard to friends or family, is an indication of a heart destitute of humanity or benevolence. But if a man reserve time sufficient for all laudable pursuits, and money sufficient for all generous purposes, he is free from every shadow of blame or reproach.

Since luxury may be considered either as innocent or blameable, one may be surprized at those preposterous opinions, which have been entertained concerning it; while men of libertine principles bestow praises even on vicious luxury, and represent it as highly advantageous to society; and on the other hand, men of severe morals blame even the most innocent luxury, and represent it as the source of all the corruptions, disorders, and factions, incident to civil government. We shall here endeavour to correct both these extremes, by proving, *first*, that the ages of refinement are both the happiest and most virtuous; *secondly*, that wherever luxury ceases to be innocent, it also ceases to

---

eighteenth century amongst such terms as 'luxury,' 'refinement,' 'polish,' and 'civilize,' see Jean Starobinski, *Blessings in Disguise; or The Morality of Evil*, trans. by A. Goldhammer (Cambridge: Harvard University Press, 1993), pp. 1–35. See n. 35.]

be beneficial; and when carried a degree too far, is a quality pernicious, though perhaps not the most pernicious, to political society.

To prove the first point, we need but consider the effects of refinement both on *private* and on *public* life. Human happiness, according to the most received notions, seems to consist in three ingredients; action, pleasure, and indolence: And though these ingredients ought to be mixed in different proportions, according to the particular disposition of the person; yet no one ingredient can be entirely wanting, without destroying, in some measure, the relish of the whole composition. Indolence or repose, indeed, seems not of itself to contribute much to our enjoyment; but, like sleep, is requisite as an indulgence to the weakness of human nature, which cannot support an uninterrupted course of business or pleasure. That quick march of the spirits, which takes a man from himself, and chiefly gives satisfaction, does in the end exhaust the mind, and requires some intervals of repose, which, though agreeable for a moment, yet, if prolonged, beget a languor and lethargy, that destroys all enjoyment. Education, custom, and example, have a mighty influence in turning the mind to any of these pursuits; and it must be owned, that, where they promote a relish for action and pleasure, they are so far favourable to human happiness. In times when industry and the arts flourish, men are kept in perpetual occupation, and enjoy, as their reward, the occupation itself, as well as those pleasures which are the fruit of their labour. The mind acquires new vigour; enlarges its powers and faculties; and by an assiduity in honest industry, both satisfies its natural appetites, and prevents the growth of unnatural ones, which commonly spring up, when nourished by ease and idleness. Banish those arts from society, you deprive men both of action and of pleasure; and leaving nothing but indolence in their place, you even destroy the relish of indolence, which never is agreeable, but when it succeeds to labour, and recruits the spirits, exhausted by too much application and fatigue.[262]

Another advantage of industry and of refinements in the mechanical arts, is, that they commonly produce some refinements in the liberal; nor can one be carried to perfection, without being accompanied, in some degree, with the other. The same age, which produces great philosophers and politicians, renowned generals and poets, usually abounds with skilful weavers, and ship-carpenters. We cannot reason-

262. [On this matter, see Hume's *An Enquiry Concerning the Principles of Morals*, p. 89 (this edition).]

ably expect, that a piece of woollen cloth will be wrought to perfection in a nation, which is ignorant of astronomy, or where ethics are neglected. The spirit of the age affects all the arts; and the minds of men, being once roused from their lethargy, and put into a fermentation, turn themselves on all sides, and carry improvements into every art and science. Profound ignorance is totally banished, and men enjoy the privilege of rational creatures, to think as well as to act, to cultivate the pleasures of the mind as well as those of the body.

The more these refined arts advance, the more sociable men become: nor is it possible, that, when enriched with science, and possessed of a fund of conversation,[263] they should be contented to remain in solitude, or live with their fellow-citizens in that distant manner, which is peculiar to ignorant and barbarous nations. They flock into cities; love to receive and communicate knowledge; to show their wit or their breeding; their taste in conversation or living, in clothes or furniture. Curiosity allures the wise; vanity the foolish; and pleasure both. Particular clubs and societies are every where formed: Both sexes meet in an easy and sociable manner; and the tempers of men, as well as their behaviour, refine apace. So that, beside the improvements which they receive from knowledge and the liberal arts, it is impossible but they must feel an encrease of humanity, from the very habit of conversing together, and contributing to each other's pleasure and entertainment. Thus *industry, knowledge,* and *humanity,* are linked together by an indissoluble chain, and are found, from experience as well as reason, to be peculiar to the more polished, and, what are commonly denominated, the more luxurious ages.

Nor are these advantages attended with disadvantages, that bear any proportion to them. The more men refine upon pleasure, the less will they indulge in excesses of any kind; because nothing is more destructive to true pleasure than such excesses. One may safely affirm, that the TARTARS are oftener guilty of beastly gluttony, when they feast on their dead horses, than EUROPEAN courtiers with all their refinements of cookery. And if libertine love, or even infidelity to the marriage-bed, be more frequent in polite ages, when it is often regarded only as a piece of gallantry; drunkenness, on the other hand, is much less common: A vice more odious, and more pernicious both to mind and body. And in this matter I would appeal, not only to an OVID or

263. [The importance of conversation in Hume's understanding of how human beings become civilized cannot be overrated.]

a PETRONIUS,[264] but to a SENECA or a CATO.[265] We know, that CAESAR, during CATILINE'S conspiracy, being necessitated to put into CATO'S hands a *billet-doux,* which discovered an intrigue with SERVILIA, CATO'S own sister, that stern philosopher threw it back to him with indignation; and in the bitterness of his wrath, gave him the appellation of drunkard, as a term more opprobrious than that with which he could more justly have reproached him.

But industry, knowledge, and humanity, are not advantageous in private life alone: They diffuse their beneficial influence on the *public,* and render the government as great and flourishing as they make individuals happy and prosperous. The encrease and consumption of all the commodities, which serve to the ornament and pleasure of life, are advantageous to society; because, at the same time that they multiply those innocent gratifications to individuals, they are a kind of *storehouse* of labour, which, in the exigencies of state, may be turned to the public service. In a nation, where there is no demand for such superfluities, men sink into indolence, lose all enjoyment of life, and are useless to the public, which cannot maintain or support its fleets and armies, from the industry of such slothful members.

The bounds of all the EUROPEAN kingdoms are, at present, nearly the same they were two hundred years ago: But what a difference is there in the power and grandeur of those kingdoms? Which can be ascribed to nothing but the encrease of art and industry. When CHARLES VIII. of FRANCE invaded ITALY, he carried with him about 20,000 men: Yet this armament so exhausted the nation, as we learn from GUICCIARDIN,[266] that for some years it was not able to make so great an effort. The late king of FRANCE, in time of war, kept in pay above 400,000 men;[267] though from MAZARINE'S death to his own, he was engaged in a course of wars that lasted near thirty years.

264. [Ovid (43 B.C.–A.D. 17) is best known for his love poems and the *Metamorphoses*. Petronius was the arbiter of good taste or refinement under Emperor Nero (Emperor from A.D. 54 to 68).]

265. [Seneca (between 4 B.C. and A.D. 1–A.D. 65) was a Stoic philosopher. Cato the Younger (95–46 B.C.) supported Pompey against Caesar in the Roman Civil War.]

266. [Francesco Guicciardini (1483–1540) describes the invasions of Charles VIII (King of France from 1483 to 1498) in *The History of Italy*, trans. by S. Alexander (New York: The Macmillan Co., 1969), pp. 23–127.]

267. The inscription on the PLACE-DE-VENDOME says 440,000.

This industry is much promoted by the knowledge inseparable from ages of art and refinement; as, on the other hand, this knowledge enables the public to make the best advantage of the industry of its subjects. Laws, order, police, discipline; these can never be carried to any degree of perfection, before human reason has refined itself by exercise, and by an application to the more vulgar arts, at least, of commerce and manufacture. Can we expect, that a government will be well modelled by a people, who know not how to make a spinning-wheel, or to employ a loom to advantage? Not to mention, that all ignorant ages are infested with superstition, which throws the government off its bias, and disturbs men in the pursuit of their interest and happiness.

Knowledge in the arts of government naturally begets mildness and moderation, by instructing men in the advantages of humane maxims above rigour and severity, which drive subjects into rebellion, and make the return to submission impracticable, by cutting off all hopes of pardon. When the tempers of men are softened as well as their knowledge improved, this humanity appears still more conspicuous, and is the chief characteristic which distinguishes a civilized age from times of barbarity and ignorance. Factions are then less inveterate, revolutions less tragical, authority less severe, and seditions less frequent. Even foreign wars abate of their cruelty; and after the field of battle, where honour and interest steel men against compassion as well as fear, the combatants divest themselves of the brute, and resume the man.

Nor need we fear, that men, by losing their ferocity, will lose their martial spirit, or become less undaunted and vigorous in defence of their country or their liberty. The arts have no such effect in enervating either the mind or body. On the contrary, industry, their inseparable attendant, adds new force to both. And if anger, which is said to be the whetstone of courage, loses somewhat of its asperity, by politeness and refinement; a sense of honour, which is a stronger, more constant, and more governable principle, acquires fresh vigour by that elevation of genius which arises from knowledge and a good education. Add to this, that courage can neither have any duration, nor be of any use, when not accompanied with discipline and martial skill, which are seldom found among a barbarous people. The ancients remarked, that DATAMES[268] was the only barbarian that ever knew the art of war.

268. [Persian commander who led a rebellion against Artaxerxes II (see n. 23), which ended with his assassination in 362 B.C.]

And PYRRHUS,[269] seeing the ROMANS marshal their army with some art and skill, said with surprize, *These barbarians have nothing barbarous in their discipline!* It is observable, that, as the old ROMANS, by applying themselves solely to war, were almost the only uncivilized people that ever possessed military discipline; so the modern ITALIANS are the only civilized people, among EUROPEANS, that ever wanted courage and a martial spirit. Those who would ascribe this effeminacy of the ITALIANS to their luxury, or politeness, or application to the arts, need but consider the FRENCH and ENGLISH, whose bravery is as uncontestable, as their love for the arts, and their assiduity in commerce. The ITALIAN historians give us a more satisfactory reason for this degeneracy of their countrymen. They shew us how the sword was dropped at once by all the ITALIAN sovereigns; while the VENETIAN aristocracy was jealous of its subjects, the FLORENTINE democracy applied itself entirely to commerce; ROME was governed by priests, and NAPLES by women. War then became the business of soldiers of fortune, who spared one another, and to the astonishment of the world, could engage a whole day in what they called a battle, and return at night to their camp, without the least bloodshed.

What has chiefly induced severe moralists to declaim against refinement in the arts, is the example of ancient ROME, which, joining, to its poverty and rusticity, virtue and public spirit, rose to such a surprizing height of grandeur and liberty; but having learned from its conquered provinces the ASIATIC luxury, fell into every kind of corruption; whence arose sedition and civil wars, attended at last with the total loss of liberty. All the LATIN classics, whom we peruse in our infancy, are full of these sentiments, and universally ascribe the ruin of their state to the arts and riches imported from the East: Insomuch that SALLUST represents a taste for painting as a vice, no less than lewdness and drinking.[270] And so popular were these sentiments, during the later ages of the republic, that this author abounds in praises of the old rigid ROMAN virtue, though himself the most egregious instance of modern luxury and corruption; speaks

269. [Pyrrhus (319–272 B.C.), the most famous king of Epirus, assisted Tarentum (in the south of Italy) against the Romans in 280, and he continued to fight against them until 275.]

270. [Sallust (probably 86–35 B.C.), *The War with Catiline*, sec. X–XIII (especially, XI).]

contemptuously of the GRECIAN eloquence, though the most elegant writer in the world; nay, employs preposterous digressions and declamations to this purpose, though a model of taste and correctness.

But it would be easy to prove, that these writers mistook the cause of the disorders in the ROMAN state, and ascribed to luxury and the arts, what really proceeded from an ill modelled government, and the unlimited extent of conquests. Refinement on the pleasures and conveniencies of life has no natural tendency to beget venality and corruption. The value, which all men put upon any particular pleasure, depends on comparison and experience; nor is a porter less greedy of money, which he spends on bacon and brandy, than a courtier, who purchases champagne and ortolans. Riches are valuable at all times, and to all men; because they always purchase pleasures, such as men are accustomed to, and desire: Nor can any thing restrain or regulate the love of money, but a sense of honour and virtue; which, if it be not nearly equal at all times, will naturally abound most in ages of knowledge and refinement.

Of all EUROPEAN kingdoms, POLAND seems the most defective in the arts of war as well as peace, mechanical as well as liberal; yet it is there that venality and corruption do most prevail. The nobles seem to have preserved their crown elective for no other purpose, than regularly to sell it to the highest bidder. This is almost the only species of commerce, with which that people are acquainted.

The liberties of ENGLAND, so far from decaying since the improvements in the arts, have never flourished so much as during that period. And though corruption may seem to encrease of late years; this is chiefly to be ascribed to our established liberty, when our princes have found the impossibility of governing without parliaments, or of terrifying parliaments by the phantom of prerogative. Not to mention, that this corruption or venality prevails much more among the electors than the elected; and therefore cannot justly be ascribed to any refinements in luxury.

If we consider the matter in a proper light, we shall find, that a progress in the arts is rather favourable to liberty, and has a natural tendency to preserve, if not produce a free government. In rude unpolished nations, where the arts are neglected, all labour is bestowed on the cultivation of the ground; and the whole society is divided into two classes, proprietors of land, and their vassals or tenants. The latter are necessarily dependent, and fitted for slavery and subjection; especially where they possess no riches, and are not valued for their knowledge in agriculture; as must always be the case where the arts are neglected. The former naturally erect themselves into petty tyrants; and must either submit to an absolute master, for the sake of peace and order; or if they will preserve their independency, like the ancient barons, they must fall into feuds and contests among themselves, and throw the whole society into such confusion, as is perhaps worse than the most despotic government. But where luxury nourishes commerce and industry, the peasants, by a proper cultivation of the land, become rich and independent; while the tradesmen and merchants acquire a share of the property, and draw authority and consideration to that middling rank of men, who are the best and firmest basis of public liberty. These submit not to slavery, like the peasants, from poverty and meanness of spirit; and having no hopes of tyrannizing over others, like the barons, they are not tempted, for the sake of that gratification, to submit to the tyranny of their sovereign. They covet equal laws, which may secure their property, and preserve them from monarchical, as well as aristocratical tyranny.

The lower house is the support of our popular government; and all the world acknowledges, that it owed its chief influence and consideration to the encrease of commerce, which threw such a balance of property into the hands of the commons. How inconsistent then is it to blame so violently a refinement in the arts, and to represent it as the bane of liberty and public spirit!

To declaim against present times, and magnify the virtue of remote ancestors, is a propensity almost inherent in human nature: And as the sentiments and opinions of civilized ages alone are transmitted to posterity, hence it is that we meet with so many severe judgments pronounced against luxury, and even science; and hence it is that at present we give so ready an assent to them. But the fallacy is easily perceived, by comparing different nations that are contemporaries; where we both judge more impartially, and can better set in opposition those manners, with which we are sufficiently acquainted. Treachery and cruelty, the most pernicious and most odious of all vices, seem peculiar to uncivilized ages; and by the refined GREEKS and ROMANS were ascribed to all the barbarous nations, which surrounded them. They might justly, therefore, have presumed, that their own ancestors, so highly celebrated, possessed no greater virtue, and were as much inferior to their posterity in honour and humanity, as in taste and science. An ancient FRANK or SAXON may be highly extolled: But I believe every man would think his life or fortune much less secure in the hands of a MOOR or TARTAR, than in those of a FRENCH or ENGLISH gentleman, the rank of men the most civilized in the most civilized nations.

We come now to the *second* position which we proposed to illustrate, to wit, that, as innocent luxury, or a refinement in the arts and conveniencies of life, is advantageous to the public; so wherever luxury ceases to be innocent, it also ceases to be beneficial; and when carried a degree farther, begins to be a quality pernicious, though, perhaps, not the most pernicious, to political society.

Let us consider what we call vicious luxury. No gratification, however sensual, can of itself be esteemed vicious. A gratification is only vicious, when it engrosses all a man's expence, and leaves no ability for such acts of duty and generosity as are required by his situation and fortune. Suppose, that he correct the vice, and employ part of his expence in the education of his children, in the support of his friends, and in relieving the poor; would any prejudice result to society? On the contrary, the same consumption would arise; and that labour, which, at present, is employed only in producing a slender gratification to one man, would relieve the necessitous, and bestow satisfaction on hundreds. The same care and toil that raise a dish of peas at CHRISTMAS, would give bread to a whole family during six months. To say, that, without a vicious luxury, the labour would not have been employed at all, is only to say, that there is some other defect in human nature, such as indolence, selfishness, inattention to others, for which luxury, in some measure, provides a remedy; as one poison may be an antidote to another. But virtue, like wholesome food, is better than poisons, however corrected.

Suppose the same number of men, that are at present in GREAT BRITAIN, with the same soil and climate; I ask, is it not possible for them to be happier, by the most perfect way of life that can be imagined, and by the greatest reformation that Omnipotence itself could work in their temper and disposition? To assert, that they cannot, appears evidently ridiculous. As the land is able to maintain more than all its present inhabitants, they could never, in such a UTOPIAN state, feel any other ills than those which arise from bodily sickness; and these are not the half of human miseries. All other ills spring from some vice, either in ourselves or others; and even many of our diseases proceed from the same origin. Remove the vices, and the ills follow. You must only take care to remove all the vices. If you remove part, you may render the matter worse. By banishing *vicious* luxury, without curing sloth and an indifference to others, you only diminish industry in the state, and add nothing to men's charity or their generosity. Let us, therefore, rest contented with asserting, that two opposite vices in a state may be more advantageous than either of them alone; but let us never pronounce vice in itself advantageous. Is it not very inconsistent for an author to assert in one page, that moral distinctions are inventions of politicians for public interest; and in the next page maintain, that vice is advantageous to the public?[271] And indeed it seems upon any system of morality, little less than a contradiction in terms, to talk of a vice, which is in general beneficial to society.

I thought this reasoning necessary, in order to give some light to a philosophical question, which has been much disputed in ENGLAND. I call it a *philosophical* question, not a *political* one. For whatever may be the consequence of such a miraculous transformation of mankind, as would endow them with every species of virtue, and free them from every species of vice; this concerns not the magistrate, who aims only at possibilities. He cannot cure every vice by substituting a virtue in its place. Very often he can only cure one vice by another; and in that case, he ought to prefer what is least pernicious to society. Luxury, when excessive, is the source of many ills; but is in general preferable to sloth and idleness, which would commonly succeed in its place, and are more hurtful both to private persons and to the public. When sloth reigns, a mean uncultivated way of life prevails amongst individuals, without society, without enjoyment. And if the sovereign, in such a situation, demands the service of his subjects, the labour of the state suffices only to furnish the necessaries of life to the labourers, and can afford nothing to those who are employed in the public service.[272]

Essay XIX: *Idea of a Perfect Commonwealth*

[h]It is not with forms of government, as with other artificial contrivances; where an old engine may be rejected, if we can discover another more accurate and commodious, or where trials may safely be made, even

271. Fable of the Bees. [Bernard Mandeville (1670–1733), *The Fable of the Bees: or, Private Vices, Publick Benefits*, ed. by F.B. Kaye, 2 vols. (Oxford: At the Clarendon Press, 1924).]

272. [It is worth comparing Hume's views in this essay to those of Jean-Jacques Rousseau (1712–78), especially his *Discourse on the Origin of Inequality*. See n. 35.]

though the success be doubtful. An established government has an infinite advantage, by that very circumstance of its being established; the bulk of mankind being governed by authority, not reason, and never attributing authority to any thing that has not the recommendation of antiquity. To tamper, therefore, in this affair, or try experiments merely upon the credit of supposed argument and philosophy, can never be the part of a wise magistrate, who will bear a reverence to what carries the marks of age; and though he may attempt some improvements for the public good, yet will he adjust his innovations, as much as possible, to the ancient fabric, and preserve entire the chief pillars and supports of the constitution.

The mathematicians in EUROPE have been much divided concerning that figure of a ship, which is the most commodious for sailing; and HUYGENS,[273] who at last determined the controversy, is justly thought to have obliged the learned, as well as commercial world; though COLUMBUS had sailed to AMERICA, and Sir FRANCIS DRAKE[274] made the tour of the world, without any such discovery. As one form of government must be allowed more perfect than another, independent of the manners and humours of particular men; why may we not enquire what is the most perfect of all, though the common botched and inaccurate governments seem to serve the purposes of society, and though it be not so easy to establish a new system of government, as to build a vessel upon a new construction? The subject is surely the most worthy curiosity of any the wit of man can possibly devise. And who knows, if this controversy were fixed by the universal consent of the wise and learned, but, in some future age, an opportunity might be afforded of reducing the theory to practice, either by a dissolution of some old government, or by the combination of men to form a new one, in some distant part of the world? In all cases, it must be advantageous to know what is most perfect in the kind, that we may be able to bring any real constitution or form of government as near it as possible, by such gentle alterations and innovations as may not give too great disturbance to society.

273. [Christiaan Huygens (1629–95) was an extremely important Dutch mathematician, astronomer, and inventor. Hume may be referring to Huygens's work in France in the early 1660s on a cycloidal-pendulum clock for the determination of longitude at sea. In 1665, Huygens published an instruction manual for pilots for the use of such a clock.]

274. [Sir Francis Drake (1545–95) sailed around the world from 1577 to 1580.]

All I pretend to in the present essay is to revive this subject of speculation; and therefore I shall deliver my sentiments in as few words as possible. A long dissertation on that head would not, I apprehend, be very acceptable to the public, who will be apt to regard such disquisitions both as useless and chimerical.

All plans of government, which suppose great reformation in the manners of mankind, are plainly imaginary.[275] Of this nature, are the *Republic* of PLATO, and the *Utopia* of Sir THOMAS MORE.[276] The OCEANA is the only valuable model of a commonwealth, that has yet been offered to the public.[277]

The chief defects of the OCEANA seem to be these. *First,* Its rotation is inconvenient, by throwing men, of whatever abilities, by intervals, out of public employments. *Secondly,* Its *Agrarian* is impracticable. Men will soon learn the art, which was practised in ancient ROME, of concealing their possessions under other people's name; till at last, the abuse will become so common, that they will throw off even the appearance of restraint. *Thirdly,* The OCEANA provides not a sufficient security for liberty, or the redress of grievances. The senate must propose, and the people consent; by which means, the senate have not only a negative upon the people, but, what is of much greater consequence, their negative goes before the votes of the people. Were the King's negative of the same nature in the ENGLISH constitution, and could he prevent any bill from coming into parliament, he would be an absolute monarch. As his negative follows the votes of the houses, it is of little consequence: Such a difference is there in the manner of placing the same thing. When a popular bill has been debated in parliament, is brought to maturity, all its conveniencies and inconveniencies, weighed and balanced; if afterwards it be presented for the royal assent, few princes will venture to reject the unanimous desire of the people. But could the King crush a disagreeable bill in embryo (as was the case, for some time, in the SCOTTISH parliament, by

275. [Compare Machiavelli's (1469–1527) remark that, "Many have imagined republics and principalities that have never been seen or known to exist in truth; for it is so far from how one lives to how one should live that he who lets go of what is done for what should be done learns his ruin rather than his preservation" (*The Prince*, trans. by H. Mansfield {Chicago: University of Chicago Press, 1985}, p. 61).]

276. [Sir Thomas More (1478–1535) coined the term 'utopia' in *Utopia* (1516); see the edition in *The Complete Works of St. Thomas More*, ed. by E. Surtz and J. H. Hexter (New Haven: Yale University Press, 1979), vol. IV.]

277. [Hume is referring to James Harrington's (1611–77) *Oceana*.]

means of the lords of the articles[278]), the BRITISH government would have no balance, nor would grievances ever be redressed: And it is certain, that exorbitant power proceeds not, in any government, from new laws, so much as from neglecting to remedy the abuses, which frequently rise from the old ones. A government, says MACHIAVEL, must often be brought back to its original principles.[279] It appears then, that, in the OCEANA, the whole legislature may be said to rest in the senate; which HARRINGTON would own to be an inconvenient form of government, especially after the *Agrarian* is abolished.

Here is a form of government, to which I cannot, in theory, discover any considerable objection.

Let GREAT BRITAIN and IRELAND, or any territory of equal extent, be divided into 100 counties, and each county into 100 parishes, making in all 10,000. If the country, proposed to be erected into a commonwealth be of more narrow extent, we may diminish the number of counties; but never bring them below thirty. If it be of greater extent, it were better to enlarge the parishes, or throw more parishes into a county, than encrease the number of counties.

Let all the freeholders of twenty pounds a-year in the county, and all the householders worth 500 pounds in the town parishes, meet annually in the parish church, and chuse, by ballot, some freeholder of the county for their member, whom we shall call the county *representative.*

Let the 100 county representatives, two days after their election, meet in the county town, and chuse by ballot, from their own body, ten county *magistrates,* and one *senator.* There are, therefore, in the whole commonwealth, 100 senators, 1100 county magistrates, and 10,000 county representatives. For we shall bestow on all senators the authority of county magistrates, and on all county magistrates the authority of county representatives.

Let the senators meet in the capital, and be endowed with the whole executive power of the commonwealth; the power of peace and war, of giving orders to generals, admirals, and ambassadors, and, in short, all the prerogatives of a BRITISH King, except his negative.

Let the county representatives meet in their particular counties, and possess the whole legislative power of the commonwealth; the greater

278. [See Hume's discussion of the lords of articles in *The History of England*, vol. V, pp. 333–34.]

279. [Niccoló Machiavelli, *Discourses on Livy*, trans. by H. Mansfield and N. Tarcov (Chicago: University of Chicago Press, forthcoming), bk. 3, ch. 1.]

number of counties deciding the question; and where these are equal, let the senate have the casting vote.

Every new law must first be debated in the senate; and though rejected by it, if ten senators insist and protest, it must be sent down to the counties. The senate, if they please, may join to the copy of the law their reasons for receiving or rejecting it.

Because it would be troublesome to assemble all the county representatives for every trivial law, that may be requisite, the senate have their choice of sending down the law either to the county magistrates or county representatives.

The magistrates, though the law be referred to them, may, if they please, call the representatives, and submit the affair to their determination.

Whether the law be referred by the senate to the county magistrates or representatives, a copy of it, and of the senate's reasons, must be sent to every representative eight days before the day appointed for the assembling, in order to deliberate concerning it. And though the determination be, by the senate, referred to the magistrates, if five representatives of the county order the magistrates to assemble the whole court of representatives, and submit the affair to their determination, they must obey.

Either the county magistrates or representatives may give, to the senator of the county, the copy of a law to be proposed to the senate; and if five counties concur in the same order, the law, though refused by the senate, must come either to the county magistrates or representatives, as is contained in the order of the five counties.

Any twenty counties, by a vote either of their magistrates or representatives, may throw any man out of all public offices for a year. Thirty counties for three years.

The senate has a power of throwing out any member or number of members of its own body, not to be re-elected for that year. The senate cannot throw out twice in a year the senator of the same county.

The power of the old senate continues for three weeks after the annual election of the county representatives. Then all the new senators are shut up in a conclave, like the cardinals; and by an intricate ballot, such as that of VENICE or MALTA, they chuse the following magistrates; a protector, who represents the dignity of the commonwealth, and presides in the senate; two secretaries of state; these six councils, a council of state, a council of religion and learning, a council of trade, a council of laws, a council of war, a council of the admiralty, each council consisting of five persons; together with six commissioners of the treasury and a first commissioner. All these must be senators. The senate also names all the ambassadors to foreign courts, who may either be senators or not.

The senate may continue any or all of these, but must re-elect them every year.

The protector and two secretaries have session and suffrage in the council of state. The business of that council is all foreign politics. The council of state has session and suffrage in all the other councils.

The council of religion and learning inspects the universities and clergy. That of trade inspects every thing that may affect commerce. That of laws inspects all the abuses of law by the inferior magistrates, and examines what improvements may be made of the municipal law. That of war inspects the militia and its discipline, magazines, stores, &c. and when the republic is in war, examines into the proper orders for generals. The council of admiralty has the same power with regard to the navy, together with the nomination of the captains and all inferior officers.

None of these councils can give orders themselves, except where they receive such powers from the senate. In other cases, they must communicate every thing to the senate.

When the senate is under adjournment, any of the councils may assemble it before the day appointed for its meeting.

Besides these councils or courts, there is another called the court of *competitors;* which is thus constituted. If any candidates for the office of senator have more votes than a third of the representatives, that candidate, who has most votes, next to the senator elected, becomes incapable for one year of all public offices, even of being a magistrate or representative: But he takes his seat in the court of competitors. Here then is a court which may sometimes consist of a hundred members, sometimes have no members at all; and by that means, be for a year abolished.

The court of competitors has no power in the commonwealth. It has only the inspection of public accounts, and the accusing of any man before the senate. If the senate acquit him, the court of competitors may, if they please, appeal to the people, either magistrates or representatives. Upon that appeal, the magistrates or representatives meet on the day appointed by the court of competitors, and chuse in each county three persons; from which number every senator is excluded. These, to the number of 300, meet in the capital, and bring the person accused to a new trial.

The court of competitors may propose any law to the senate; and if refused, may appeal to the people, that is, to the magistrates or representatives, who examine it in their counties. Every senator, who is thrown out of the senate by a vote of the court, takes his seat in the court of competitors.

The senate possesses all the judicative authority of the house of Lords, that is, all the appeals from the inferior courts. It likewise appoints the Lord Chancellor, and all the officers of the law.

Every county is a kind of republic within itself, and the representatives may make bye-laws; which have no authority 'till three months after they are voted. A copy of the law is sent to the senate, and to every other county. The senate, or any single county, may, at any time, annul any bye-law of another county.

The representatives have all the authority of the BRITISH justices of peace in trials, commitments, &c.

The magistrates have the appointment of all the officers of the revenue in each county. All causes with regard to the revenue are carried ultimately by appeal before the magistrates. They pass the accompts of all the officers; but must have their own accompts examined and passed at the end of the year by the representatives.

The magistrates name rectors or ministers to all the parishes.

The Presbyterian government is established; and the highest ecclesiastical court is an assembly or synod of all the presbyters of the county. The magistrates may take any cause from this court, and determine it themselves.

The magistrates may try, and depose or suspend any presbyter.

The militia is established in imitation of that of SWISSERLAND, which being well known, we shall not insist upon it. It will only be proper to make this addition, that an army of 20,000 men be annually drawn out by rotation, paid and encamped during six weeks in summer; that the duty of a camp may not be altogether unknown.

The magistrates appoint all the colonels and downwards. The senate all upwards. During war, the general appoints the colonel and downwards, and his commission is good for a twelvemonth. But after that, it must be confirmed by the magistrates of the county, to which the regiment belongs. The magistrates may break any officer in the county regiment. And the senate may do the same to any officer in the service. If the magistrates do not think proper to confirm the general's choice, they may appoint another officer in the place of him they reject.

All crimes are tried within the county by the magistrates and a jury. But the senate can stop any trial, and bring it before themselves.

Any county may indict any man before the senate for any crime.

The protector, the two secretaries, the council of state, with any five or more that the senate appoints, are possessed, on extraordinary emergencies, of *dictatorial* power for six months.

The protector may pardon any person condemned by the inferior courts.

In time of war, no officer of the army that is in the field can have any civil office in the commonwealth.

The capital, which we shall call LONDON, may be allowed four members in the senate. It may therefore be divided into four counties. The representatives of each of these chuse one senator, and ten magistrates. There are therefore in the city four senators, forty-four magistrates, and four hundred representatives. The magistrates have the same authority as in the counties. The representatives also have the same authority; but they never meet in one general court: They give their votes in their particular county, or division of hundreds.

When they enact any bye-law, the greater number of counties or divisions determines the matter. And where these are equal, the magistrates have the casting vote.

The magistrates chuse the mayor, sheriff, recorder, and other officers of the city.

In the commonwealth, no representative, magistrate, or senator, as such, has any salary. The protector, secretaries, councils, and ambassadors, have salaries.

The first year in every century is set apart for correcting all inequalities, which time may have produced in the representative. This must be done by the legislature.

The following political aphorisms may explain the reason of these orders.

The lower sort of people and small proprietors are good judges enough of one not very distant from them in rank or habitation; and therefore, in their parochial meetings, will probably chuse the best, or nearly the best representative: But they are wholly unfit for county-meetings, and for electing into the higher offices of the republic. Their ignorance gives the grandees an opportunity of deceiving them.

Ten thousand, even though they were not annually elected, are a basis large enough for any free government. It is true, the nobles in POLAND are more than 10,000, and yet these oppress the people. But as power always continues there in the same persons and families, this makes them, in a manner, a different nation from the people. Besides the nobles are there united under a few heads of families.

All free governments must consist of two councils, a lesser and greater; or, in other words, of a senate and people. The people, as HARRINGTON observes, would want wisdom, without the senate: The senate, without the people, would want honesty.

A large assembly of 1000, for instance, to represent the people, if allowed to debate, would fall into disorder. If not allowed to debate, the senate has a negative upon them, and the worst kind of negative, that before resolution.

Here therefore is an inconvenience, which no government has yet fully remedied, but which is the easiest to be remedied in the world. If the people debate, all is confusion: If they do not debate, they can only resolve; and then the senate carves for them. Divide the people into many separate bodies; and then they may debate with safety, and every inconvenience seems to be prevented.

Cardinal de RETZ says, that all numerous assemblies, however composed, are mere mob, and swayed in their debates by the least motive.[280] This we find confirmed by daily experience. When an absurdity strikes a member, he conveys it to his neighbour, and so on, till the whole be infected. Separate this great body; and though every member be only of middling sense, it is not probable, that any thing but reason can prevail over the whole. Influence and example being removed, good sense will always get the better of bad among a number of people.

There are two things to be guarded against in every senate: Its combination, and its division. Its combination is most dangerous. And against this inconvenience we have provided the following remedies. 1. The great dependence of the senators on the people by annual elections; and that not by an undistinguishing rabble, like the ENGLISH electors, but by men of fortune and education. 2. The small power they are allowed. They have few offices to dispose of. Almost all are given by the magistrates in the counties. 3. The court of competitors, which being composed of men that are their rivals, next to them in interest, and uneasy in their present situation, will be sure to take all advantages against them.

The division of the senate is prevented, 1. By the smallness of their number. 2. As faction supposes a combination in a separate interest, it is prevented by their dependence on the people. 3. They have a power of expelling any factious member. It is true, when another member of the same spirit comes from the county, they have no power of expelling him: Nor is it fit they should; for that shows the humour to be in the

280. [See Cardinal de Retz (1614–79), *Memoires*, in *Oeuvres*, nouvelle ed. (Paris: Hachette, 1870–96), vol. II, p. 422.]

people, and may possibly arise from some ill conduct in public affairs. 4. Almost any man, in a senate so regularly chosen by the people, may be supposed fit for any civil office. It would be proper, therefore, for the senate to form some *general* resolutions with regard to the disposing of offices among the members: Which resolutions would not confine them in critical times, when extraordinary parts on the one hand, or extraordinary stupidity on the other, appears in any senator; but they would be sufficient to prevent intrigue and faction, by making the disposal of the offices a thing of course. For instance, let it be a resolution, That no man shall enjoy any office, till he has sat four years in the senate: That, except ambassadors, no man shall be in office two years following: That no man shall attain the higher offices but through the lower: That no man shall be protector twice, &c. The senate of VENICE govern themselves by such resolutions.

In foreign politics the interest of the senate can scarcely ever be divided from that of the people; and therefore it is fit to make the senate absolute with regard to them; otherwise there could be no secrecy or refined policy. Besides, without money no alliance can be executed; and the senate is still sufficiently dependant. Not to mention, that the legislative power being always superior to the executive, the magistrates or representatives may interpose whenever they think proper.

The chief support of the BRITISH government is the opposition of interests; but that, though in the main serviceable, breeds endless factions. In the foregoing plan, it does all the good without any of the harm. The *competitors* have no power of controlling the senate: They have only the power of accusing, and appealing to the people.

It is necessary, likewise, to prevent both combination and division in the thousand magistrates. This is done sufficiently by the separation of places and interests.

But lest that should not be sufficient, their dependence on the 10,000 for their elections, serves to the same purpose.

Nor is that all: For the 10,000 may resume the power whenever they please; and not only when they all please, but when any five of a hundred please, which will happen upon the very first suspicion of a separate interest.

The 10,000 are too large a body either to unite or divide, except when they meet in one place, and fall under the guidance of ambitious leaders. Not to mention their annual election, by the whole body of the people, that are of any consideration.

A small commonwealth is the happiest government in the world within itself, because every thing lies under the eye of the rulers: But it may be subdued by great force from without. This scheme seems to have all the advantages both of a great and a little commonwealth.

Every county-law may be annulled either by the senate or another county; because that shows an opposition of interest: In which case no part ought to decide for itself. The matter must be referred to the whole, which will best determine what agrees with general interest.

As to the clergy and militia, the reasons of these orders are obvious. Without the dependence of the clergy on the civil magistrates, and without a militia, it is in vain to think that any free government will ever have security or stability.

In many governments, the inferior magistrates have no rewards but what arise from their ambition, vanity, or public spirit. The salaries of the FRENCH judges amount not to the interest of the sums they pay for their offices. The DUTCH burgo-masters have little more immediate profit than the ENGLISH justices of peace, or the members of the house of commons formerly. But lest any should suspect, that this would beget negligence in the administration (which is little to be feared, considering the natural ambition of mankind), let the magistrates have competent salaries. The senators have access to so many honourable and lucrative offices, that their attendance needs not be bought. There is little attendance required of the representatives.

That the foregoing plan of government is practicable, no one can doubt, who considers the resemblance that it bears to the commonwealth of the United Provinces, a wise and renowned government. The alterations in the present scheme seem all evidently for the better. 1. The representation is more equal. 2. The unlimited power of the burgo-masters in the towns, which forms a perfect aristocracy in the DUTCH commonwealth, is corrected by a well-tempered democracy, in giving to the people the annual election of the county representatives. 3. The negative, which every province and town has upon the whole body of the DUTCH republic, with regard to alliances, peace and war, and the imposition of taxes, is here removed. 4. The counties, in the present plan, are not so independent of each other, nor do they form separate bodies so much as the seven provinces; where the jealousy and envy of the smaller provinces and towns against the greater, particularly HOLLAND and AMSTERDAM, have frequently disturbed the government. 5. Larger powers, though of the safest kind, are intrusted to the senate than the States-General possess; by which means, the former may become more expeditious, and secret in their resolutions, than it is possible for the latter.

The chief alterations that could be made on the BRITISH government, in order to bring it to the most perfect model of limited monarchy, seem to be the following. *First,* The plan of CROMWELL'S parliament[281] ought to be restored, by making the representation equal, and by allowing none to vote in the county elections who possess not a property of 200 pounds value. *Secondly,* As such a house of Commons would be too weighty for a frail house of Lords, like the present, the Bishops and SCOTCH Peers ought to be removed: The number of the upper house ought to be raised to three or four hundred: Their seats not hereditary, but during life: They ought to have the election of their own members; and no commoner should be allowed to refuse a seat that was offered him. By this means the house of Lords would consist entirely of the men of chief credit, abilities, and interest in the nation; and every turbulent leader in the house of Commons might be taken off, and connected by interest with the house of Peers. Such an aristocracy would be an excellent barrier both to the monarchy and against it. At present, the balance of our government depends in some measure on the abilities and behaviour of the sovereign; which are variable and uncertain circumstances.

This plan of limited monarchy, however corrected, seems still liable to three great inconveniencies. *First,* It removes not entirely, though it may soften, the parties of *court* and *country. Secondly,* The king's personal character must still have great influence on the government. *Thirdly,* The sword is in the hands of a single person, who will always neglect to discipline the militia, in order to have a pretence for keeping up a standing army.

We shall conclude this subject, with observing the falsehood of the common opinion, that no large state, such as FRANCE or GREAT BRITAIN, could ever be modelled into a commonwealth, but that such a form of government can only take place in a city or small territory. The contrary seems probable. Though it is more difficult to form a republican government in an extensive country than in a city; there is more facility, when once it is formed, of preserving it steady and uniform, without tumult and faction. It is not easy, for the distant parts of a large state to combine in any plan of free government; but they easily conspire in the esteem and reverence for a single person, who, by means of this popular

281. [Oliver Cromwell (1599–1658) was a leading member of the parliamentary opposition to Charles I in the English Civil War (1642–52). In 1653, after the fall of the monarchy and the establishment of the Protectorate, Cromwell was named Protector of England. See Hume's depiction of Cromwell in *The History of England*, vol. V and VI.]

favour, may seize the power, and forcing the more obstinate to submit, may establish a monarchical government. On the other hand, a city readily concurs in the same notions of government, the natural equality of property favours liberty, and the nearness of habitation enables the citizens mutually to assist each other. Even under absolute princes, the subordinate government of cities is commonly republican; while that of counties and provinces is monarchical. But these same circumstances, which facilitate the erection of commonwealths in cities, render their constitution more frail and uncertain. Democracies are turbulent. For however the people may be separated or divided into small parties, either in their votes or elections; their near habitation in a city will always make the force of popular tides and currents very sensible. Aristocracies are better adapted for peace and order, and accordingly were most admired by ancient writers; but they are jealous and oppressive. In a large government, which is modelled with masterly skill, there is compass and room enough to refine the democracy, from the lower people, who may be admitted into the first elections or first concoction of the commonwealth, to the higher magistrates, who direct all the movements. At the same time, the parts are so distant and remote, that it is very difficult, either by intrigue, prejudice, or passion, to hurry them into any measures against the public interest.

It is needless to enquire, whether such a government would be immortal. I allow the justness of the poet's exclamation on the endless projects of human race, *Man and for ever!* The world itself probably is not immortal. Such consuming plagues may arise as would leave even a perfect government a weak prey to its neighbours. We know not to what length enthusiasm, or other extraordinary movements of the human mind, may transport men, to the neglect of all order and public good. Where difference of interest is removed, whimsical and unaccountable factions often arise, from personal favour or enmity. Perhaps, rust may grow to the springs of the most accurate political machine, and disorder its motions. Lastly, extensive conquests, when pursued, must be the ruin of every free government; and of the more perfect governments sooner than of the imperfect; because of the very advantages which the former possess above the latter. And though such a state ought to establish a fundamental law against conquests; yet republics have ambition as well as individuals, and present interest makes men forgetful of their posterity. It is a sufficient incitement to human endeavours, that such a government would flourish for many ages; without pretending to bestow, on any work of man, that immortality, which the Almighty seems to have refused to his own productions.

VARIANTS

Variant Readings for David Hume, *Political Writings*

"Of the Liberty of the Press"

a. This was included in the essay in editions from 1741 to 1768.

Since therefore that liberty is so essential to the support of our mixed government; this sufficiently decides the second question, *Whether such a liberty be advantageous or prejudicial;* there being nothing of greater importance in every state than the preservation of the ancient government, especially if it be a free one. But I would fain go a step farther, and assert, that this liberty is attended with so few inconveniencies, that it may be claimed as the common right of mankind, and ought to be indulged them almost in every government: except the ecclesiastical, to which indeed it would prove fatal. We need not dread from this liberty any such ill consequences as followed from the harangues of the popular demagogues of ATHENS and tribunes of ROME. A man reads a book or pamphlet alone and coolly. There is none present from whom he can catch the passion by contagion. He is not hurried away by the force and energy of action. And should he be wrought up to ever so seditious a humour, there is no violent resolution presented to him, by which he can immediately vent his passion. The liberty of the press, therefore, however abused, can scarce ever excite popular tumults or rebellion. And as to those murmurs or secret discontents it may occasion, 'tis better they should get vent in words, that they may come to the knowledge of the magistrate before it be too late, in order to his providing a remedy against them. Mankind, it is true, have always a greater propension to believe what is said to the disadvantage of their governors, than the contrary; but this inclination is inseparable from them, whether they have liberty or not. A whisper may fly as quick, and be as pernicious as a pamphlet. Nay, it will be more pernicious, where men are not accustomed to think freely, or distinguish between truth and falshood.

It has also been found, as the experience of mankind increases, that the *people* are no such dangerous monster as they have been represented, and that it is in every respect better to guide them, like rational creatures, than to lead or drive them, like brute beasts. Before the United Provinces set the example, toleration was deemed incompatible with good government; and it was thought impossible, that a number of religious sects could live together in harmony and peace, and have all of them an equal affection to their common country, and to each other. ENGLAND has set a like example of civil liberty; and though this liberty seems to occasion some small ferment at present, it has not as yet produced any pernicious effects; and it is to be hoped, that men, being every day more accustomed to the free discussion of public affairs, will improve in the judgment of them, and be with greater difficulty seduced by every idle rumour and popular clamour.

It is a very comfortable reflection to the lovers of liberty, that this peculiar privilege of BRITAIN is of a kind that cannot easily be wrested from us, but must last as long as our government remains, in any degree, free and independent. It is seldom, that liberty of any kind is lost all at once. Slavery has so frightful an aspect to men accustomed to freedom, that it must steal upon them by degrees, and must disguise itself in a thousand shapes, in order to be received. But, if the liberty of the press ever be lost, it must be lost at once. The general laws against sedition and libelling are at present as strong as they possibly can be made. Nothing can impose a farther restraint, but either the clapping an IMPRIMATUR upon the press, or the giving to the court very large discretionary powers to punish whatever displeases them. But these concessions would be such a bare-faced violation of liberty, that they will probably be the last efforts of a despotic government. We may conclude, that the liberty of *Britain* is gone for ever when these attempts shall succeed.

"That Politics may be reduced to a Science"

b. This was included in the essay in editions from 1748 (seven years after its original publication) to 1772.

, and such, in a great measure, was that of England, till the middle of the last century, notwithstanding the numerous panegyrics on ancient English liberty.

"Of the Independency of Parliament"

c. This began the essay in editions from 1741 to 1760.

I have frequently observed, in comparing the conduct of the *court* and *country* parties, that the former are commonly less assuming and dogmatical in conversation, more apt to make concessions; and tho' not, perhaps, more susceptible of conviction, yet more able to bear contradiction than the latter; who are apt to fly out upon any opposition, and to regard one as a mercenary designing fellow, if he argues with any coolness and impartiality, or makes any concessions to their adversaries. This is a fact, which, I believe, every one may have observed, who has been much in companies where political questions have been discussed; tho', were one to ask the reason of this difference, every party would be apt to assign a different reason. Gentlemen in the *Opposition* will ascribe it to the very nature of their party, which, being founded on public spirit, and a zeal for the constitution, cannot easily endure such doctrines, as are of pernicious consequence to liberty. The courtiers, on the other hand, will be apt to put us in mind of the clown mentioned by lord SHAFTSBURY. "A clown," says that excellent author, "once took a fancy to hear the *Latin* disputes of doctors at an university. He was asked what pleasure he could take in viewing such combatants, when he could never know so much, as which of the parties had the better. *For that matter,* replied the clown, *I a'n't such a fool neither, but I can see who's the first that puts t'other into a passion.* Nature herself dictated this lesson to the clown, that he who had the better of the argument would be easy and well-humoured: But he who was unable to support his cause by reason would naturally lose his temper and grow violent."

To which of these reasons shall we adhere? To neither of them, in my opinion; unless we have a mind to enlist ourselves and become zealots in either party. I believe I can assign the reason of this different conduct of the two parties, without offending either. The country party are plainly most popular at present, and perhaps have been so in most administrations: So that, being accustomed to prevail in company, they cannot endure to hear their opinions controverted, but are as confident on the public favour, as if they were supported in all their sentiments by the most infallible demonstration. The courtiers, on the other hand, are commonly so run down by popular talkers, that if you speak to them with any moderation, or make them the smallest concessions, they think themselves extremely beholden to you, and are apt to return the favour by a like moderation and facility on their part. To be furious and passionate, they know, would only gain them the character of *shameless mercenaries;* not that of *zealous patriots,* which is the character that such a warm behaviour is apt to acquire to the other party.

In all controversies, we find, without regarding the truth or falshood on either side, that those who defend the established and popular opinions, are always the most dogmatical and imperious in their stile: while their adversaries affect almost extraordinary gentleness and moderation, in order to soften, as much as possible, any prejudices that may lye against them. Consider the behavior of our *free-thinkers* of all denominations, whether they be such as decry all revelation, or only oppose the exorbitant power of the clergy; *Collins, Tindal, Foster, Hoadley.* Compare their moderation and good manners with the furious zeal and scurrility of their adversaries, and you will be convinced of the truth of my observation. A like difference may be observed in the conduct of those French writers, who maintained the controversy with regard to ancient and modern learning. *Boileau,* Monsieur and Madame *Dacier,* l'Abbe de *Bos,* who defended the party of the ancients, mixed their reasonings with satire and invective; while Fontenelle, la Motte, Charpentier, and even Perrault, never transgressed the bounds of moderation and good breeding; though provoked by the most injurious treatment of their adversaries.

I must, however, observe, that this Remark with regard to the seeming Moderation of the *Court* Party, is entirely confin'd to Conversation, and to Gentlemen, who have been engag'd by Interest or Inclination in that Party. For as to the Court-Writers, being commonly hir'd Scriblers, they are altogether as scurrilous as the Mercenaries of the other Party; nor has the *Gazeteer* any Advantage, in this Respect, above *Common Sense.* A man of Education will, in any Party, discover himself to be such, by his Good-breeding and Decency; as a Scoundrel will always betray the opposite Qualities. *The false Accusers accus'd,* &c. is very scurrillous, tho' that Side of the Question, being least popular, shou'd be defended with most Moderation. When L—d B—e, L—d M—t, Mr. L—n take the Pen in Hand, tho' they write with Warmth, they presume not upon their Popularity so far as to transgress the Bounds of Decency. [This paragraph is only found in Editions A and B.]

I am led into this train of reflection, by considering some papers wrote upon that grand topic of *court influence and parliamentary dependence,* where, in my humble opinion, the country party, besides vehemence and satyre, shew too rigid an inflexibility, and too great a jealousy of making concessions to their adversaries. Their reasonings lose their force by being carried too far; and the popularity of their opinions has seduced them to neglect in some measure their justness and solidity. The following reason will, I hope, serve to justify me in this opinion.

"Of the Parties of Great Britain"

d. This was included in the essay in editions from 1741 to 1768.

I must be understood to mean this of persons who have motives for taking party on any side. For, to tell the truth, the greatest part are commonly men who associate themselves they know not why; from example, from passion, from idleness. But still it is requisite, that there be some source of division, either in principle or interest; otherwise such persons would not find parties, to which they could associate themselves.

e. This was included (with some minor variations) in the essay in editions from 1741 to 1768.

'Tis however remarkable, that tho' the principles of WHIG and TORY were both of them of a compound nature; yet the ingredients, which predominated in both, were not correspondent to each other. A TORY loved monarchy, and bore an affection to the family of STUART; but the latter affection was the predominant inclination of the party. A WHIG loved liberty, and was a friend to the settlement in the PROTESTANT line; but the love of liberty was professedly his predominant inclination. The TORIES have frequently acted as republicans, where either policy or revenge has engaged them to that conduct; and there was no one of that party, who, upon the supposition, that he was to be disappointed in his views with regard to the succession, would not have desired to impose the strictest limitations on the crown, and to bring our form of government as near republican as possible, in order to depress the family, which, according to his apprehension, succeeded without any just title. The WHIGS, 'tis true, have also taken steps dangerous to liberty, under colour of securing the succession and settlement of the crown, according to their views: But as the body of the party had no passion for that succession, otherwise than as the means of securing liberty, they have been betrayed into these steps by ignorance, or frailty, or the interests of their leaders. The succession of the crown was, therefore, the chief point with the TORIES; the security of our liberties with the WHIGS. Nor is this seeming irregularity at all difficult to be accounted for, by our present theory. *Court* and *country* parties are the true parents of TORY and WHIG. But 'tis almost impossible, that the attachment of the court party to monarchy should not degenerate into an attachment to the monarch; there being so close a connexion between them, and the latter being so much the more natural object. How easily does the worship of the divinity degenerate into a worship of the idol? The connexion is not so great between liberty, the divinity of the old *country* party or WHIGS, and any monarch or royal family; nor is it so reasonable to suppose, that in that party, the worship can be so easily transferred from the one to the other. Tho' even that would be no great miracle.

'Tis difficult to penetrate into the thoughts and sentiments of any particular man; but 'tis almost impossible to distinguish those of a whole party, where it often happens, that no two persons agree precisely in the same maxims of conduct. Yet I will venture to affirm, that it was not so much PRINCIPLE, or an opinion of indefeasible right, which attached the TORIES to the ancient royal family, as AFFECTION, or a certain love and esteem for their persons. The same cause divided ENGLAND formerly between the houses of YORK and LANCASTER, and SCOTLAND between the families of BRUCE and BALIOL; in an age, when political disputes were but little in fashion, and when political *principles* must of course have had but little influence on mankind. The doctrine of passive obedience is so absurd in itself, and so opposite to our liberties, that it seems to have been chiefly left to pulpit-declaimers, and to their deluded followers among the vulgar. Men of better sense were guided by *affection;* and as to the leaders of this party, 'tis probable, that *interest* was their chief motive, and that they acted more contrary to their private sentiments, than the leaders of the opposite party. Tho' 'tis almost impossible to maintain with zeal the right of any person or family, without acquiring a good-will to them, and changing the *principle* into *affection;* yet this is less natural to people of an elevated station and liberal education, who have had full opportunity of observing the weakness, folly, and arrogance of monarchs, and have found them to be nothing superior, if not rather inferior to the rest of mankind. The *interest,* therefore, of being heads of a party does often, with such people, supply the place both of *principle* and *affection.*

Some, who will not venture to assert, that the *real* difference between WHIG and TORY was lost at the *revolution,* seem inclined to think, that the difference is now abolished, and that affairs are so far returned to their natural state, that there are at present no other parties amongst us but *court* and *country;* that is, men, who by interest or principle, are attached either to monarchy or to liberty. It must, indeed, be confest, that the TORY party seem, of late, to have decayed much in their numbers; still more in their zeal; and I may venture to say, still more in their credit and authority. There are few men of knowledge or learning, at least, few philosophers, since Mr. LOCKE has wrote, who would not be ashamed to be thought of that party; and in almost all companies the name of OLD WHIG is mentioned as an uncontestable appellation of honour and dignity. Accordingly, the enemies of the ministry, as a reproach, call the courtiers the true TORIES; and as an honour, denominate the gentlemen in the *opposition* the true WHIGS. The TORIES have been so long obliged to talk in the republican stile, that they seem to have made converts of themselves by their hypocrisy, and to have embraced the sentiments, as well as language of their adversaries. There are, however, very considerable remains of that party in ENGLAND, with all their old prejudices; and a proof that *court* and *country* are not our only parties, is, that almost all the dissenters side with the court, and the lower clergy, at least, of the church of ENGLAND, with the opposition. This may convince us, that some biass still hangs upon our constitution, some intrinsic weight, which turns it from its natural course, and causes a confusion in our parties.

I shall conclude this subject with observing that we never had any TORIES in SCOTLAND, according to the proper signification of the word, and that the division of parties in this country was really into WHIGS and JACOBITES. A JACOBITE seems to be a TORY, who has no regard to the constitution, but is either a zealous partizan of absolute monarchy, or at least willing to sacrifice our liberties to the obtaining the succession in that family to which he is attached. The reason of the difference between ENGLAND and SCOTLAND, I take to be this: Political and religious divisions in the latter country, have been, since the *revolution,* regularly correspondent to each other. The PRESBYTERIANS were all WHIGS without exception: Those who favoured *episcopacy,* of the opposite party. And as the clergy of the latter sect were turned out of the churches at the *revolution,* they had no motive for making any compliances with the government in their oaths, or their forms of prayers, but openly avowed the highest principles of their party; which is the cause why their followers have been more violent than their brethren of the TORY party in ENGLAND.[1]

As violent Things have not commonly so long a Duration as moderate, we actually find, that the *Jacobite* Party is almost entirely vanish'd from among us, and that the Distinction of *Court* and *Country,* which is but creeping in at LONDON, is the only

1. Some of the opinions, delivered in these Essays, with regard to the public transactions in the last century, the Author, on more accurate examination, found reason to retract in his *History* of GREAT BRITAIN. And as he would not enslave himself to the systems of either party, neither would he fetter his judgment by his own preconceived opinions and principles; nor is he ashamed to acknowledge his mistakes.

one that is ever mention'd in this *kingdom.* Beside the Violence and Openness of the JACOBITE party, another Reason has, perhaps, contributed to produce so sudden and so visible an Alteration in this part of BRITAIN. There are only two Ranks of Men among us; Gentlemen, who have some Fortune and Education, and the meanest slaving Poor; without any considerable Number of that middling Rank of Men, which abounds more in ENGLAND, both in Cities and in the Country, than in any other Part of the World. The slaving Poor are incapable of any Principles: Gentlemen may be converted to true Principles, by Time and Experience. The middling Rank of Men have Curiosity and Knowledge enough to form Principles, but not enough to form true ones, or correct any Prejudices that they may have imbib'd: And 'tis among the middling Rank, that TORY Principles do at present prevail most in ENGLAND.

"Of Civil Liberty"

f. This was the title of the essay in printings from 1741 to 1754.

Of Liberty and Despotism.

"Of Protestant Succession"

g. This was included in the essay from the first edition of it in 1752 to 1768.

For my part, I esteem liberty so invaluable a blessing in society, that whatever favours its progress and security, can scarce be too fondly cherished by every one who is a lover of human kind.

"Idea of a Perfect Commonwealth"

h. This was included in the essay from the first edition of it in 1752 to 1768.

Of all mankind there are none so pernicious as political projectors, if they have power; nor so ridiculous, if they want it: As on the other hand, a wise politician is the most beneficial character in nature, if accompanied with authority; and the most innocent, and not altogether useless, even if deprived of it.